PENGUIN BOOKS

That's

Derryn Hinch wears many hats. In his last book it was a chef's hat for the bestselling *Derryn Hinch Diet*. Twice he has pulled on the thinking cap of a novelist with *Death At Newport* and *Death in Paradise*. He has written about Scrabble and one of the early-warning books about AIDS. In a media career embracing more than thirty years he has worked for newspapers, both here and abroad, and on radio. Currently he is host, writer, and executive producer of his five-nights-a-week current affairs programme on the Ten Network. He still worries about his vineyard and his favourite hobby is still lunch.

By the same author

FICTION

Death at Newport
Death in Paradise

NON-FICTION

The Scrabble Book
AIDS – Most of the questions/Some of the answers
The Derryn Hinch Diet

That's Life

DERRYN HINCH

PENGUIN BOOKS

Penguin Books Australia Ltd
487 Maroondah Highway, PO Box 257
Ringwood, Victoria 3134, Australia
Penguin Books Ltd
Harmondsworth, Middlesex, England
Viking Penguin, A Division of Penguin Books USA Inc.
375 Hudson Street, New York, New York 10014, USA
Penguin Books Canada Limited
10 Alcorn Avenue, Toronto, Ontario, Canada M4V 3B2
Penguin Books (N.Z.) Ltd
182–190 Wairau Road, Auckland 10, New Zealand

First published by Penguin Books Australia, 1992
2 4 6 8 10 9 7 5 3 1

Typeset in 11/13 Goudy Old Style by Midland Typesetters, Maryborough, Vic.
Made and printed in Australia by The Book Printer, Maryborough, Vic.
National Library of Australia
Cataloguing-in-Publication data:

Hinch, Derryn, 1944– .
That's Life.
ISBN 0 14 016986 5.
1. Hinch, Derryn, 1944– . 2. Hinch, Derryn, 1944– – Political and social views.
3. Television news anchors – Australia – Biography. I. Title.
070.195092

For my mum, Betty Hinch (1920–90)
And, as always, for Jacki.

Contents

Acknowledgements

Thanks to the Penguin team – Bob Sessions, Linda Ristow, Jo Bramble and Sally Fricker.

As usual, thanks to 'Hinch's human sandbag' Suzy Jaeger-Hughes, who keeps my professional life in some sort of order and to Jacqueline Hinch who knows what to expect in the months ahead after her initial, accusatory charge: 'You're writing in your head, again.'

Excerpts from the jail diaries were first published in the Melbourne *Sun* newspaper. My fee was given to VOCAL – that worthy organisation that cares about the victims of crime more than some judges do. Peter Smark's column appears with the permission of the author. Some other thoughts and opinions appeared, in different form, in the Melbourne *Weekend Herald* and the Melbourne *Sun*.

Introduction

This has to be paradise or damn near close to it.

The sun is out, the air is sweet with the smell of Hawaiian flowers, the rum-powered mai tais are bullish, towering coconut palms sway and Bali Hai, the mystical, mythical island used in *South Pacific* looms, green and lush, in the distance across Hanalei Bay. I say 'mythical' because the Bali Hai that dominates the Kaua'i skyline from the open air 'Happy Talk' lounge at the Hanalei Bay Resort is a peninsular, not an island. *South Pacific* was filmed there but they cheated.

As I sit here, contemplating an introduction to the most personally frank piece of writing I have ever attempted, a bird shits on my head at 3.05 on a Sunday afternoon. At 3.30 p.m. a gecko poops on my tablecloth from the exposed rafters in the bar. Maybe somebody is trying to tell me something. Not an auspicious start as I sit with a blank notebook and start to write a book. This book.

It is strange that the thought of writing eighty thousand words of a novel does not faze me. I relish the challenge. I enjoy the plot variations as the book progresses through the maze of my imagination. I like making fictional life and death decisions. I enjoy the conversations I have with my characters when I am in the shower. But a book like this one, a book of essays, pages from my life, is daunting. In fiction you can include as much or as little truth as you like. It has been said that the first novel is always, and must be, autobiographical. What else do you know to write about? But the second or third can be, and perhaps should be, more removed from your own world. Get out there into the brave new world of total fiction. Test your aim and your arm in a world of myths and mayhem.

A book of non-fiction essays is another thing altogether. It can expose flanks you didn't even know existed, or have long kept hidden. As you probe other people's perceived foibles and frailties suddenly you are probing your own. And you don't always like what you find.

I have said for years, and meant it, that I had no plans, no interest, in writing an autobiography. Did not appeal to me. It is true that over more than thirty years as a print journalist, broadcaster and author I have been like a squirrel keeping reams of paper and clippings and notes and tapes. So much of it that a few years ago I had to hire a commercial storeroom in Melbourne. But, to be honest, I don't know why I was keeping it because I had no plans, and still have no plans, to ever write my memoirs.

In the middle of writing *The Derryn Hinch Diet* which, not incidentally, ripped around 20 kilos off my chubby frame and became a bestseller, I told Bob Sessions, the chief honcho at Penguin books, that he had conned me: I never planned or intended to write about my personal life but more than I had bargained for came out in the diet book.

At a later lunch Sessions dangled a literary carrot. 'Anecdotes,' he said. 'You've got forty years of personal anecdotes from all over the world. Put them on paper. Write me some essays.' It was a word I hadn't thought of in years. Essays. Quaint. Old-fashioned. It brought back memories of teenage years, when English was the only subject I was any good at in school – maybe because it was the only subject I showed any dedication to, or enthusiasm for. In exam after exam, test after test, English (essays, compositions, comprehension) hauled my marks back from the pits. A headstrong, ambitious kid – although unsure of what he was ambitious about – who apparently as my mother said had 'a way with words.'

That day in paradise in 1991, when the bird defecated on my head, I scribbled in the notebook something along the lines of: how will I fill a book of essays? It was scratched out in seconds. Good reason. I have, for years, been niggled by guest columnists, non-writers, non-journalists, trying to fill a page in a national Sunday paper or a weekly glossy magazine. I could repeat the formula column with my eyes closed.

They start off by saying 'Hi. Gee whiz. Imagine little old me being given such a responsibility. Whatever will I write about. I can't, for the LIFE of me, think of a single, sensible, coherent thing to say. (Not surprising). I could talk about this . . . or that . . . or a dozen other topics.' In the end they don't. They feign surprise when the required several hundred words of drivel gets them to the end of the column without anything really having been said at all.

It is Hinch on Life. And I guess Life on Hinch. Like the diet book's anecdotes it has drawn more out of me than I had planned or expected. But it peels away some protections from more than thirty years of adult life, plus some childhood memories, and maybe also makes a few cogent points about why and where I am at in the 1990s because of where I came from in the '40s and '50s. Maybe the autobiography I didn't want – but had to have.

But that's life.

Those Scary, Tortured Teenage Years

We had a colourful character in my home town called Slim Jim the Pudding Strangler. I knew his nickname from an early age but did not realise, didn't have a clue, that 'pudding strangling' meant masturbation. How would I know? Heading into those mysterious, pubescent, teenage years in the 1950s we didn't get a skerrick of sex education from our parents or from teachers at school. The closest we got to talking about it with an adult was when the high school science master taught us about the pistil, the reproduction organ in plants (with its ovary, style and stigma) and there was always the behind-the-hand sniggering and giggling in biology class while discussing frogs at our all-boys school. My parents told me nothing although I assume my mother talked to my sisters about sex or at least about periods and body changes.

As an adult I asked her why we weren't told anything

about sex as children. At first my mother said, 'Of course we told you.' When I disagreed with that memory she fell back on the old cop out that by the time they were going to tell us 'You already knew'! And of course we didn't. All we really knew was that we liked girls and that, somehow, babies came out of Mummy's tummy. It was real 'cabbage bush' time.

There were plenty of signs and signals around but we were too ignorant to pick up on them or even know what we were looking for. My dad had a couple of special adult records hidden away (or so he thought) in the bottom of the radiogram and some nights at a party he and his mates would sit around on the padded, floral lounge suite and listen to them. They'd guffaw when one of those 'nudge, nudge, wink, wink, know what I mean', vaudeville comics like Max Miller would sing about bringing Horlicks up to bed 'to stop your night starvation'.

On the train on high school footy trips and on the bus heading for the St John's Ambulance Brigade cadet championships we'd raucously sing dirty ditties like 'Oh, Sir Roger do not touch me'. I never really knew if the maiden slipped, slept, or slapped between the sheets 'with nothing on at all'. Every trip we would always sing 'I know 'cos I've seen it, been right up between it, the hairs on her mickey-do-di hang down to the ground.' We knew that was a rude one but would have fainted if someone had pointed out we were singing about female pubic hair. Sounds naive . . . but true.

When I was about eleven I bought a birthday card to send to a friend. It shocked my mother and she wouldn't let me send it. It depicted a buxom red-head, her huge mammaries spilling out of a tight red dress.

From memory a lot of cleavage and a lot of thigh – at least for those days. The message on the front said 'Ashes to ashes, dust to dust,' and continued inside, 'If the wine don't get you, the women must.' (Remember, I was eleven). When my mother confiscated it and I asked her why she said it was 'too grown up'.

One of the biggest, most hotly debated, events in my home town in about 1955 was the screening of a sex film for parents. Not a father-and-son night or a mother-and-daughter night like they had in some of the bigger towns. This was a sex education film to tell adults where babies came from and what caused them. Some of the town burghers wanted the film banned. In a compromise the council decided it was too permissive for adult males and females to see under the same roof at the same time. So husbands and wives were forbidden to go to the same screening. Children, even sixteen and seventeen-years-olds, were not allowed to go at all. The husbands all went one night, after a few beers and some ribald, rib-poking jokes at the pub and the wives went the next night. Presumably they still slept together in the same bed on both nights.

While all this was going on we were discovering masturbation. Over the years there have been all sorts of names and expressions for, and jokes about, self-gratification: jerking off, pulling yourself, wanking – before that became an accepted public word for verbal or mental masturbation. We all did it, bathroom, lavatory, bedroom, and all felt guilty about it. Would have died if our parents had known what shameful things a teenage boy was doing to himself and what disgusting thoughts he was having about girls behind the bedroom door. I didn't even think of talking about it with my father, and certainly not my mother, even though through those teenage years I talked to her about most things. But this was sex. And anything that felt that good had to be bad. Had to be dirty. It was in PK days. Not chewing gum – pre-Kleenex days. Nothing was ever said but, unless she knew the truth, my mother must have thought that I had a cold for about five years judging by the number of handkerchiefs I used every day and every night. I couldn't wait to get to bed. And because I shared a bedroom with an older brother it meant the under-the-blankets self-sex had to be silent, urgent and fast. I quickly got used to holding my breath. We all wanked . . . sometimes pulling at newly-awakened teenage penises until they bled.

We never discussed this private sexual world with our friends. There were jokes but no personal confessions. Instead we talked, in detail, about real or imagined sexual conquests with teenage girls. And, in those prudish days, a hand inside a blouse was a sexual conquest.

By the time I was twelve I was at an all-male public school (public as in state school) where all 1100 students swam in the nude. For the first time you got to see a mass of male bodies and penises of all shapes and sizes. Ninety-nine per cent were circumcised. Boys with small penises were mocked cruelly and unmercifully particularly by older bullies who would flick at their buttocks and genitals with wet towels.

Once, just before swim time when we all stripped naked on the pool terrace, I had to surreptitiously remove a Band-aid from my penis.

I heard all those schoolboy stories about the boarders

having 'jerking off' contests in the dormitories at night. But we were day boys, 'day bugs' and the idea of spending the night at school under any circumstances was bizarre. I believed twenty or thirty teenage boys in a dormitory could get involved in public farting contests but public masturbation sounded grotesque.

There was that great wanking line pointing out that, 'The one thing about masturbation is that you don't have to look your best'. And in *Hannah and Her Sisters*, when Woody Allen and Mia Farrow are having trouble conceiving because of his low sperm count, she starts probing his sexual past and his masturbatory habits. His defensive response: 'Are you going to start knocking my hobbies?' We didn't even think about female masturbation. I mean, they couldn't. They didn't have dicks. Years later I believed the story about Queen Victoria's England where the laws forbade homosexuality between males but didn't mention women because the Queen allegedly told her politicians not to be silly because 'women didn't, even couldn't, do that sort of thing.'

I recall first masturbating (or to be more accurate first ejaculating) by accident while having a bath. I was innocently washing my penis with soap and suddenly experienced this amazing new sensation and this strange emission. Felt guilty and a bit dirty. For some time I would only masturbate in the bath or, later, by soaping myself and lying on the bathroom floor. (It certainly caused some logjams in the bathroom and some desperate hammerings on the bathroom door because our bath and lavatory were in the same room).

From there the sexual experiments (still solo) moved to the bedroom where I had graduated from pin-up pictures of the New Zealand All Blacks – Superboot fullback Don Clarke and dive-passing half-back Kevin Briscoe – to Elizabeth Taylor. My favourite magazine picture sticky-taped to my bedroom wall showed her with lots of cleavage in a lace petticoat sitting on a big bed and wrapped sexily around the brass bed ends in a publicity shot from *Cat on a Hot Tin Roof*.

When I was thirteen or fourteen I lied about my age (for the first of a thousand times) to get into the movies to see a new, young, French actress called Brigitte Bardot in a restricted film called *And God Created Woman*.

I was instantly in love. Certainly in lust. That mouth. The long, tousled blonde hair. We even saw her naked derriere when the sheet fell away from her body. Keep in mind that sex in movies was so rare that the biggest talking point in *Rock Around the Clock* was not Bill Haley and his Comets but the black knickers we got a glimpse of (pre-pantyhose) when the dark-haired girl let it rip on the dance floor. And when television finally arrived Dick Van Dyke and Mary Tyler Moore slept in voluminous, flannel night attire and separate beds.

The Hinch family was a typical 1950s family where nobody walked around in the nude. I never saw my mother naked until I nursed her on her death bed. I stopped wearing clothes to bed as a twelve year old. It upset my mum. She had all the right reasons: unclean, not seemly. And the kicker: what if there is a fire? I remember saying that I couldn't care less, if I were caught naked in a fire I would shamelessly run, bare bum and all, into the street.

Our social life revolved around local dances – places where you got a real chance, virtually your only chance, to feel female flesh. In such bizarre rites as the 'Twilight Foxtrot' and the 'Blackout Waltz' you maybe got to even kiss a girl. Clumsily. The boys got to know through the teenage male grapevine the two or three girls who would 'do tongues' and the girls quickly got to know the dozen or so mouth-probing boys to avoid.

After the dance the lights would come up and fifty teenage boys, trying to look nonchalant, would walk off the dance floor with one hand in a pocket to disguise a tell-tale bulge . . . no matter how small.

Those dances were barbaric: girls in their white socks or first nylons and all that taffeta and rope petticoats lined up on one side of a huge dance floor, boys lined up on the other. 'Hot to trot' young males jockeying for position (but pretending not to) on one side of the hall so that when the next dance was announced you were perfectly placed to sprint across no man's land to snare the girl of your choice. You wanted to cover the ground as fast as possible but look as if you were in no hurry at all. And the dance floor's lubricating powder called Glide made the crossing increasingly treacherous. Deadly in fact, in slippery, no-traction, leather-soled shoes. We all, at some stage, ended humiliatingly flat on our backs like cast sheep after skidding on the deceptive powder.

If the girl you wanted to dance with was taken you would have a split second to make it look like you were actually targeting another nubile student. And if she had been snaffled by a faster, or inevitably better-looking, male then you had even less time to grab a consolation prize or a dog (we WERE sexist pigs) or be stranded on the wrong side of no man's land with no dance partner at all. It was a long walk back. God, it was sexist. It must have been horrific for the taffeta princesses lining the girls' side of the floor waiting for the gormless male onslaught. Especially for the 'plain Janes'. And it happened dance after dance, week after week.

By the time we queued for supper – the orange cordial and the cakes and mini-pies and ham, almost hamless, sandwiches – most couples had sorted themselves out.

If you had snared a partner by then your chances of a grope in the dimly lit final dances were substantially enhanced. Back at school on the Monday, after the Friday or Saturday night dance, it was as if nothing had happened. As if the pelvic-grinding had happened on the moon. In truth nothing much had happened. The girls were coralled by anxious fathers who waited outside the dance halls to rescue their darling virgin daughters from teenage satyrs, some still in short pants.

It was in those bewildering, explorative, uninformed years when you would go into your older sister's bedroom and open her dresser drawers just to look at her bras. They were exotic, forbidden, unknown sexual garments.

Nobody told us anything. You'd have to take furtive looks at the bras and girdles and corsets on plaster models in shop windows.

The sexiest literature available was *Man* magazine in the barber shop. *Playboy* and *Penthouse* hadn't happened and when *Playboy* did come out in the 1960s it was banned in New Zealand and Queensland (but then Joh Bjelke-Petersen, the old bible bashing hypocrite, was born in Dannevirke, NZ). In New Zealand they even stopped a planned visit by Mandy

Rice-Davies, who, with Christine Keeler, gained fame or notoriety from the Profumo Affair. And in my home town the local morning newspaper, the *Taranaki Daily News*, was fined for obscenity for having the audacity to print the Lord Astor 'man in the apron' evidence in the Stephen Ward court case. The newspaper did not even appeal. Did not have the guts to make it a test case, a cry for journalistic freedom, a *cause célèbre*.

Most of my generation's sexual education came from the movies and IN the movies. The Friday night feelies. We could never afford to take girls to the pictures. Didn't even really think about it. You were lucky to amass one or two shillings in pocket money garnered from mowing lawns, chopping kindling or selling scavenged beer bottles. And yet every Friday night, in a strange teenage mating ritual we would all queue at the local movie theatre, the 'flea house'. Somehow in this moving picture mating game, we would end up sitting next to the girl of our choice – or hopes or dreams – for a couple of hours in the unsupervised dark. That was the big bit: the UNSUPERVISED dark. A chance to be (sort of) alone. Often it became several hours of unsupervised struggle. Sometimes the whole night – the shorts, the serial, the feature, became a contortionist's struggle. Only the older, more knowledgeable filmgoers got to deliberately, calculatingly, boldly sit and 'pash' in the back row.

For a girl to volunteer to sit in the back row was almost like taking an ad saying 'I don't wear knickers'. Down the front you had to be more contrived. Hands would inch across that mile-wide divide between your seat and her lap. Eye contact was avoided at all cost.

In fact it was usually a case of breath held and eyes glued to the screen. Fingers had to meet and somehow entwine almost by accident. Sometimes a head resting, tentatively, on a shoulder would lead to exploratory kissing. But no tongues! All of this accompanied by tut-tutting disgust from adults in the seats behind. Adults who could, and usually did, know your parents – and they'd tell them.

Bare arms would be stroked. Sometimes a hand was allowed to rest on the outside of a breast. Occasionally, very occasionally, the fingers were not stopped as they burrowed and strained against 'sensible' teenage bras. A touch of a nipple, albeit a flaccid one, was worth ten Friday nights at the pictures.

More often than not, flesh stroked at the movie theatre, was not what it seemed. Every male who saw, or read, *Summer of '42* could identify with the poor, frustrated teenage explorer who thought he had scored – got all the way to first base playing with a girl's firm, forbidden breast in the darkened movie theatre – when, in fact, all night he had been assiduously probing under the shirred elastic of her sleeve and desperately stroking her small but smooth bicep.

For young males at the pictures the thigh was always a new and daunting battleground after the breasts were conquered. (In the 1950s all sexual contact was seen as a contest, a battleground. How much new territory can I cover and hold? How much resistance? Is it serious, genuine, resistance?) It was literally virgin territory – harder territory to take and hold than Gallipoli. At least to an irreverent teenager. The terrain was scary and unknown. The first, supposedly casual, hand on the leg would trigger a knee freeze. A tension. Not a rejection as such but a tension. After all no girl would ever take your hand and push it up her dress. Never.

Teenaged boys had to learn the meaning of the word 'stealth'. You'd have to creep up there. Slowly, slowly, catchee monkey. Inch by inch by inch. Gotcha. To touch bare flesh above a stocking top was nirvana.

Maybe one Friday night a year, at the pictures, you would be permitted to go 'all the way' and we're not talking about fucking here. Far from it. We thought it was heaven if a girl let us French kiss her. Put a tongue in her mouth, in the dark, in an uncomfortable flea-house of a picture theatre while probing wildly, desperately, ignorantly (and not to mention often inaccurately) beneath the formidable elastic of her bloomers. That was home base. Then, at the end of the feature, clothing would be rearranged (seconds before the lights came up) and everybody would shuffle out with a 'bye, see ya' to catch buses or trams to various suburbs. As if nothing had ever happened. That was sex. That and the sensation on the bus on the ride home when the engine vibrations would give you another hard-on. And of course there was the crude and grubby comparing of notes with mates next day. 'How far did YOU get?'

I remember, still, the first time I ever made a woman come. A far cry from Friday nights at the pictures. These days I would say 'helped' or 'assisted' a woman to have an orgasm. I was still a teenager, she was much older, and it was an accident. Somehow I touched one, or all, of those nobs and ridges and female crannies and the woman became orgasmic. It scared the living daylights out of me. I didn't know what I had done, what I had touched, as she bucked and writhed, almost broke my fingers and obviously had more fun than I was having. But it was magic. She arched her back, shuddered and screamed so loudly I thought I must be hurting her. Something I would never do to a woman. And then she exploded. She swore. Used language that, as a teenager, I had never heard a woman use before and then drenched me.

I did not know exactly what I had done right but we were both bathed in sweat and the car, borrowed from an older friend, had a redolent, inexplicable smell. And all the windows were fogged.

This exploration and growing up happened in a bureaucratically-oppressed small town that was often shut. It seemed to me it was ALWAYS shut with not much to do. Shops couldn't open early or close late. Inspectors came snooping to see if my dad was selling illegal goodies at weekends in the grocery shop and milk bar that he owned. A phone book-sized list of regulations said that we could sell people a packet of Band-aids on a Sunday but not a bandage; a can of ham but not fresh bacon; biscuits but not bread. On Sundays my town was shut. Sealed. The shops weren't open; the movies weren't playing; sport was banned. No restaurants were open because there weren't any (apart from a couple of grease-pits called fish and chip shops and they were closed by law on Sundays). Even if there had been restaurants open, we couldn't possibly have afforded to patronise them.

On good, sunny Sundays, if you were really brave, sophisticated (and lucky) you would contrive to meet a girl 'for a walk'. There would always be four or five males – including a couple of gormless mates who these days would be called nerds – and two or three girls. We would actually go for long Sunday afternoon walks and the males would show off shamelessly. Practical jokes. Dares fulfilled. Mild vandalism. Sometimes even shop-lifting of Mars bars.

If our beer bottle scavenging had been successful the previous week we could sometimes afford to hire a rowing boat on the fern-shrouded lake at Pukekura Park. After an hour of straining at the rowlocks you would hear the persistent, authoritative loudspeaker voice 'Come in Number 46 . . . your time is up.' In those cockle shell boats with a girlfriend in the stern we would clown around, ram other boats, scud the oars and drench each other. Real teenage hoons, for those days.

After the boat ride we would contrive to end up at a remote spot in the park: a dell, a glen, a fernery, where there was a chance you would get a kiss or a feel while trying to ignore the braying of the members of the pack who hadn't paired off.

Occasionally, one of us would hit pay dirt: parents having gone away for a holiday, a business trip or a long weekend. On those days we would all troop over to the empty house to play spin the bottle or postman's knock.

One such game at a chaperoned teenage party sticks in my mind. There were about fifteen teenagers there. My 'date' was a pretty 14-year-old I had made contact with by showing off, 'hot-dogging', riding my school bike with no hands on the handle bars, behind her school bus.

At the party we were playing some silly parlour game which involved rapid changes of pieces of clothing. My 'date' (and I write it like that because we never publicly tagged relationships no matter how intense or how innocent) was struggling to get a shirt over her head.

As she reached up and twisted to get out of it, against the clock, her contortions made her grey skirt ride up her young thighs. With her head shrouded in cloth she didn't know that she had exposed her stocking tops and the first suspenders I had ever seen. I was mesmerised. Absolutely mesmerised.

The other girls at the party were embarrassed and a chaperoning parent moved ultra-quickly to haul the hemline down.

The moment is etched in my memory thirty-five years later. Maybe that is why I instantly understood what President Lyndon Johnson meant when he once said that a piece of legislation in Congress 'did for progress what pantyhose did for finger-fucking.'

When you think of it the first moments of sexual awareness come when you are a baby. At first it is encouraged and then it is punished. Oh, look! She's found her toes. Oh, look! He's playing with his nose (ears, belly button). Isn't it cute. Then it's, Peter take your hands off that. It's dirty. Or, Deborah, nice girls don't put their fingers in there.

You wonder, do parents – having been teenagers once – remember the sort of thoughts that course through their own teenagers' potent, troubled and sexual minds? Do adults forget so quickly? Probably. Apparently.

For this book, for this essay, I have dug deep and resurrected memories that have not surfaced in decades. Memories I have never, ever, shared with my stepson or nieces and nephews. Some I have never shared with anyone. And maybe shouldn't now.

At eleven I wrote to a female penpal dissecting (in literary fashion of course) a photo of us she had sent me after we had holidayed at the same relatives' house.

It was a totally innocent, candid, shot from a Kodak box Brownie. In my teenaged innocence (frustration?) I analysed the grainy picture in my next letter to her: how my hand around her waist was only an inch below the obvious bulge of her breast. I never heard from her again. I suspect her mother forbade her from writing to a 'pervert'.

Around that time I had my first flight on a plane. A 'lean forward for takeoff' DC3 from New Plymouth to Christchurch. (It was back in the days when women passengers would not dream of flying without gloves and probably a hat. In those days women in Sydney or Melbourne would feel naked if they ever went to town without gloves.)

I was going to visit my only aunty and uncle, Edna and Ken. I was so naive, so 'small town', so working class, that when they picked me up at the airport and we drove to their house I thought we were stopping for ham sandwiches and tea at the local hotel/restaurant. It was so grand. It was their house.

I wasn't the only guest. In this huge two-storey house with sun-rooms and an attic there was also a pretty blonde woman. Looking back she was probably only 23–25. She had a pert, three-year-old daughter named Claire who became my mate.

All I knew about the situation was that a stranger with a young daughter was staying at my aunt and uncle's house. We used to all go for walks along the banks of the Avon River. There were some conversations that I didn't grasp and wasn't expected to comprehend. Cryptic stuff. But I recall a pretty, but forlorn, woman, stoic, deserted, coping, with a brave face.

The little girl followed me like a puppy maybe because of the trauma of the loss of a father whose name was never uttered.

This holiday led to a big moment in my sexual development. Even though I did not know it at the time. Several times while we were all staying with my aunt and uncle, Claire's mother would come downstairs and stuff a newspaper-wrapped package in the garbage bin. Just like my teenage sister did at home! I didn't know they were such avid readers.

My holiday chore was to diligently burn the garbage. I did it daily. One day, surreptitiously – with the adrenalin pumping – I went behind my uncle's shed near the summer house (the pergola I called the pagoda) and unwrapped the other guest's newspaper parcel. I knew it was mystical, feminine, illicit. Remember I was only 11 with no sex education. I only knew it was something to do with how the 'other side' lived and operated. Something about female magic. It was a case of knowing, but not really knowing, that I was doing something exciting, something dirty.

In the newspaper parcel I found an alien cotton pad that looked and smelled strange of blood and something else. I was excited. I looked furtively over my shoulder. I couldn't understand where it came from, what it was used for, or why it was wrapped so thoroughly. But I knew, instinctively – in that blind, groping, ignorant sexual world we grew up in – that it was important. I had never heard of 'the curse' or of 'that time of the month' or of somebody having 'the rags on'. I didn't know about, or ask about, the hieroglyphics that my mother and older sister scribbled on the calendar each month.

But, at my uncle's incinerator, I knew I was learning something monumental about life. I actually sniffed the evidence and, heart-pounding, wrapped it up again. But I didn't burn it. In fact, bemused, really puzzled, I went back several times with my heart aflutter to unwrap it and examine it again. I knew it was important but I didn't have the faintest idea why.

I couldn't relate a dank, smelly, stained pad to the pretty blonde woman with the cute daughter a few feet away in my relatives' house.

I could not know then that the experience would tie in with another one only a few years later.

Somehow in my small town I got to know an attractive, married woman. I've never been able to accurately recall not so much how we met but how we 'crossed the Rubicon' and, incongruously, became lovers. Her husband played in a band at the local teenage dances.

In a town with a population of around 30,000 we had probably passed in the street but she was a married woman and I was hardly – I was going to say barely – out of short pants. From the minute I set eyes on her I thought she was so sexy. As a teenager I couldn't really define it, probably still can't, but the chemistry was there. Even though I was so young and she was married, maybe because she WAS married – that meant she had done 'it'.

One night at the end of a dance where her husband had been belting it out in the band, we bumped into each other outside the dance hall. She was old: maybe 25 or 26. She said something like, 'Isn't it cold?' and, spontaneously, gave me an innocent and quick-warming cuddle. The fleeting squeeze was followed by a clumsy kiss but, unlike the teenage girls in taffeta and chiffon inside the dance hall, her kiss was not prim, tight, suspicious or troubled. It was open-mouthed, full on the mouth. It was fleeting but it left me stunned and breathless. No tongues, and it was brief, but it was a kiss I hadn't had to ask for or fight for in those tortured years. It was real, upfront, come and get me, passion. I was knocked out.

Somehow we eventually managed moments together. It was all secret, surreptitious and dangerous. This was a time when adulterers were caught by private investigators leaping out of wardrobes with cameras flashing on naked thighs. We would drive to a park, a reserve, at the base of a local sugarloaf mountain known as Paritutu. We talked (God knows about what) and then we spread a blanket on the ground and kissed and cuddled. Suddenly, for a teenage boy yearning for, desperate for, sexual contact it wasn't a war. No resistance. Suddenly breasts weren't off-limits. I could explore and roam at random. With teenagers every kiss, every touch of the knee, every approach to even the outside of a 'lead-lined' pointy bra was a battle. With a married woman it was different. Forget, or ignore, the moral issue, sexually it was a smorgasbord. She even kissed with her mouth open. She didn't stop a hand under her skirt but made it easier. There was even a willing, subtle, widening of the thighs. Holy Shimoly! A long way from Friday nights at the pictures. I remember having trouble with her bra clip but also remember, even more vividly, that she helped me with it! It was all incredibly dangerous, adrenalin-pumping and grown-up. Or at least I thought it was. It was certainly major league sex.

One day we went to the park behind the monolith, spread the blanket and stretched out on it. There was the usual open-mouthed, full-on, kissing. The same non-protesting reaction to young fingers naively exploring breasts. But when a confident hand went under the skirt another adult hand came down in a vice-like grip.

'I can't,' she said. 'I'm sorry . . . but it's that time of the month.'

Feigning adult knowledge and tons of savoir faire (and not even giving a thought to that day by the incinerator in Christchurch doing research on female periods) I rolled away and said something like 'I understand,' while understanding nothing.

Two days later we were back behind Paritutu. Same monolith. Same blanket. Same desires. Emboldened (great word) and with a teenaged hard-on aching in my trousers I confidently crossed the knee barrier and – without even pausing at the hem – went straight up under the dress to the smooth skin between stocking top and crotch. Her hand again suddenly came down like a clamp. Again like a vice. 'Don't. I told you. It's the wrong time of the month.' I rolled away, stared up at Paritutu, that amazing natural phenomenon, and thought: 'How long does this go on for?'

Holden Caulfield, eat your heart out.

A Time For Dying

Apart from the death of my mother, shrivelled and suffering in her bed, the memory of death that sticks in my mind more than any other, in more than three decades of observing the vagaries of this world, is a tableau of helplessness and horror halfway across the world in Africa, just outside the dustbowl of a town called Allamatta, north of Addis Ababa, in Ethiopia.

There were about 25,000 people, 25,000 desperate and starving people, sitting in the dust and dirt outside a medical centre run by an Australian doctor called Tony Atkins. A refugee army of gaunt mothers, fathers and dying children. They had been there for days, perhaps weeks, hoping and praying that Atkins and his medical team would give them the thumbs up rather than the thumbs down. Thumbs up meant primitive medical treatment; a turnaway was a certain death sentence for most, if not all, of the family.

Atkins admitted to me at the time that, although he didn't like it, although it tore him apart inside, he had to play God. There was no point giving scarce food or medical supplies to a baby he knew would not survive. The ultimate example of the 'lifeboat' theory.

To see thousands upon thousands of grotesquely gaunt, starving, people huddled around their match-stick babies with huge saucer-shaped, pus-infected eyes and bloated air-filled bellies must test anybody's religious faith. I often think about those 25,000 people and realise they must now be dead. Hundreds of thousands, maybe even millions more, are now dead. Dr Atkins, to me an Australian hero, made so many life and death decisions that nobody should ever be called upon to make. Imagine standing at the door, actually a flimsy gate, of a pretty basic medical centre saying to traumatised and emaciated mothers 'yes' or 'no' in a decision that everybody knew (doctor, nurses, parents) meant a child would live or die. Tony Atkins did not have a nervous breakdown, but he came close. It was so emotional, so traumatic, that even though my team had taken cardboard packs of orange juice to the area and even though we were thirsty we couldn't drink them. The three of us admitted, back in our comfortable hotel in the Ethiopean capital, that not a drop of fruit juice had passed our lips, even behind closed doors, in the hours we were in Allamatta, because, in good conscience, you just could not open your throat.

On the same African trip I visited a foul-smelling, disease-ridden camp, set aside from the rest of the suffering and administered by the most dedicated band of Mother Teresa's nuns. Everybody in that camp had been virtually given a death sentence. Turned away, rejected, denied food or medical treatment by every other aid agency, on the grounds that the precious food and the scarce medicine could be put to better use on a child with a chance of survival. In the squalid brick huts we saw people within hours of dying: the unsalvagable. The stench was unbelievable. My young sound man, Darren James, who had been with me through the poverty camps in India, had to go outside and throw up.

The thing about Allamatta that will be forever burned in my mind is that even when people are involuntarily knocking on death's door and daily see their children and other relatives gasp their last breath, they still try to cling to some shreds of a real life. I saw that starving mass of humanity still striving to retain some semblance of a family unit. Some continuum. If they had one precious, tattered, stained blanket or wrap they spread it out on the barren ground, put stones on the corners to hold it down, and called it 'home'.

The memories, the images, of Ethiopia stuck much longer than other stories that I have reported on. I went there just before Christmas and returned to an Australia with shop windows stuffed with toys and goodies. Indulgences that could feed and save a village. Through Melbourne's 3AW I launched a rash, emotional, and impromptu fundraiser. I knew that the dustbowl of Africa was a long way from most Australian minds, especially in the boom years of the mid-1980s. Especially at Christmas. I called the money chase the STIC appeal, an acronym for 'So This Is Christmas'. Backed by John Lennon's haunting and pleading song I asked my listeners to buy their kids one less toy that year, explain why, and give me the unspent money. And, bless them, they did. In a couple of weeks we raised nearly half a million dollars. I used my Christmas holidays to buy blankets, high-protein biscuits, cooking oil and powdered milk. I personally chartered a Boeing 707 to take the food and blankets to Ethiopia. (That in itself was a challenge. Where do you find a 707 at short notice? The quotes ranged up to $150,000. I finally found a Rumanian cargo plane for $70,000.)

About a year later I went to see it all again, in the Sudan. This time, near the Mali border, soldiers with whips beat starving people, forcing them away from railway carriages carrying aid agency grain. We saw starving children crawling through the dust searching for individual grains of spilled wheat and rice to take home to their families. Distraught mothers used twigs to try to flick grain through the cracks in the doors of ramshackle railway carriages. And kept on doing it even as soldiers' whips cut into their shoulders.

This trip to the Sudan was undertaken partly as a favour for one of the world's best charities, the Save the Children Fund. Former Melbourne Lord Mayor, Ron Walker, a generous and enthusiastic supporter of SCF, implored me to go after the success of the So This Is Christmas Appeal. Without sounding too 'holy-moley' I really didn't want to. I had seen famine. Seen the suffering. Seen starving people in India and in Africa. I was promised the chance to interview the organisation's hard-working world president, Princess Anne. It started with a few frustrating days in Khartoum. The interview I thought I had been promised with Princess Anne (and for which three of us had forfeited our holidays to go to Africa to get) seemed to be moving increasingly out of reach. Anne's marriage (mock-marriage) to 'Fog' Captain Mark Phillips, was again on the front pages of the tabloids in Fleet Street because of a rumoured liaison between Anne and one of her equerries, Commander Tim Laurence, a rumour that, in the 1990s, turned out to be true. The Palace minders were, understandably, not keen to put Princess Anne face to face with any journalists, especially for a one-on-one interview. In fact, day after day, as we trudged through the dust and the deprivation of Africa, Princess Anne did not even acknowledge that the 'reptiles of the Press' existed. Even though we slept in an open-sided, rickety, cholera hospital somewhere in the middle of Africa.

I did get the interview eventually, the only interview she gave on that tour, after I sat down late at night in a shack in some God-forsaken village in Africa, with my typewriter perched on my knee, and wrote her a personal note that probably breached Royal protocol. Once the green light was given my team (Hinch, producer Paul Barber and sound man Darren James) had to literally commandeer a Landrover in the middle of Africa, join the Royal cavalcade, and bounce over desert roads and dried, corrugated, bum-jarring, river beds for about forty minutes. But we made it to the hidden Royal oasis which consisted of one large, freshly-painted mud hut with a thatched roof, a lumpy bed, a table, and a pitcher of water. It stood apart from the rest of the village compound.

Thinking back, it sounds incongruous. There I was after ten days of trying to get an interview – and after a Monty Pythonesque Landrover ride in which I spent most of my time lying flat on my back, legs in the air, on a semi-seat – suddenly standing in the dust in the middle of Africa waiting for the Queen's daughter.

There were no equerries, no secretaries, no ladies-in-waiting, no security guards, no gofers. Donkeys brayed in the distance, smoke rose from the village square, and suddenly she appeared behind me in a white shirt and dusty jodphurs. She was clutching a can of soft drink. Understandably she looked a little wrung out having just come through the same bone-jarring, bum-bruising day of wretched 'roads' and corrugated wadis – dry river beds that can be so sharp that they can cause umpteen flat tyres. Even to Royal jeeps. As the sun went down, and the day's oppressive heat finally subsided, I started one of the most unusual interviews of my career. It also produced the put-down of my career. In one of the early questions I started to say 'As patron of Save the Children . . .' In a dusty village in the middle of Africa, the Queen's daughter interrupted to correct me, 'I am president of Save the Children. Not the patron. Mother is.'

Reminiscing about Princess Anne, Africa, and the Save the Children Fund, brings me closer to death and suffering at home.

One of my favourite restaurants used to be Gowing's in Melbourne. No more. The restaurant has gone. Dennis Gowing, one of the most generous men when it came to donating money or services to charitable causes, is dead. One of my fondest memories of him is at a lunch in his restaurant before the 1986 Melbourne Cup. I had recently returned from Africa and Gowing, his millionaire friend, Lloyd Williams, and cocky jockey Mick Dittman were adamant that their horse, What a Nuisance, would win. By the end of that lunch

Williams had agreed to donate ten per cent of his winnings to Save The Children and Gowing had agreed to donate ten per cent of his winnings to the Variety Club. What A Nuisance came from behind to win. I felt like I had been riding it. My two favourite charities collected $130,000 that first Tuesday in November.

The larrikinism, the largesse and the luxury of that Melbourne Cup triumph is hard to equate with the emaciated, drained, colostomy bag-wearing and doomed cancer victim that Dennis Gowing quickly became. And, as with my mother, it brought death very close to home.

In an eighteen-month period in recent years I have been reminded again and again and again about how fragile existence is on this planet. How easy it is, as they say, to slip the mortal coil. Within months my mother suffered an agonising, debilitating, cruel death; my mother-in-law did not survive heart surgery; a craggy old mate lost a long battle against bowel cancer; an actress friend of my wife died suddenly from a brain haemorrhage; and my sister's best mate, for whom I had carried a teenage torch, had her life snuffed out by a ravaging, speeding, cancer. It all affected me more at the time than I probably acknowledged, even to myself.

When I was thirteen I attempted to write my first novel. Actually it was more of a short story – an exceedingly short story. I can still remember, pretty accurately, the first couple of paragraphs:

> 'Kurt was dying. He only had 14 minutes to live if the pills he had taken worked.'

(How as a teenage author I could pinpoint the timing

of a pill-induced suicide to 14 minutes I haven't the faintest idea!)

> 'His life flashed before his eyes, his memory files flipping over and over as he sat at his parents' formica-topped table.'

Thirty-five years later I remember that the formica-topped table was important for writing realism then. I also remember that when my father read my first attempt at raw, realistic writing he was perplexed. Even numbed: Kurt had a drunken, violent father.

I have been writing about death – or trying to write about it – for decades. And not really coming to grips with it. Even when killing people off in novels.

For example when I heard the news that Dennis Gowing had died I was in Hawaii. I said something banal like, 'It's for the best' and went for my daily walk along the island cliff tops. That morning I paid special attention to all the old, grey or balding, American men in their ridiculous plaid or virulently-coloured golf trousers, darting around the Princeville course in their electric buggies. All of them older than my just dead friend. And I thought, why him? I watched them whack a small white ball across the green sward and wondered about life and, to be perfectly honest, even wondered where the word 'sward' came from.

As you get older, and as family and friends die, you find yourself saying to yourself 'he wasn't that old'. Although, in these 'been there, done that' years if you can make it to fifty or sixty you've had a pretty good and exciting trot.

As a teenager I read a book called *A Stone For Danny*

Fisher. I think that was where I first read the line, later pinned on heart-throb young actor James Dean: 'Live fast, die young and have a good-looking corpse.' I used to quote it. Endlessly. It was insecure, teenage, juvenile rubbish. When you think about it if you are dead who gives a tinker's cuss if you are a good-looking corpse. Look at Marilyn Monroe's.

My father's mum lived until she was a shade under 97. Lived alone until she was 91. And, at 96, still had a pretty good head of black hair. Maybe that's why I expect people to live through their seventies and eighties. Maybe that's why a mother dying in her sixties came as an inexplicable shock. I just did not expect it.

But then, no matter what age, death by cancer is a jolt for everybody. It is a ghastly way to die and – having seen my own mum succumb in less than ten weeks – I think I would rather take a tablet and avoid the final indignities. It is little wonder that people consider it a death sentence the minute their doctor passes on the diagnosis. It doesn't matter that some cancers can be and are cured. Safely removed. Words like cancer, tumour, lump, malignant, cyst, still send shivers down the spine.

In my mother's case, to be journalistically blunt and clinical, she didn't really die from cancer. She starved to death. A sixty-nine-year-old woman with mouth ulcers, cold sores and thrush in her throat, trying to keep a body alive on an occasional teaspoon of ice cream or yoghurt. No wonder she ended up looking like a stranded, vulnerable, parchment-covered bird. It wasn't living. There was absolutely no quality to my mother's life in her final two months. A proud and private woman lost all privacy, all dignity.

I arrived back in New Zealand the night before she died. I had been warned I would not recognise her – the decline had been so fast, so drastic. Only two months earlier I had raced back from Australia when she was first told she had cancer and maybe only had six months to live. She was having radiotherapy which was knocking her about and was already having trouble swallowing anything except a few spoons of ice cream. Although weak she was as sharp as ever. One night, that I will treasure forever, we sat up yarning and reminiscing until nearly two o'clock in the morning. Somebody had got to her and told her that, under no circumstances, should she have chemotherapy. A close friend had had it, had suffered grievously and still died. Stubborn to the end Mum spurned the treatment, talking about the quality of life compared to no life at all. She was ready to die. When I arrived home the last time, she turned to me, squeezed my hand, and said: 'I'll be alright, boy. All I need is a little fine tuning.' It was the last thing she ever said. It was almost as if she had held on until I made it home.

On my mother's final night on this earth, I perched hour after hour on the edge of her 'glory box' that was one of the few material possessions she took into her marriage. I still have, and cherish, one other thing: a tubular map case made of lead and containing a portrait of my mother on silk. A sailor, visiting New Zealand, painted it for my grandmother. My mum would have been about three. She looked like Myrna Loy.

The glory box – or 'hope chest' as the sexists used to call it – sticks in my mind because I had sat on that box every Friday or Saturday night for years. If not perched on the fading velvet nap I would sit on the end of my parents' bed to wrap up a night out. Didn't always tell them the truth. Didn't always understand what had or had not happened. Usually Dad would be asleep, although he would occasionally contribute a grunt to the nocturnal conversation. Mum always stayed awake until we were home. She would follow the trials and tribulations of our courtships and puppy love.

It was on her side of the bed I sat, ashen-faced and shaking, the night she had to prod my father awake and tell him that his sixteen-year-old son, showing off, had crashed the family car (a Morris Minor) only hours after it had been released from the panelbeaters after repairs from my sister's identical bingle. And it was my mum who hushed his anger by asking a chastened and frightened son, 'Are you OK . . . are you hurt?'

In my mother's case I watched the agonised 'help me' eyes of a pain-wracked, trapped, human and it crossed my mind around four o'clock in the morning that I would be doing a loved one a favour if I put a pillow over her face and ended it. Would have been the biggest act of love I could have shown to my mother. That fleeting, but admittedly serious, thought ended up as a cover line on *New Idea* magazine, stripped of all decency, compassion and love and dressed up, shrilly, sensationally as 'HINCH: I wanted to kill my mum'.

In fact I just wanted to end her pain. Such awful pain. Such needless, cruel, undignified, gasping, final hours of cruddy existence. That wasn't my mother. Nobody knows how close I came to reaching for the pillow to smother her. If she had been a racehorse somebody would have legally shot her. I actually sat there and watched a human being starved and tortured to death. And it was my own mum. It just doesn't make sense.

Maybe not much does. My old mate Dennis Gowing went out only weeks before he died and bought a brand new Jaguar. He also took a five year lease on a Toorak mansion when his doctor (and friend) Richard Ward was hardly advising him to buy a new shirt. It was like, 'I don't believe any of the experts. I'm going to prove you all wrong.' And that is understandable. When the big knife of death hovers over you who can say how you will react?

Gowing's offspring took turns to be with him and sleep on cots in his hospital room as the end, inexorably, got closer. I suspect that, like my family, the suffering experience brought them closer together. I know the death throes of my mother drew me closer to my family – especially to my stalwart of an older sister, Barbara.

Actually that respect, and love, had really grown and been nurtured through an earlier Hinch family tragedy as I watched my sister grapple and cope with a mother's nightmare, the loss of a son, her beloved Rodney, in a shooting accident on a New Zealand farm. A great knockabout, generous kid, chopped down at sixteen years of age when he was about to start his first real job in the adult world. He was out on the farm with his best mates, hunting rabbits like they had done a hundred times. They were country kids, used to guns and country living. One of his friends, my namesake Derryn, wearing gumboots and carrying a loaded shotgun, jumped over a log as they walked, single file, across a paddock. As he landed he jarred the gun. It went off and removed half of my nephew's head.

My sister did not only cope . . . she held a stunned

and grieving family together after having her son's head blown apart. I watched her in awe. My love for her grew. When Mum died such a ghastly death Barbara, Dad and I were there. One tiny tear formed in the corner of Mum's left eye . . . and she was gone. I took her wedding ring off and gave it to my dad. Then, a father and two of his kids just clung to each other for a few minutes.

From that experience of having my mother die at home, in her own bed, the laying out of the body in the parlour makes a lot of sense to me. Before my mother's death, I used to think it was, well, ghoulish. But I also thought that hospitals didn't exactly have it right either. When people died in hospital it was almost as if their families did not exist. I don't, and won't, denigrate the passionate, gruelling and emotional work that professional nurses put themselves through, but sometimes bureaucracy takes over. He, or she, is dead – pull the curtain. Reach for the shroud. Somebody in a white coat or a uniform has control. Suddenly there is a barrier of machines and tubes and efficiency between the aching family and the victim. Suddenly a loved one is gone. The physical body is gone. The void so vast.

When my own mother died I called the undertaker and asked him not to come to the house for several hours. The home nurses had done whatever, physically, they had to do and crossed my mum's hands. Then, throughout the next few hours, my family, in groups or singly, would move down the familiar corridor to my parents' bedroom – as we had done so many times over all those years to tell Mum about nights out that had gone so well or so badly. I'd talk about fun times, disastrous teenage faux pas times, awkward moments. Not the real heavy sweating, groping stuff of a teenage boy determined to get a sexual education – although, in restrospect, my mother seemed to be almost prescient about what I was doing with whom and where. For a while I thought she had to have the best network of smalltown spies in the world.

As I sat on the end of her bed again, with her body still in it, she seemed to grow younger as if she could relax now the struggle was finally over. With all that pain finally gone the combat lines in her face softened and actually disappeared. That expression about death being a 'merciful release', that it finally sets somebody free and leaves them in peace, is, I know now, the truth. I saw it.

Around 11 p.m. on the night my mother died – and she went just before 7.30 p.m. – the undertaker told me it was time to take her. In one of those Keystone Cops cockups (that she would have shrieked over) we discovered that the professionals could not get the clunky metal corpse stretcher down the narrow corridor to the bedroom.

Suddenly, and it was not planned, I had this feeling that in death I did not want a stranger touching my mother's body. That there was one more thing that I could, and should, do for her. From memory I got quite persistent. There was something pushing me there to make sure I did something I felt I had to do myself. So I carried her out of the bed that I had sat on the end of so many times for so many years.

Although she looked a bird-like waif she was surprisingly heavy. Incongruously I thought at the time of that expression 'dead weight'. My stalwart of a brother-in-law, Les Swanson, a real brick as they say, had taken her feet. We carried her out and put my mother in a heavy, black plastic shroud with big zippers and a lot of straps. I said goodbye and zipped it up but then unzipped it when somebody got agitated about her jewellery. Was she or wasn't she wearing it all? With finality I unzipped the black plastic bag containing my mother's body, checked the jewellery and knew I had said 'goodbye' forever.

It was a moment so final, so tough, that it made acceptance of her death perhaps, in retrospect, a little bit easier for me. I didn't give a shit about the jewellery.

My mother's death brought home to a (now foreign) journalist how things had changed in New Zealand in recent years. In a town of less than 50,000 people we were warned not to let anyone know that my mother was a cancer victim, very ill, and on a morphine drip at home. Naively, even though I had more than thirty years experience as a journalist including years on police rounds, I asked why. I only needed to read the various funeral notices in the paper to work it out: 'Died at home. All drugs have been returned to the hospital.' Apparently it was quite common, even in such a small town, for drug addicts to check the death notices and raid houses during the funeral. Coincidentally, my younger sister, Sandra, worked in a chemist shop and recognised a car with several known drug users cruise past my parents' house. Police took it seriously enough to leave two guarding our house, actually sitting inside our house, while we went to my mother's funeral. A sign of the times even in little New Zealand.

That family decision to have my mother's body left at home for some hours made acceptance of her death much easier for me. And made me realise why the practice of bringing loved ones home from hospital to die in their own house makes sense. So does the viewing at home. When my much-loved nephew, Rodney, died suddenly in that shooting accident we went to say goodbye at the funeral parlour. My dad didn't go and I know that made it harder for him to accept his grandson's death. In fact he still really hasn't.

I am not a religious person. Far from it . . . even though, or maybe because, I was a cassock and surplice-clad choir boy in a Church of England choir in my youth. (We used to hold mock weddings in the church during mid-week rehearsals and grope for the breasts of the female choristers).

As a non-religious being who thought, and still thinks, that bodies become worm fodder I have for decades been a campaigner for cremation. And yet my mother-in-law's funeral changed my views on that. Jacki's Mum, Ede, was buried in a cemetery. There was something old-fashioned, even comforting, about it all. Something good, and solid, and even reassuring, about it.

I know people say, and I have said it many times, that if you are religious you believe the soul has long departed before a 'carcass' is burned or buried. And, if you are not, what does it matter? But as an agnostic-all-but-atheist I was mesmerised by the funeral of assassinated Indian leader Rajiv Gandhi. I watched in macabre awe as his body was set alight and burned in front of international television cameras, as his wife and children set fire to the funeral pyre – a bier that I guess by necessity is larded with incense so you can't smell a loved one cooking.

It was very late at night in Australia and I watched the Gandhi barbecue for about five hours into the early hours of the morning. I wondered about the religious strength that prompted people to put a torch to the body of a loved one. But then I thought about cremation in crematoriums and funeral parlours where we let somebody else do it. In the same way we hope, sometimes pray, that a doctor will make a euthanasia decision for us.

My family has felt the pain from the loss of a child through an accidental death. Even worse is the heartache when a son or daughter makes the decision that he or she can't go on and commits suicide. I have seen at close range a lot of parents beaten, crushed, mentally and physically destroyed, as the gnawing questions eat at their hearts: Why? Could we have done more? Why didn't we spot the disturbing signs? Surely, as parents, we were to blame?

I had a character in one of my novels contemplate suicide once (in *Death At Newport*) and so, in a writer's sense, I gave the idea of killing yourself some detailed thought. In real life I have also talked some people out of killing themselves, during my years of talk-back radio in Melbourne. I remember tracing the identity of one tortured and hurting woman, contemplating suicide, through some flowers she sent my secretary.

But, incongruously, I have also always preached that suicide is your ultimate civil right. And it is. It is a terrible, indulgent, selfish waste but it is your right. There was a time when suicide was not a crime (after all the offender was dead) but *attempted* suicide was a serious crime. I always thought that was sick. Imagine a successful bank robbery being less of a crime than an attempted bank robbery.

When I was about 12 our next-door neighbour committed suicide. Family and friends talked in hushed tones about the incident and it took some hours for the kids to find out what had actually happened. We lived behind the shop next door. When the hearse arrived all the kids were sent to play out the back while the body was removed from the butcher shop's back room. I still don't know if he hanged himself (the usual method of exit in those days) or fell on one of those huge threatening knives that every butcher had rattling around in a scabbard, or put his head in the gas oven.

My first wife's neighbour, who lived with two 'middle-aged' spinster daughters (they were probably 31 or 32) put his head in the gas oven and killed himself one day. My mother-in-law couldn't understand how the daughters could cook their usual Sunday roast leg of lamb in the same oven only a couple of days after his funeral. I figured that the guy had gassed himself, not cooked himself to death, so it didn't offend me. It did remind me of the Simon and Garfunkel song: '*. . . he put his head in the oven and he went to sleep and he never woke up . . . and somebody said there was a brother somewhere who must be notified soon. He really was a most peculiar man.*'

Sadly, for many young women, the first death they experience is the death of their own child. Cot Death. It must be a mother's nightmare. To tuck your child into his or her cot, with dummy and a fluffy toy and come back hours later to find your beloved baby blue, cold and dead must be absolutely dreadful. After the shock comes the guilt. Did I do something wrong? Could

I have done something differently? Could I have saved my baby's life?

I admire the annual Red Nose appeal campaign to raise money for research into the Sudden Infant Death Syndrome (SIDS) and the gold hearts on the sleeve for the Variety Club, but I wonder about the motives of donators who leave the plastic red noses on their car grilles for weeks or months. Is it laziness? Or is it a case of somebody saying, 'Look at me. I give to charity.' If I had lost a child to that brutal syndrome those red noses on cars would be a daily reminder. I could brace myself and live with it for one day because of the income going towards vital research but not eight months later.

A mother losing a baby to cot death, or having a baby still-born, must face a trauma that no man, no matter how close or loving, can understand or comprehend. After all those body changes, the backache, the nausea, the morning sickness, the soreness, to have a child die must be horrific. Imagine having all those things happen to your body and then to have a little baby that is still-born. Dead without a chance at life.

I do not believe in the vagaries of fate. I don't actually believe in fate at all. I don't believe in those rugged quotes about your card being dealt, your number being up or a bullet having your name on it. Don't believe it. Never have. I believe in coincidence, unless you are a novelist. In real life I think things just happen. A good example about 'deadly whimsy' in Melbourne recently. A middle-aged, average sort of couple took their Jack Russell terrier out for an after-dinner stroll. A normal, usual, after-dinner thing to do. While they were walking, around half past nine at night, two joy-riders in a stolen car happened to pick their street to hoon around in or at least to try to avoid the pursuing police cars.

The stolen car mounted the footpath and ploughed into the couple in a mesh of metal and blood. Both were killed instantly. The dog lived. A stolen car with two joyriders goes out of control and two innocents die. They never went home again. I call it the Luby's Syndrome. The Killeen Fields. Being in the wrong place at the wrong time. I named it after Luby's Restaurant in Killeen, Texas, where a disgruntled American from a nearby town decided one lunch time to create the Killeen Fields in Texas. He 'wasted' a restaurant. Drove his pickup truck through the front window and started shooting. Imagine going to your local fast food joint for lunch. You pick up a hamburger and a 'side order of fries'. 'Hiya, Buck . . . Good to see you, Jed' and then all hell breaks loose. A looney with a grudge, a powerful truck and a high-powered rifle crashes through the window and starts shooting people.

Imagine being in Sydney, having a cappuccino with your mother and a friend in a coffee shop in a shopping plaza. A quiet Saturday afternoon after picking up a video or buying your wife or husband a birthday present. You are sitting there in the comfy world of coffee and cakes and suddenly a young girl at the next table is dead with a huge knife blade slammed into her back. And suddenly there's a loony, a loner, who had been sitting at a nearby table, spitting death at the world from a variety of high-powered, semi-automatic weapons. That's exactly what happened at the Strathfield Shopping Plaza. A crazy loner who spent most of his money with prostitutes for 'talk sessions' and then guilty anal sex, started killing anything that moved.

Maybe, to preserve your own sanity, it is best to subscribe to that simplistic theory about your number being up. I personally do not believe there is some Grand Plan. Some great, giant lottery of life where the ringmaster behaves like Jack Nicholson's Joker in the first Batman movie. I do not believe there is some person, or some force, out there that plans people's behaviour like marionettes on a string. 'Tonight this young couple will die in a car crash on their wedding night. Now, who should the drunk groom crash into. Let's make it a head-on. Let's make it that nice Mr Aldershot who just picked up his three young kids from a school camping trip. And let's kill them all.' I don't believe that. I'll concede there is a lottery element to it all. Ten months after my mother-in-law died my wife and I were having a drink (I was, she wasn't) at a resort in Hawaii. She looked around and said, 'All these people are much older than my mother. It's not fair.' And it wasn't . . . life isn't. When I was about ten or eleven years old my sister used to bring her schoolgirl friends home in the afternoon. There were some I used to have pubescent tinglings for even though their teenage bodies were imprisoned in heavy, grey flannel tunics. One was a girl called Karen Armstrong. She was Hollywood beautiful. I was eleven and she was about fourteen and she sat on the concrete front steps at our house talking to my sister. After she went home one day my mother cried. Beautiful Karen had a thing called leukemia. She was dead within weeks.

Being around death gives you a feeling not only of impermanence but sometimes a 'Seize the Day' mentality. Live for the day and let the devil take the hindmost. As friends, and lovers die you find yourself becoming increasingly selfish, increasingly self-indulgent, even reckless, which when you think of it is silly, even childish, in a world where we are merely gnats, fleas, insects, if there is a Great Order Of Things.

As the Irish say: The longer you live, the sooner you die.

The Foreign Correspondent

Probably the worst, but most telling line, about the strange breed of person called a 'foreign correspondent', surfaced in Africa, in Kenya, during the Mau Mau uprisings. After a village had been razed and nuns slaughtered a breathless Fleet Street reporter roared up in a jeep and asked: 'Has anybody here been raped and speaks English?'

Now, it may not have been Kenya. It might have been Leopoldville or Sharpeville. The fact is somebody said it . . . and around the world for decades foreign correspondents have guffawed about it. And repeated it. Ad nauseum.

'A weird mob' as Nino Culotta would say. At times a dangerously weird mob. I've seen the mob at work. Seen it close up. Tasted it. Been part of it. Seen it at its best and at its worst. Seen its contortions and its concoctions. Been part of the travelling road show in the

United States, Canada, Mexico, Brazil, the Caribbean.

And when you have been part of that circus you can totally believe that William Randolph Hearst did cable a photographer around the time of the Spanish-American conflict and say: 'You supply the photographs. I'll supply the war.'

Why not believe it? Journalists and publishers have done a lot worse. On the other side of the Atlantic, Fleet Street has done amazing things in the name of journalism and competition. At a time when they somehow regarded Australian newspapers and Australian journalists as beneath them.

I was a foreign correspondent for many years. Some of it makes me understand what Ernest Hemingway was saying about the world of newspapers when he gave this bit of advice: 'Get in, get wise, get out.'

And yet it can be one of the greatest and most honourable of professions. Journalism took a kid from a town of 30,000 people in New Zealand on a journalistic rocket ride that led to a reserved seat in Florida in July 1969 when the men of Apollo 11 first climbed aboard their giant spaceship and went and landed on the moon. Only four years earlier, at 21 years of age, I had been chasing fire engines in Sydney. Sometimes, when it comes to journalism, I feel like I have been alive forever. I got out of the starting blocks of adult life very, very fast. Could not wait. Left school at 15. Found an adult swagger within weeks. Maybe even days. My first press card photograph shows an arrogance, a confidence, a psychologist could have a field day with. I thought I was shit-hot and going places years before I discovered that I WAS shit-hot and going places.

At fifteen I was a young cadet reporter in New Zealand. That meant on Saturdays I would have to scrape the green mould out of the cups and make tea for the reporters and the sub-editors working on the Saturday night sports edition. On the Monday I could be substituting for the drunken, vindictive, gay chief reporter, covering a Supreme Court trial, even though I couldn't do (and never learned) shorthand. Or I'd be sent off on the office motor-scooter or in the office wreck of a car (only senior reporters got to drive the new Austin) to cover a Rabbit Board meeting, or a County Council meeting (for which we got five shillings expenses for a lunch we didn't have). And all the council, and harbour board, and dairy board, and county meetings, were so structured and ultimately so dishonest that if, and when, anybody raised any issue that was remotely interesting they went 'into committee' and threw us out. And if they didn't – if somebody let something slip in our presence, they went into committee retrospectively. If you managed to get a smidgeon, a tad, a sniff of a story, the board chairman would call the editor and the story would get killed anyway. That's how small town politics and newspapers worked.

I couldn't wait to get away from it. By the time I was eighteen I was in Sydney, Australia.

Australia! The big league. Living in King's Cross (where shops were actually open at the weekend – unlike some parts of Melbourne even in the 1990s.) I was lying about my age, adding between three and five years and covering police rounds for the *Sun*. I had a spindly Harry Messell beard but no moustache. I don't think I could grow one. A gruff and growling police sergeant at the 6 a.m. CIB conference told me to grow some hair on my top lip and 'make a real cunt of yourself'.

Apart from police rounds I also had a stint in a rotten job covering the Coroner's Court down in The Rocks area of Sydney. Next to the Seamen's Mission.

It was a ghastly blood and gore job for a young reporter. The clerk took some perverse pleasure in guiding you through the morgue where flies crawled over naked bodies. Where autopsy victims had their skins roughly laced back together from throat to scrotum. Where tops of skulls had been taken off with electric saws like the lopping of a boiled breakfast egg. Where stories abounded about necrophilia and the tabloid police roundsman who ate his sandwiches in the morgue whenever a pretty young accident victim was brought in.

The smell of death and decay and formaldehyde stuck in my nostrils for hours after my first morgue visit. And for years I remembered the refrigerated drawer being opened and an eye dribbling down the cheek of a shattered corpse after a morgue attendant showed me the remains of a suicide victim who checked himself into the Salvation Army's 'People's Palace' under the name of Mr Body – and blew his brains out.

The only bright moment in covering the suffering of the Coroner's Court was the occasional appearance in the Press box of a pretty blonde with great, tanned legs, poking out from under a short yellow dress. She worked for my opposition – the Sydney *Daily Mirror* – and ultimately did marginally better than me out of print journalism. Her name was Anna Torv. She married Rupert Murdoch and became an author in her own right. So did another beautiful, blonde Sydney cadet from that time. A skilled female writer who would go on to write the definitive biography of Bob Hawke: Blanche d'Alpuget.

All of this contributed to the thick skin, the callouses, of the foreign correspondent, which should always be written as Foreign Correspondent ('cap F, cap C' as you would tell a copytaker) because that is the way we saw ourselves. Hired guns. Typewriters that could be as deadly, as devastating, as pistols. Hit a town. Trash it. Bleed it dry. Move on. Anybody here been raped and speaks English?

And yet, on the other side of the coin, we would and could really live life (albeit usually at somebody else's expense). We'd sometimes experience the pain, feel the anguish, but always record it with that rush of blood to the head. There was that huge journalistic/morality furore in 1992 when political thugs invaded the Iranian Embassy in Canberra, and beat people, stabbed people, trashed an office. The pain and the passion was caught forever and went out on the five o'clock and six o'clock news. The graphic pain raised an obvious question: why didn't the SBS crew drop their cameras and try to help the victims? Always a tough question for any newsman, woman, or camera crew in any riot, in any war. I believe the SBS crew did the right thing. And if their footage, ultimately, put people in jail, then so be it. But if the observers are meant to let down their guard and become participants, then you are never going to get dispassionate news observers to record the 'what' or the 'why'. Never going to get chroniclers of history whether it is Tiananmen Square or Kent State.

The SBS film of the 1992 Iranian Embassy attack left me chilled. For me it brought back memories of the early 1960s, when I was a young, naive Sydney police roundsman. One morning my crew had been assigned to Wollongong, NSW to try for an interview with a pretty young woman who had survived a bullet in the head from a jealous ex-boyfriend.

We headed south from the Fairfax concrete bunker – an architect's nightmare on Broadway – before the city was really up and breathing for the day. There was Hinch the reporter (around 18 pretending to be 23 or 25) a pock-marked photographer who wouldn't work in an iron lung and 'Wally' the avuncular driver.

We were halfway to Wollongong, around 7 o'clock in the morning bouncing along in an uncomfortable bone-jarring snub-nosed, dark green machine, that we called the 'pie truck' and that could somehow send picturegrams back to head office via some machinery I never understood in the back. As we rounded a corner on the highway we almost crashed into a car that had just failed the turn. It had slewed to the left, flipped on its roof and its wheels were still spinning. That's how fresh the accident was. Petrol was pouring out of the upturned car and sparks were flying. Wally swerved around it and parked at a safe distance. I jumped out, ran back and prised open the driver's door. He was unconscious and upside down. It was in the days before seat belts. I got him out safely and we radioed for an ambulance. The whole saga took about fifteen/twenty minutes out of my life. We went on to the story about the shooting victim in Wollongong, got the interview, filed an exclusive story, but missed the first edition. When we got back to Sydney I was carpeted. Severely. The News Editor told me (using a lot of four-letter words) that I was an incompetent journalist, a pathetic police roundsman, an early-start dickhead and a wimp. Or whatever the word was for 'wimp' in the early 1960s.

I remember, edition missed, standing in front of his battered, stained wooden desk with a cracked glass top being flailed while his loyal secretary Rita (whom I'm now sure didn't like or respect him) kept her head down.

I copped such a scathing editorial 'serve' that I virtually forgot that, earlier that morning, I had saved a man's life. And, to a degree, risked my own. Didn't matter – it hadn't sold a paper.

There was a ton of hypocrisy. For example: in July, 1969 a Kennedy dream came true. John F. Kennedy had pledged, in a stirring speech early in his presidency, that his nation would commit itself 'before this decade is out' to put a man on the moon and return him safely to earth. The United States, in the late 1950s and early 1960s was losing the Space Race and the Cold War. The big bad Russians had put Sputnik up there and then Yuri Gargarin. The Americans had the failed, blowing-up-on-the-launch-pad Vanguard programme and the captured U-2 spy pilot Gary Powers. John Kennedy would not live to see his dream come true. And in one of those Greek tragedies that haunted his family his 1969 men-on-the-moon triumph was soon smeared by his brother's plunge off Dyke bridge in Massachusetts and the death of Mary Jo Kopechne.

The Kopechne drowning was a gem for journalists, especially foreign correspondents. The antics in Chappaquiddick in the summer of '69 had it all: a bunch of young women – the so-called 'Boiler Room girls' – booze, a team of mostly married older men, and a Kennedy. What more could the world's Press ask for? They descended on Kennedy territory with all moral guns blazing. Some of them wrote some outrageous things even though I have to stress that I believe Teddy Kennedy behaved abominably. Behaved like a selfish, self-preserving, spoiled, rich, cowardly brat. I doubt he could have saved Mary Jo Kopechne's life. We'll never know. I doubt he even tried. He saved his own life and Senate – but not presidential – career.

One night, with a belly full of bourbon, I celebrated my scoop of an exclusive interview with Mary Jo's parents, the exclusive interview the American reporters couldn't get. I didn't, in all honesty, give much lasting thought to the Kopechnes, an ordinary, god-fearing, grieving couple from a small town near Scranton, Pennsylvania. I got the scoop, filed the story. As I said I did not linger over the fact that those people would probably never get justice.

And they didn't get it. They never really got answers as to how their precious, only daughter died. How a man who fled from the scene of a fatal accident could finally plead guilty to a paltry charge and not spend a minute behind bars. More than twenty years later, to my mind, Senator Edward Moore Kennedy has still not told the truth about that night.

I mentioned hypocrisy. In Massachusetts, at one of the interminable court hearings that followed the 'Kennedy-Kopechne scandal' (see how you can reduce it to three words) a married journalist who had been as outspoken as anyone about Kennedy's wealth, power and immoral behaviour, waited until another foreign correspondent had gone to the lavatory before adroitly white-anting his colleague. A New York Jewish princess who had been expensively wined and dined by the other reporter all night was suddenly targetted and moved in on. Persuaded, impetuously, to leave immediately for a cognac and a late night swim. They ended up humping in the sand not twenty yards from the borders of the Kennedy estate at Hyannisport. The hungover foreign correspondent saw no irony, bore no shame, when he wrote a scathing article next day about Teddy Kennedy's tom-catting habits. About his morals or lack of them. And having written a lurid Page Four piece with a ringing Page One pointer, he phoned his wife in New York and told her he was a bit seedy because he'd had a few cognacs with a couple of other foreign correspondents before hitting the sack around one o'clock the night before.

The lies were everywhere. In Edgartown, Massachusetts, there was a Police Chief called Dominic Arena. In the early days it was a joke. 'Dominic Arena? I thought it was a skating rink?' By the end of the week every foreign correspondent had bought him a meal. At least that's what the expense accounts said. The joke was that Dominic Arena had eaten 3000 meals in a week. Journalists write savagely about bureaucratic rorts. And, of course, there's a moral 'out' that a foreign correspondent 'fudging' on an expense account does not involve taxpayers' money.

Foreign correspondents bleed each other, eat each other, mislead each other, suck each other dry. Interview each other, steal from each other, quote each other. Exaggerate. Obfuscate. And sometimes it backfires.

It certainly backfired on me and the Melbourne *Herald*'s New York correspondent, Peter Costigan, on the Kennedy story in Massachusetts in 1969. We had driven up there late at night. A three-and-a-half hour drive, plus car ferry ride, from New York. I was covering for the *Sun* and the *Sydney Morning Herald*. Steve Dunleavy, the legendary, indefatigable, tabloid king with Roy Orbison hair, was reporting for the Murdoch stable in Australia and London.

After Mary Jo's death there was much speculation about how Teddy Kennedy had actually got off the island and back to Edgartown. Remember the ferry had stopped running for the night. The official story was that Teddy swam back to Edgartown after trying repeatedly to get Mary Jo out of the upturned Oldsmobile in the dark, cold waters of Pucha Pond. He, somehow, made his way back to the Shiretown Inn. He didn't report the accident to the police. Didn't raise the alarm. He didn't try to find Mary Jo's parents in Pennsylvania and say their daughter had died, or had been lost, presumed dead, in a ghastly accident. Kennedy did none of those decent things. Instead he went to his room. He changed into dry clothes and then deliberately went downstairs to seek out the hotel duty manager to complain about the noise of a party in a nearby room. I asked, and wrote at the time, and ask again: Was this a genuine complaint from a man who couldn't sleep (a man who had left a woman's body submerged in his car) or an attempt to build a fragile, pathetic, late-night 'I'm home, I'm safe' alibi?

Kennedy did not in fact call the police for more than eight hours. The body of an innocent woman swayed and bumped against the floor of an upturned luxury car in that cold, murky pond for all that time. In fact, an accident alert had gone out in the dawn hours and police divers were hauling the car and Mary Jo's body out of the pond. They also found the zany-coloured purse of 'Cricket' Keogh, another 'Boiler Room' girl. That discovery of her purse prompted the first, erroneous, reports that she was the victim. A wild report that jarred her family. Another report claimed Cricket was Kennedy's date that night and Mary Jo had died because she was unwittingly asleep in the back when the car went off the wooden bridge.

The phone records now show that in the crucial hours after the accident Kennedy did not sleep at the Shiretown Inn in Edgartown, Massachusetts. Instead he made heaps of phone calls to his minders, his image-makers, his lawyers, his speechmakers. The Kopechnes in Pennsylvania weren't exactly high-priority.

In all of this something backfired against me and Peter Costigan. We were not in head-to-head, city-to-city, combat but we still fought each other for scoops. Sometimes we would share a hire car or a hotel room when accommodation was tough. In Edgartown, during Kennedygate, it was tough. The place was usually full anyway in July and August with parents and students who holidayed there. In July 1969, with men walking on the moon, Edgartown attracted, as waitresses, a lot of young, attractive college students with great bodies and a Boston twang. The foreign correspondents who swamped the small holiday town were not only different, not only foreign, but were good tippers. It wasn't our money.

One night several of the student/waitresses at the Shiretown Inn invited a couple of foreign journos to a party. One of the gatecrashers was Steve Dunleavy, a now legendary Australian export of tabloid journalism. Dunleavy had, uncharacteristically, got to this story of sex, booze, and Kennedys, a mite later than some of us. Playing 'catchup' makes you hungry and desperate. He still managed to wangle an invitation to the pretty students' party. A few beers. A few laughs. But Dunleavy never stopped working. Never.

That night I caught him in the most blatant, the most naked, eavesdrop. Deliberately, to Peter Costigan, I started to boast about a great contact in the Edgartown community who had confirmed to me that only hours after Kopechne's death somebody had stolen a boat from near the death site and taken it across the bay to Edgartown. It was total fantasy. 'I must follow it up tomorrow,' I said. 'Sounds plausible.' All the time knowing it was rubbish.

Dunleavy immediately made some lame excuse about why he had to leave in a hurry. And Costigan and I laughed like drains. I was still gloating next morning until my editor phoned me and blistered me for not having the 'scoop' that was leading the opposition's first edition. 'Kennedy mystery boat'. It was no mystery to me. I had made it up.

That Kennedy saga gave me a real insight into the way that the so-called Fleet Street hotshots worked. If they had a genuine scoop they would give 'blacks' (carbon copies of their stories) to their opposition as soon as the first edition deadline had passed and their story was in print. Australians wouldn't. It caused a lot of flack when Australian and British newspapers started to deal with each other after the Dirty Digger, Rupert Murdoch, grew his international tentacles. The Australians wouldn't play the back-scratching game, Wouldn't deal in protectionism. Apparently it was a golden rule on Fleet Street. It meant that when irate editors phoned from across the Atlantic to complain about being scooped and to demand an instant 'matcher' their 'hotshots' could safely say 'I'm on to it. I've got it. I'm sorry I couldn't firm it up for the first edition.'

It was a custom so ingrained on Fleet Street that some big name British journalists couldn't comprehend when reporters, raised on the 'take no prisoners' Sydney tabloid scene, refused to play the game. And a game it often was.

In retrospect, the rumour I started about a stolen runabout was probably closer to the truth than Kennedy's 'official' tale about diving off the dock and swimming from the ferry to Edgartown. In fact, more than twenty years later I am sure it is.

The Bag Ladies

When I was a kid I worked on my father's milk run every day before I went to school. Up at five o'clock, a quick Weetbix breakfast (or claggy porridge which I hated) and then I would ride my push bike into town to rendezvous with my dad to do the 'town run' – deliver half-pint and pint bottles of milk and cream to the shops in Devon Street. He would have already, alone, delivered milk and cream to suburban houses in Vogeltown and Frankleigh Park. At weekends I would put on the first pair of denim jeans my parents ever allowed me to own. Coarse, blue denim. We weren't allowed to have black ones because that is what bikies and bodgies and widgies wore. Every Saturday and Sunday morning I would get out of bed at one o'clock to help my father do the weekend deliveries. The first weekend he owned the milk round – to my crushing disappointment – I wasn't allowed to go with him, despite many tears. My older brother, Des went the first night. Then, my older sister, Barbara. I finally copped weekend three. And every weekend thereafter. My brother and sister didn't like the hard yakka in the cold, wet, wintry, dead of night. Didn't like it when you had to jam your young hand into a sodden hedge, grope for the milk bottle, and separate the new-fangled plastic milk tokens from the snails and slugs that infested the bottom of the milk bottle. I can still remember that feeling. Pitch dark, cold, drizzly, spooky. The slimy slugs and the half-inch of icy water that everybody seemed to leave in their milk bottles.

I guess it brought me close to my dad. Closer than I realised at the time. We really were a team. And when times got tough and my mother threatened, or attempted, to leave him, my brother and sisters lined up on her side. I always said I'd go with him. Not because I loved my mother less (I sympathised with her) but because I figured it was only fair that someone gave Dad some public sign of support.

As we emptied the old milk truck, barking knuckles on the metal crates in the mid-winter cold, I would stack the back of the truck with discarded beer bottles I'd found along the route. Bottles worth a penny (a cent) each, once I had washed them and stacked them behind Dad's shed. Thirty bottles on a Saturday night meant 2/6 (half a crown) which was good money for a poor kid's piggy bank in the early '50s.

My dad and I would shout warnings to each other as a late-night Saturday drunk weaved his car towards us in the danger days when breathalysers and .05 rules did not exist. Everybody got drunk and drove – every Saturday night. And when things got really dangerous we would sprint away from the milk truck, run across somebody's front yard and cower on their front verandah until a drunken driver had swerved off into the night.

That was weekends. During the week I pedalled into town to do the milk drop outside the local shops. Didn't get paid for it. Didn't expect to. It was something you did for your dad. Unquestioning.

It was around that time, and under those strange circumstances that I got to meet so many of the local characters. There was Brown-Eyed Betty – a woman who wore Dame Edna Everidge-type sparkly glasses, a tartan skirt, and always, as I put it, had her fetlocks bandaged. I didn't realise, in my youth, what people meant when they called her the town bike and when my parents joked about her 'favours' being worth a dozen cakes or two bottles of beer.

And then there was Miss Marks. Used to dread meeting her on the milk run. So did my dad. Miss Marks had taken a shine to my father. Every night she would lie in wait for him in her flannel nightdress, muttering and mumbling, and urge him to take the breakfast she had prepared for him: two Sao crackers, dry, and wrapped in lavatory paper. She was mad as a cut snake. The offering was made night after night.

Maybe that is what nurtured or triggered my interest in 'bag ladies', those tortured souls of the night.

I am reminded of one of my favourite bag lady stories of all time. It goes like this.

She was a New York bag lady. He was an urbane, clever, well-off, Broadway director. Their paths crossed one Christmas day in New York City. He was a man of poetic expression and theatrical dreams who directed greasepaint productions on Broadway for people like Neil Simon. She was an obsessively private person, of private passions and solitary dreams, who appeared daily on Broadway with her wordly possessions in a couple of supermarket shopping bags.

His name was Philip Cusack. He had directed actors like Sally Struthers, Rita Moreno, Jacki Weaver and had been a theatrical doctor to a lot of Neil Simon plays. He had lunched, a languid Christmas lunch, at Sardi's, the show business mecca on New York's West 44th Street. He waved to George, the maitre d', and left the restaurant, heading out on to 44th Street past the hat-check lady and past the Shubert Theatre.

A salute to the Sardi's doorman, who makes more in Christmas tips than some people make in a year, and then the footsteps point towards the Algonquin Hotel for an after-lunch cocktail. Why not? It's Christmas. A post-lunch cocktail in an antique-filled lounge has a charm, an appeal.

The bag lady had walked a different path, from the overflowing garbage bins outside 'Nathan's Famous' hotdog restaurant on 43rd and Broadway past the gilded doorway of the old Paramount theatre building. She started to sing as she rummaged through a bin outside the former theatre in Times Square. Well-off New Yorkers usually, calculatingly, ignore bag people. Affluent New Yorkers, mink-wrapped, fur-clad, galoshes-shod New Yorkers, daily ignore the pathetic army of human scavengers.

'It's only a paper moon . . .hanging over a cardboard sea . . .'

The director had eaten and drunk well. Had had two extra-dry martinis. And as he stood at the traffic lights on 44th and Broadway and waited for the lights to change the bag lady's voice was bell-like:

'hanging over a cardboard sea, and it wouldn't be make believe . . .'

It WAS Christmas week. He WAS waiting for the lights to change after an indulgent Christmas lunch. He DID have a belly full of martinis. And the bag lady's voice was bewitching, pure.

'And it wouldn't be make believe'

She rummaged so deeply, so desperately, through the papers and the cans and the pizza cardboard that, when her voice soared, it seemed like her garbage bin was wired for sound. The man from the world of passionate theatre, the world of make believe, felt a lump in his throat. The bag lady's mid-afternoon voice was a rose in New York's increasingly oppressive and thorny reminder of poverty.

Standing at the corner of 44th and Broadway Cusack thought warmly about his life and his craft.

'And it wouldn't be make believe'

Here was proof that no matter if the feet are chilblained, no matter if the shoes are held together with string, no matter if your next meal desperately depends on what somebody else throws away, a voice cannot EVER be stilled.

Theatrical director Philip Cusack ignored the WALK sign that flashed a command at him. In the deep pocket of his expensive cashmere overcoat he felt some notes. He dug deeper, in that cautious way that New Yorkers deal with greenbacks, and found a twenty-dollar bill. The man of the theatre, beguiled by the dulcet tones, was just about to make a donation when, suddenly, the lady of the leftovers, the songstress of the sewers, caught his eye. And, abruptly, stopped singing.

'What are you looking at, arsehole?' The look was bitter, challenging, final.

New Yorkers don't like confrontation. The director put his money back in his pocket and went home.

Give my regards to Broadway.

Bag ladies have always intrigued me – in New York, Sydney, Melbourne, New Zealand. In Sydney there was Bea Miles, the fog-horned mountain of a woman who used to quote Shakespeare on street corners and tear doors off taxis if the cab driver questioned her demand to be driven to Perth – without payment.

From my sixth floor office in the Paramount Theatre building on the fringe of New York's Times Square I would watch the sly, daily antics of one eccentric who waved an old, furled umbrella like a sword. She would sit for hours on the edge of a concrete tree-holder that grew garbage and would spit at people as they walked past her. Anyone foolish enough to challenge the spittle attack would face a flailing with the umbrella.

At the Port Authority building on Eighth Avenue platoons of bag ladies shuffled their worldly belongings in and out of coin lockers and vied for the warmth of the ladies' public toilets. They muttered in a language only they could comprehend.

In Melbourne's Albert Park once I watched a bag lady, talking that language, and carrying all her possessions, hopes and dreams, in two plastic shopping bags. The bags still had the faint, faded names of famous stores. And I wondered if she had found them, bought them or stole them. She was wearing the remnants of about three cardigans or sweaters, and her skirt, or sarong, was a grubby strip of calico with only a hint of a design. It was held together like a tattered kilt with two or three safety pins. The slippers were in tatters but then the bunions would have complained about any other sort of footwear and, incongruously, her grey and blonde and greasy hair was held off her face by a bright, almost luminous pink, plastic hairclip.

I looked at her as we passed and thought: Where did you come from? Where are you going? Did the bulbous, arthritic feet in the frayed slippers once glide across the dance floor at the Windsor?

It is always the way with that shuffling, lonely, ghostly army. You look at them and think: where did you come from? Where are you going? Where have you been? What is your future?

In a New York bus station or in a Sydney or Melbourne park, bag ladies prompt that rash of questions. Where is your husband? Did you ever have one? DO you still have one . . . somewhere? Where are your children? Did you ever have happiness in your life? Did you ever have love in your life? Was that lank hair now held together by a pink, plastic hairclip, ever stroked by a lover's comb before or after sex on a cloud? Where do you sleep? How do you eat? How do you live? How will you survive a winter? Do you have grandchildren?

I look at these women and wonder if a brave husband, father, or fiancé, went off to a war and didn't come back. I look at them and think of the Bette Midler/Helen Reddy song 'Delta Dawn'. Women left, stranded, abandoned, in a country town by a smooth-talking man who never intended coming back.

Their ages are so indiscriminate, their faces so raddled, you don't know, can't know, if a lover died at Dieppe or Dienbienphu. As a journalist . . . shit, as a person . . . you sometimes want to intrude. Want to hand out a verbal branch to get them to share their story. But the look is always aloof and challenging. There is no extended palm to make a conversation possible. And so you keep walking. Like Philip Cusack did with his twenty dollar note still buried in his coat pocket. And you never know, and will never know, how a whole life of dreams dwindled, shrivelled, and wound up in two tattered old shopping bags on the street. And you never know how some women got old before their time. Destined to spend their twilight years ingloriously with a few street pigeons for friends, a monologue for conversation.

You watch them, and ache, as they rummage. Defenceless. Down. Degraded. Under siege from real and imagined demons. Suffering from real and imagined illnesses. Surrounded by their flotilla of fantasy friends and enemies. Their crime: not that they got old, but that some of them got so old and so lonely . . . so young. So very young.

Would the last person out of Detroit please turn out the lights

In 1992, from the safety of a television studio in Australia, I told the Ten Network's correspondent, Ken Burslem, reporting from the streets of Los Angeles, during the first hours of the urban riots, to keep his head down because 'you never know when or where it is going to flare next'.

I mentioned that I had covered the Detroit riots in 1967 in which more than forty people were killed.

In the end the death toll in Los Angeles was worse than Detroit, worse than Watts in the same city in 1965. In fact the worst, most costly, race riot in terms of deaths, injuries and property damage in American history.

A couple of hours after my on-camera warning our reporter and his crew were set upon and knocked to the ground while filming the looting of LA shops. They were kicked in the head and had $50,000 worth of camera gear stolen. Burslem came on air the next night with an egg-sized lump on his head, a stressed nervous giggle, and a worry about what the future meant if this was LA in 1992.

Jeff Kramer from the *Boston Globe* gave the world a first-hand insight into the anarchy. Kramer was driving his rental car through moderately-moving traffic on Normandie Avenue in Los Angeles' South Side. As he put it:

'At first things seemed fine. Then I started to get into a rundown business district and the traffic slowed. Suddenly five to ten people swarmed around my car.'

The mob smashed all his windows, they then tried to drag him out of the car but he was luckily imprisoned by the seat belt.

'I felt as if I was going to die. Oddly I kept thinking how wrong that jury was which maybe seems a strange way to think when your own situation is so bad.

'Maybe I was in shock, but I almost didn't blame these people. I certainly wasn't angry at them.

'I just felt very, very sad. I felt sad for myself, for the city, for the country.'

Then one of the rioters reached through the smashed window and punched Kramer in the head. He decided, on the spur of the moment, to pretend he had been knocked unconscious. Slumped forward, Kramer strained against the seat belt the rioters kept trying to open. One anarchist, angry and frustrated, suddenly pulled a gun and shot Kramer twice in the legs. Bravely, amazingly, the defenceless victim still played dead. Until, with motor still running, he took a chance, gunned his engine and with a bloodied, shattered leg on the accelerator drove off in a screaming U-turn.

There were more gunshots. Another bullet hit him, this time in the shoulder but Kramer kept driving, desperately, nightmarishly. He finally got help from a suburban black family and made it to hospital and safety.

In a minor way, a much, much, smaller way, I know what Kramer was going through and what he was feeling. Peter Costigan and I were in Atlanta, Georgia, in April 1968. We had been in Memphis, Tennessee, covering the assassination of civil rights leader Martin Luther King by James Earl Ray, a knockabout, vagabond, mini-crim, supposedly acting alone. After the death the media scrum moved to Atlanta, where King's funeral service was to be held in his tiny, red-brick church, the Ebenezer Baptist Church, in a ceremony conducted by his father, Martin Luther King Senior, and his chubby, plodding, earnest and brave disciple, the Rev. Ralph Abernathy.

Costigan and I checked into the Heart of Atlanta motel, on Peachtree Street in downtown Atlanta. Sounded great. Real Southern charm and style. We did not know that our motel was owned by the red-necked, racist Governor of Atlanta, a 'nigra' hating bigot named Lester Maddox. We found out next morning when a bullet came through the foyer window of the motel – it made a bit of a joke of the motel's monogrammed souvenirs: glasses with cutesy hearts on them.

Maddox rose to fame for owning a restaurant called the Pickrick. He used to have a barrel of pick axe handles by the door for white customers after several blacks had tried to test the new civil rights laws by eating there.

When Martin Luther King's body, and that emotional funeral cortege, passed the Georgian State Capitol building the flag was not flying at halfmast. Governor Maddox personally ordered it to remain at full mast.

I shuffled past Martin Luther King's body, in the midst of an emotional vigil at Montgomery University, on the night before his funeral. The coffin was open, people were wailing. In death that courageous giant looked small, and, I hate to say it, but he also looked green. I felt intrusive and embarrassed to be there: a foreign white, socially and financially successful, New York-based Antipodean with an expense account at Sardi's, could not ever comprehend the depth of the rage.

It was my first visit to Georgia. We had rented a big red Yank Tank and Costigan and I went cruising for the always requested 'colour piece' that would fill a hole in the Saturday magazine pages of the *Sydney Morning Herald* and, in Melbourne, for me, the *Age*. We drove through groves of heavily-scented dogwood trees, through suburbs full of mansions with sweeping lawns, weeping willows, more columns than a newspaper's classified section. And black servants. Real *Gone With the Wind* stuff.

Like Kramer – or the poor schmuck in Tom Wolfe's *Bonfires of the Vanities* – we ended up in a poor suburb. Suddenly the big red rented Cadillac (which had seemed a good joke on our employers) was surrounded by about ten disillusioned and angry black Americans. Their hero was dead, their hopes dashed. I remember their faces, filled with understandable hate and hurt. They spat on the windscreen and pummelled the car's windows. The chants, the threats, outside the locked car were muted by the doors and windows.

I was 24 and pretending to be a world-weary, experienced, foreign correspondent. The only angry blacks I had met previously was when a couple of under-the-weather Maoris had been pushed back in the queue at a charity fundraising, dirt oven, *hangi* in New Zealand.

I turned to Costigan and said something encouraging like 'Let's get the fuck out of here.' As the former motoring editor of the *Herald* Costigan wasn't bad on the pedal. He hit it hard and we did career out of there, but not before two protesters dragged up a slab of concrete about two feet wide and one foot deep and caved in the boot of the rental car. We got out of there, just, amidst screams of anger.

The next day, Martin Luther King's funeral was an extraordinary experience. Apart from the tangible, touchable, grief, it was one of the most amazing days in my life. Because of a bureaucratic bungle my Press pass was decreed null and void, a fact I discovered thirty minutes before the funeral. So did Murdoch's representative, Ray Kerrison. To make things worse Vice President Hubert Humphrey had just arrived at the Ebenezer Baptist Church and the Secret Service had, we were told, 'sealed' the area. Glad-wrapped it. Nobody in or out.

Kerrison and I were suddenly outside and in the cold. Amidst the 250,000 people, 99 per cent black, who were lining the streets outside the church.

Professionally thwarted I saw a column of black choir members pouring through the security screen, threading into the church. I nudged Kerrison, actually pushed him. Suddenly two white Australians were shuffling into church as part of the choir.

'We'll never get away with this,' he said.

'Shut up and watch me,' I said. 'They'll think we are very old sopranos or very young baritones.'

We got in and I watched American politics at work in a presidential year.

Richard Nixon was the only person I saw wearing TV makeup. Eight years after his narrow defeat by John Kennedy – which Kennedy's corrupt father bought although a lot of people had attributed it to Nixon's deadly five o'clock shadow in the televised debates – Tricky Dicky wasn't going anywhere without his pancake.

I did see one, telling, bit of political body language at the funeral. In the middle of an emotional tribute, with a bell-like soprano's black voice ripping your heart out, Nixon tried to make personal contact with Jackie Kennedy Onassis. She cut him dead. So did Bobby Kennedy. And Teddy.

I had bull-shitted and bluffed my way into King's funeral and I found myself on a balcony wedged between heaps of mourners and a large, perspiring, black man. People kept coming up to him and saying things like 'main man' . . . 'hey, top job' . . . 'you the best . . .'

It didn't take much for a foreign reporter to figure this guy might be important. He was. He was the undertaker, the man who had rebuilt Martin Luther King's shattered head. Recrafted it to such an extent that the thousands of mourners, who shuffled past his bier, did not know what a bloodied mess they were saluting.

The end of Martin Luther King Junior's funeral was one of the most moving, but in respect, most bizarre, moments of my professional career. The Ebenezer

Baptist Church was swarming with Secret Service men. Why not? Hubert Humphrey was there, Bobby Kennedy was there, Richard Nixon was there, and heaps of other heavies. Teddy Kennedy, Jackie Kennedy, Eartha Kitt.

When it was over the Secret Service men became insensitive bovver boys – pushing and bullying mourners. Moving us like sheep. I remember being pushed and pummelled down narrow and rickety stairs into the sunlight were 250,000 black mourners were venting their anger and their grief.

There was the authoritative demand 'Move it, move it'. Those guys had guns – and so you did. By a fluke I was pushed down the stairs, thanks to a bony elbow in my back and, literally fell into a single-file nightmare of mourners being shunted out of the Ebenezer Church. I was pushed into the procession and found myself wedged between a man named Bobby Kennedy and behind me, his wife, Ethel. The grieving crowd, having lost their best black hope, suddenly swamped their only white hope. It was a day of pain, a day of sadness, but the poor black people of Georgia, shouted 'Bobby! Bobby! Bobby!' As we shuffled along and being, literally, at his shoulder I wondered how can this man carry this pressure? His grey-suited shoulders were bent and wearied but the question was never answered. Two months later, to the day, he was dead. I sat in a church pew at his funeral too.

The obvious pain of the blacks in L.A. in 1992 jolted me back to Detroit in 1967. And Newark, and Cleveland and Atlanta in 1968. When other American cities were also burning. It was a time of high unemployment, hopelessness and racism that, even in one of America's most prosperous, most capitalistic cities, prompted the savage graffiti, 'Would the last person out of Detroit please turn off the lights.' It was a slogan later used for other embattled cities around the world and Down Under it became a slogan for a whole country, New Zealand, in the late 1970s and troubled 1980s.

I was a 23-year-old reporter, who had covered pain and suffering on police rounds in Sydney but, in truth, had been sheltered from the economic and racial torture that was tearing American society apart.

I had been living in New York for about a year when I was suddenly assigned to Detroit. The fact that Detroit was burning shocked me. This was America – the land of the free! Heaven on a stick! But Detroit, the car capital of the world, the consumer capital of the world – thanks to Ford, General Motors and Chrysler – was under the surface starting to feel the economic pressures which would emerge in the bruising, and painful, recession of the early 1970s. Unemployment figures were relatively high, especially among blacks, and welfare payments were frugal – sometimes non-existent. The ghettoes were still there and Martin Luther King's dream had eluded the minds and bellies of a lot of black Americans. In 1965 in Watts, in 1967 in Detroit, in 1968 in Newark (after King's assassination) the frustration, the disillusionment, the pain, didn't require much to unleash a destructive revenge. Even when it meant burning down your own suburb. I recall bewildered Australians, and equally ignorant middle-class Americans, expressing surprise that, in a race riot, blacks would torch their own suburbs. I tried to explain that when you are down, when you feel there is no hope, when agitators cry 'Burn, baby, burn', you don't give a shit about what you burn. What you destroy. A person with nothing doesn't think that the liquor store he torches might put two black people out of work. It burns because the bottles, the cartons, of liquor are reminders of something somebody in the street doesn't have and cannot afford. The race riots came because so much change was promised and so little actually eventuated. The marches, the sit-ins, the protests, had painfully and eventually given black Americans the right to sit anywhere on the bus but they hadn't put food on the tables or created more jobs. They did provide the international moral spark that forced other countries like Australia to look at despicable racist attitudes such as the 'White Australia' Policy. In fact if America had not shown such racial bravery in the early 1960s Apartheid would not have started to crumble in South Africa in the 1990s.

One of the big problems in America was that despite Martin Luther King and Bobby Kennedy and Ruth Parks saying she wasn't going to sit at the back of the bus anymore, the word had not seeped through into the grey matter of white policemen from Selma in the south to Chicago in the north. They were, in their minds, still dealing with nigras, coons and watermelon eaters. Tolerance and racial harmony were not expressions that popped up on the police blotter.

In 1992 it was a jury's verdict to acquit four police thugs (despite brutal and damning video evidence) that provided the torch for the flames that burned America's second biggest city: the City of Angels, the City of Dreams. The place that gave birth to Hollywood. In Detroit, 25 years earlier, the riot was triggered by a police raid on a sly grog hangout, a grotty, unlicenced gin mill. I think they called them 'blind pigs' in the 1960s. A joint where you could buy illegal but cheap rotgut whisky and take an escapist ride on an alcoholic magic carpet. The 'blind pig' raid started a riot that meant blood in the streets, 42 people dead and, eventually, National Guardsmen hunched behind machine guns in the doorways of Detroit hotels like the Sheraton-Cadillac where I had to step over sand-bags (and nervous troops) in the lobby to check in.

When I was suddenly assigned to the Detroit riots in '67 I should have twigged that these were different times. I was the only passenger on the plane. The TV news was telling people that Detroit was burning, dozens of people killed and hundreds injured. I climbed on the plane carrying my typewriter, and ordered a bloody Mary. When I ordered my second the flight attendant – a pretty blonde with a mass of teeth from Kansas City – perched on the armrest of my seat and started to interrogate me about funny accents and places like Australia. By the end of the flight to Detroit she was sitting in the next seat, showing a lot of stockinged thigh and, for some reason, playing her highly-varnished guitar, and singing a lot. That's why, I guess I laughed at Helen Reddy in *Airport* – and laughed even more at the spoof in *Flying High*.

Just before we landed the plane was given a different approach pattern because rioters, according to the earnestly strumming flight attendant, were shooting at planes. Then she excused herself. A minute later a disembodied voice came over the plane's intercom: something along the lines of 'Ladies and gentlemen (and me the only passenger) as we make our approach to the Detroit Airport would you please make sure your tray tables are stowed and your seats are in an upright position.' I could wear all that in the interests of airline rules and safety regulations, but then she said, in all earnestness, 'And we hope you have an enjoyable stay in the Detroit area.'

My plane had been diverted because it had been shot at. I looked out the window and could see spirals of smoke from a town in tatters, and she was wishing me a happy holiday?

I had left Manhattan in such a hurry I had no luggage: no toothbrush, no clean shirt, just the old Remington portable typewriter. What do you do, aged 23, when assigned to a riot in a strange city in a country you don't know or understand and when, to them, you talk funny? I walked off the plane and hailed a taxi.

The driver was big and very black. I said 'Take me to the riot.' He answered with something like, 'You've got to be joking.' With a few four-letter additions in there. Finally he agreed and drove me close to Twelfth Street which was smouldering and a no man's land for police and firefighters. The driver was nervous and sweating. 'You a mad mother, you foreign, I aint goin' no further, no how.' It was hard to argue with him because the way was blocked by two of the biggest, but busted, TV sets I had ever seen.

I paid him, got out, and walked past the broken shop windows and abandoned TV sets. The looting had stopped mainly because the streets were filled with National Guardsmen. I started to pick my way through the rubble and a voice with a twang told me to 'Back up buddy'. I kept going. After all, a Press pass is a bullet-proof vest, right? The part-time patriot warned me again to freeze. I kept walking towards him and stupidly plunged my right hand into the inside left pocket of my suit jacket to get my Press pass. Didn't get far. A National Guard captain, who was probably a mechanic at Bozzo's bash and crash shop for most of the year, had a massive rifle, with bayonet affixed, right on my throat, right on the vital bleeding area, within about two seconds. It sounds melodramatic I know but that part-time soldier, that weekend warrior, *wanted* to shoot me. They all did. Remember Kent State where four kids died and nine were wounded. The National Guard in America is a Coney Island shooting gallery on the prowl but with real bullets. Lucky for me he understood my accent as I talked my way out of it. Later that night I was scared shitless again hiding behind a police car, under fire on Twelfth Street and wondering where the next bullet was coming from. And they were coming.

Next day, safely in my guarded hotel room I felt bewildered. Growing up with Maoris in New Zealand I could honestly say, though never asked in those days, that there was not a racist bone in my body. It really was not an issue. Although, in retrospect, there must have been racist remarks made against the Maoris in my school years.

Mid-riot the governor of Michigan, a Republican and presidential candidate called George Romney gave a late-night press conference. We watched an inept performance from a politician who claimed he was brainwashed in Vietnam. It taught me something – at 2 a.m., with his main city burning, Romney paused before he entered the press conference to take his jacket off and turn up his cuffs. Calculating, posing, political bullshit. In Washington President Lyndon

Johnson played it tough. Romney asked for federal troops to stop his city burning. LBJ virtually told him to 'stick his presidential aspirations up a dead bear's bum'. The presidential message was, not in so many words, 'If you can't run your town you can't run this country.' Lyndon Johnson let Governor Romney squirm. Really squirm. He refused to commit federal troops as a major city burned. And Detroit was burning. Jesus, it was burning. Johnson just held out. Detroit had to get itself out of the shit. And it did. Sort of.

Cheers?

There have been days in recent years when I have not had a drink, when, as my dear old grandmother would say, alcohol has never passed my lips. Some days . . . but not many. And I can virtually remember every one of them. Trekking through the Sudan, a dry moslem country, during a ghastly famine, on a commune in the teetotal state of Gujurat in north-west India, in hospital waiting for a nose operation, in jail (well, somebody did sneak me one tot of rum there in twelve days) and for one month when I took a pledge for a boozeless thirty days to win a bet.

But that is not a very admirable or respectable record, when you consider that I have been around for about 11,000 days in my adult life and have gone without alcohol for less than 100 of them. It is not something of which I am proud and not something that is written as a boast. I actually admire people (including my wife) who do not drink at all any more. Not that long ago they would have been derided as party-poopers, wowsers or wimps. Remember when, at a party, a person would say 'no thanks' and the host's knee-jerk reaction would be: 'Come on, one won't hurt you.' And when the first light beers came on the market that sensible, low alcohol beverage was derided. Men in pubs would order a 'real beer' as if the only reason you drank was not for the taste or to slake a thirst but for the higher alcohol content. You only drank to get drunk. Teetotallers may find this surprising, but for a lot of drinkers that is not the motive. When they first came in low alcohol beers were nicknamed 'love on the beach' because they were 'fucking near water'. Things like liver damage, road carnage, loss of brain cells, didn't come into it.

It is true that Australians are, and have long been, among the heaviest consumers of alcohol in the world. Especially beer, although that is changing. We haven't had the lifelong tradition of wine with meals like the French and did not ever embrace the gruelling three-martini lunch of the Americans but we have guzzled high-alcohol beer in a torrent unmatched by most countries. The beer guts are proof of it. So is the road toll and our sickening statistics over domestic violence, wife bashing, and gang rape.

We are a nation of heavy drinkers. It's probably safe to generalise and say we are a nation of drunks. I admit to being a drinker. I admit to being a heavy drinker. There were times in my radio days when I would drink four bottles of wine a day. Every day. Starting around lunch-time after my three and a half hour radio programme had finished and continuing, sometimes, until after midnight. Like a lot of daily drinkers I have, over the years, used the argument that I may be a drinker but I am not an alcoholic because I can stop. And I have stopped. But that doesn't necessarily exclude you from the 'alcoholic' tag. There are alcoholics who don't have a drink for a month, or a year, or five years, but still live in fear of 'going on a bender', or breaking the pledge.

As I write this my wife has not had a drink for more than ten months and I respect that. One of my best friends is a member of Alcoholics Anonymous. Her commitment to one of the best support systems I have ever encountered, and it is worldwide, underlines the complex needs of people who just want to stop. Whether it be two gin and tonics a day or ten. People who again want to totally take charge of their lives and all their actions. And, be honest, if you are a drinker, a steady drinker – or especially a binge drinker – there are times you are NOT in control of your life. Not in control of all your actions or emotions. It may be as simple as going to the pub for two drinks after work and staying for twenty. It may be a case of phoning home and saying 'hold dinner for me' and arriving home plastered at 2 a.m. It may be a case of (male or female) waking up in a strange bed with a mouth like the bottom of a birdcage and a person whose name you can't remember on a Saturday or Sunday morning. It may be a case of not only not remembering how you got home but where you were, and with whom, the night before. All of these experiences from people, especially men, who boast they can handle their liquor.

It is true that alcohol is a big part of our culture, a huge daily part of our lifestyle, the way that *peyote*, cactus juice, was to the Mexicans; lip-numbing Kava was to the Polynesians and betel nuts to the South-east Asians. Of course the Romans were heavily into wine but that's not what wiped out their empire – they probably self-destructed with all the brain damage from drinking out of lead goblets. Come to think of it, if Caligula had owned a glass, he might have been a Rotarian.

Remember Timothy Leary in the 1960s and his 'tune in, turn on, drop out' drug trip? My theory is that a lot of Australians didn't get involved in drugs because they were already tripping on strong beer and flagons of bad red wine. We were already drug addicts before funny cigarettes and speedy pills came along. I know one of the reasons I did not try marijuana (even though I was living in 'try anything' hedonistic New York in the late 1960s) was because I figured I already had a daily drug called alcohol. And also pot didn't appeal because I don't smoke.

It shouldn't surprise anybody that alcohol is so imbedded in our society and in our daily lifestyle. We are brought up with it. It is so much a part of the way we are, that it wasn't so many blinks (or drinks) ago that anybody – especially any male – who did not drink was considered a bit strange. A bit of a girl, maybe a poof. And then of course we developed that special breed called the 'social drinker'. I have never had that adequately explained to me. Is a social drinker a person who doesn't drink much or often, or is he or she like that perfect guest who eats liver at a dinner party, even though they can't stand offal, just being polite?

I know what an 'anti-social' drinker is. The hoon who drinks heavily and then gets behind the wheel of a car.

Or the lout at the football, or cricket, who ruins it for other sports fans by a can-tossing, punch-throwing, pissing-in-public, foul-mouthed spectacular.

I guess I have to admit that I started drinking around the age of three or four. A lot of Australian and New Zealand kids did – with parental assistance and approval. Nothing sinister, it was part of the game of growing up. The memory of my first taste of alcohol (although it was probably earlier) was when I was about seven or eight. Sundays: roast dinner in the middle of the day, always roast leg of lamb, baked potatoes, baked parsnips, chunks of pumpkin in their skin, delicious-smelling gravy and, while all that was cooking, huge cauldrons of peas and beans and carrots having the bejesus boiled out of them on top of the stove. Dad would come in from mowing the lawns or hacking at weeds or doing the edges and have a beer before the big midday roast that everybody had to attend under penalty of death. When times were good, and that wasn't often, Dad would open a gassy bottle of lager. Sometimes he would explode the top from a frothing and yeasty, putrid, bottle of home brew but usually he would open a flagon – a half-gallon of slops – flat, warm, soapy beer served in returnable, refillable glass jars. The drinking was always done before the meal. We never drank anything while eating, not even water. Just 'put the jug on pet' for a cuppa afterwards.

On those Sundays, after listening to the hospital request session on the radio when most of the requests were for Wilfred Pickles' 'You will never grow old', for dying pensioners – Dad would let us kids have a small shandy: a peanut butter jar of flat beer fizzed up and sweetened by a heavy dose of lemonade. Nobody thought it at all strange that seven and eight-year-old kids were drinking alcohol. In fact I remember parents and other adults gooing and gaaing when a toddler, barely able to walk, would try to emulate Dad by wrapping tiny hands around the father's beer glass and taking a sip. Lots of laughs about 'taking after your father' and 'don't get pissed, son.' Nobody said it was wrong. Nobody talked about the dangers down the track. Cirrhosis . . . can't spell it let alone pronounce it. A toddler sipping Daddy's beer was considered cute.

And in those days Mums (mine included) did not stop drinking, did not stop smoking, during pregnancy. Some, in fact many, still don't despite the now documented medical risks that a smoking, drinking pregnant mother passes on to her unborn child. We'd all heard about smoking stunting your growth but I had never heard that a mother's smoking habit could stunt the growth and development of an unborn child. I recall that years later my mum and dad would laugh about her craving for stout whenever she was pregnant, never dreaming it could be harming her unborn child.

I always told my wife that if she ever got pregnant – even though I didn't want her to – I would give up drinking for the whole nine months of the pregnancy as a support thing, assuming that she would give up too.

It is intriguing, and I am really climbing back into the dusty memory bank here, that as a baby the taste, the maltiness, the bitterness of beer, seemed to have a genuine appeal. By the time I was six or eight the childhood palate was craving sweets: in those days sherbet sucked through a licorice straw, all-day suckers, huge sugary gob-stoppers, the first bubble gum and conversation lollies. But on Sundays, before the roast lamb, we had the lemonade-sweetened shandies, and by the time I reached twelve I was trying to sneak more than one pre-roast lamb drink.

Around that time of course we were experimenting with alcohol from that forbidden shrine in the lounge room or sitting room: the highly polished, walnut, cocktail cabinet. My parents' cabinet was pretty snazzy, with a fold-out front and a mirrored back and lots of expensive-looking glasses. There was the obligatory liqueur decanter, a funny little narrow-necked bottle with a glass-stopper that couldn't keep anything fresh and a frosted painting on the body of the bottle showing men in hunting jackets and hounds and other English countryside scenes. The decanters were always arranged on a tray in the midst of a miriad of tiny, similarly frosted thimble-sized glasses. Nine times out of ten the decanter was filled with crème de menthe. It tasted like toothpaste with a kick.

That's all MY parents' cocktail cabinet contained. Across the street at the Simpsons' it was a different story. They had money. Their bull-necked, red-faced father owned a factory and drove a shiny, British Mayflower. And they had two garages. Their cocktail cabinet was full of bottles of apricot brandy and sherry and a drink that looked like custard in a bottle, an unpronouncable spelling mistake called advocaat. We tested and tasted them all and when we sipped too much we filled them back up with water. The only ones we didn't like were the real firewater bottles like cognac and whisky. We couldn't understand how grown-ups could actually enjoy such throat-burning liquids.

At 14 we were high school daredevils and into home brew. Not making it – stealing it. My neighbour, who was news editor at the local paper the *Taranaki Herald*, (he would later become my boss in my first newspaper job) used to hold loud poetry readings and Shakespeare recitations at Saturday night parties. To fuel them he would make muddy, and in retrospect, sourly undrinkable home brew. As teenagers we would steal bottles of it from under his house, drink it, throw up, and then throw stones on his roof to stop the Hamlet recitations.

It wasn't that, as teenagers, we drank to get drunk (I don't now) but it was the excitement of something illicit, something that got young male hormones moving when there weren't many young female teenagers willing to help do the same. It is important to analyse – then and now – why people drink. Often to excess. For most people, as I said, I do not believe it is to get drunk. Although some people inexorably, deliberately do. They drink for the 'click' that Paul Newman talked about, as Brick, in *Cat on a Hot Tin Roof*. His character wasn't happy, wasn't at peace, hadn't blotted out some burr from the past until the alcoholic 'click' cut in. It is true, in real life, that some people drink to drown an emotional pain, to smother a real, or imagined, inadequacy, to paper over a broken love affair. To block out what they consider a boring, mundane life and job although some high-flyers with outwardly exciting lives and time in the fast lane often drink alcohol and take other mind-altering substances with a vengeance. People drink to numb the facts of a wrecked, wretched, or about to be scuttled, marriage. But for some people booze is there to be consumed just because it makes them feel good. Makes them feel released, confident, bold, whatever.

Personally, I have to concede that any man whose

adult life has reached 11,000 days and he has had less than 100 of those days in which alcohol has not passed his lips then – no beating about the bush here – you have to classify that man as a drunk. The fact that you can go a day, a week, a month without alcohol proves nothing, except perhaps that the subject is a disciplined drunk. But a drunk, nevertheless.

Alcoholics Anonymous is full of stories, full of people, who can and have gone weeks, months, even years, without a beer, without the sniff of a whisky bottle, but they have then gone on awesome, self-destructive, blinding, blitzing benders. Job-threatening, marriage-destroying, binges.

In Australia and in New Zealand and in the United States for that matter, we are hypocritical about alcohol and its ravages and its costs to the community, to the taxpayer and to our system. That has become more obvious, more apparent, with the increasingly successful federal and state campaigns against smoking. First there was the ban in the mid 1970s on tobacco advertising on television – the death of the Marlboro Man on TV years after several real men who played the cigarette-smoking Marlboro man had died from lung cancer. Then came the bans on magazine and newspaper advertising for cigarettes and in 1992 the Federal Government's announcement that all sporting sponsorships would be phased out by the mid to late 1990s and no new tobacco company/sporting alliances would be permitted. Moves I applaud, although I do not believe that smoking should be banned. People should be allowed to indulge their addiction, and that is what it is, in the privacy of their own home or with friends. I just don't want to be subjected to it in cabs, buses, trains, food stores, my office (it is banned) my home (it's been banned for 25 years) or other confined spaces.

Although I would not ban smoking I do agree with the graphic and explicit warnings on cigarette packets as to what can and probably will happen to you if you puff incessantly. And I really believe that similar warnings should be ordered on every beer, wine and liquor can or bottle in the country to acknowledge the medical and social casualties from excessive drinking. And I say that as the owner of Victoria's Macedon Ridge vineyard.

It's funny, strange, to try to write about drinking when you are a drinker. My dad was a heavy drinker. There was a time, long ago, when he reached the blackout stage. I have memory flashes of alcohol-fuelled family rows when I was about eight or nine. I know I staged a mock hanging on a piece of string hooked on the front door knob as a desperate diversion to stop my parents shouting at each other. And throwing things. It worked. I pretended I was choking although how you could hang yourself when your feet were still on the ground is a technicality I couldn't, and didn't need to, answer.

There were family rumours, that my grandfather used to roll home from the pub drunk as a skunk, night after night. My dad, they whispered in a small town, would have to go and get him and guide him in. Like father, like son – like grandson? I've sat in a pub, before it legally opened, aged eleven, while my Dad had a scotch and milk, a 6 a.m. heart starter after his early-morning milk run. I got the best, sweetest, syrupy raspberry cordial and lemonade. I can still recall the acrid smell of stale cigarette smoke, stale beer, and peas and carrot vomit. Six o'clock on a Saturday or Sunday morning. The bartender getting ready for the day was obviously a mate of my dad's. He had huge forearms like Popeye the Sailor as he mopped down the wooden bar. I took it all in.

An even bigger treat was when my dad delivered cold fresh milk to the local fish and chip shop. There, sometimes, they would take an ice-cold, strangely shaped bottle out of the freezer, and give me a treat. It was a newfangled thing called Coca-Cola.

Don't get me wrong and don't, too quickly, get too judgemental about MY family. Look at your own. We weren't the only family of drinkers in our small town.

One of the problems about grog is that our culture lionises booze. Adores it. Especially where sport is concerned. 'So he's a pisspot but can he hit?' 'He's a drunk but his on-field percentage is breathtaking.' Darren Millane was a Collingwood footie hero. He was also a thug. A drunken reckless, loose cannon, before he died in a booze-besotted car crash that, thank the Lord, didn't also wipe out a family man and his kids coming the other way.

We have, too often in the past, not only not encouraged non-drinkers, we have conspired and worked against them, in business and in government. Non-drinkers don't get the same sort of access to the boss who drinks alcohol. Cruel. Brutal. True. I actually believe, that the man who shares a few drinks after work with the boss has a better chance of his ideas, his projects, being accepted than the man who diligently heads off home to his wife and kids. The 'homebody' may be straighter, more trustworthy in the long run, more full-on for the company, but the cuff-shooter, the crapper, the ego-stroker may (in fact will) get the boss's ear in the pub and often, almost inevitably, the other man's promotion. Providing he can hold his liquor. I know. I have been there. The way that office politics, often involving millions, even billions, of dollars are played out in smokey bars and saloons is frightening.

People say 'Never trust a man who doesn't drink'. If you were smart, surely, you'd be saying 'Better than trusting a man who does'? It's a bit like the days when women, especially single women, could never get loans from the banks. (Before the loony, throw cash at them, days of the 1980s entrepreneurs and white-shoe brigade). I remember in the 1960s how silly, not to mention how unfair, it all seemed. The women's editor of the Melbourne *Herald*, a serious, responsible, talented female called Isobel Carter got knocked back for a housing loan. A middle-aged, single woman in a position of some power and responsibility. She got rejected at the same time as a young, larrikin, single police roundsman snared a bank loan even though he pissed at least half his weekly wage up against the urinal wall at Lou Richard's pub.

And speaking of pubs. If you are my generation (born 1944) or older you will remember this scenario, pre-breathaliser: office or factory floor – Monday morning. 'Jeez. What a great weekend. Don't remember getting home Sat'y night. Pissed as a fart. Drunk as a skunk. Woke up yest'y morning and saw the bloody car in the fish pond. I thought I'd left it up a tree. Haw, haw' etc.

That happened, or something similar, Monday after Monday. To be honest, years ago I did it. The office hero was the guy who couldn't remember how he had got home or WHO he had got home with. The more outlandish the story the better. The more macho the better. 'This bird was so ugly I had to chew my arm off to get out and get home . . . ' 'I didn't know her fucking name until I read the Christmas cards on her mantelpiece . . .'

When the office lair, the office boofhead, said (back in those days) he was so pissed he didn't remember driving home people gave honks of approval. Nobody said: 'You drunken, irresponsible, dickhead. You fucking selfish idiot. You drunken fool. You dangerous, mind-scrambled fool.' They should have done. But you don't tell people that. Especially not friends. It's even harder to tell a friend, 'You could have killed an innocent person. A mother, a father, a daughter . . a whole family.'

And I say that in the knowledge that most of us have done it. To my shame I have done it. Wherever I went in the 1960s, as a foreign correspondent based in New York and doing stories from about forty American states, I went first class and often ended up drunk on somebody else's money. But shit, and you don't have to believe this, we worked hard. Worked like dogs. And, I'll admit, often drove rental cars under the influence. Madness. Life was fast, glamorous, front row seats at the big news stories. It was America. It was also madness. Reckless madness.

I remember one time covering a moon shot from Mission Control in Texas. That was out in the boondocks, on NASA Boulevard One near Galveston Bay. I was also trying to cover a comeback fight in Houston, for the irrepressible, and in those days still handsome Muhammad Ali – the former Cassius Clay. Ali was a gentleman, a gem. I think he was about to fight his former sparring partner Lester Ellis or the gutsy Irishman, Jerry Quarry. No matter, after three years out of the ring for opposing the Vietnam war and – 'I ain't got no fight with no Viet Cong' Ali had no problem with Ellis or Quarry. While travelling horrendous distances at all hours in the rented Cadillac – trying to be in two places at once – I was driving even further for late night drinks with a tall blonde model from Baton Rouge with eyes as blue as a bayou. I hate to recall how many times, dog-tired and full of bourbon, I would drive through the soupy fog rolling in off Galveston Bay at 4 a.m. The air conditioner would be on full bore. I'd have my head out the window trying to get some breeze to help the heavy eyes stay open and even then would have to slap my own face to make sure I didn't doze off behind the wheel. It was criminal irresponsibility. A few years later I would reminisce and wonder how I didn't kill myself. With all the selfishness of youth I didn't even think that I could have killed somebody else. Could have killed innocent people.

But that's the way drinkers go. That's the way heavy drinkers think. You don't think about the personal, professional, community costs. You block out the times over the years, when booze has caused a stubbed toe, a broken rib, a torn suit, cigarette burns, cars dented, punches thrown, relationships bruised or busted. The 'big drink' is really a terrible thing. Something that can, and does, destroy lives. Anybody who says that he or she has it under control is either a liar or a cheat. Sometimes I suspect I may be both.

Saluting the Anzacs

Cold mashed peas and Vegemite sandwiches: I think of them one day every year even though I haven't tasted any since I was about twelve years old. And don't intend to. Cold, claggy, green peas smeared on to thin slices of white bread already coated with butter and Vegemite.

I think of that weird culinary 'treat', and taste them in my mind, every April 25. Every Anzac Day. They remind me of my dad and his mates and the prices they paid, the sacrifices they made, so that I am still here, living in precious freedom, to do and write and say the things I want to. Even in this book.

Mashed pea and Vegemite sandwiches probably sound revolting to most people. Understandably. But to me they bring back warm memories of Australasian heroes. Diggers. Anzacs. For years, every Anzac Day, my dad would get up in the dark and head off into town for the dawn service. He would then march in the parade with his World War II mates, go to the Returned Servicemen's club for a few (or inevitably a lot of) drinks and, at some hour as darkness approached, would roll home with his wartime cronies.

It was the one night when my mother would not snipe at him over his unsteadiness of step or his slurring of speech. The veterans would all roll home, florid of face and beery of breath, and talk about the time that 'Simmo got the big one', and how, if my dad hadn't dived behind an old truck at Guadalcanal, the gunfire that tore the vehicle apart would have torn him and his mate apart, and how my dad had ended up in the 'hoosegow', the stockade, because he had gone AWOL to see my mother and me when I was born in February, 1944.

Anzac Day was the only day in the year that we saw some of them. Every April 25 they would come to our house, medals clanking and voices rasping after a day of emotional, hard-talking, reunions. Sharing thoughts about the ones, the teenagers, who didn't make it home. They would swap the same stories, the same old stories, and crack the same old jokes. We would sit, sometimes uncomprehendingly, on the sidelines and listen. And every year my mum would put out the plate of cold mashed peas and Vegemite sandwiches: 'mock asparagus' sandwiches. We called them 'mock asparagus' because we didn't have enough money to buy real asparagus. In fact, we didn't have enough money to buy canned asparagus let alone the real thing. To be honest, having never seen asparagus raw, I thought it actually did come in cans. It certainly didn't look like a real vegetable to kids raised on cabbage, peas and beans.

To a kid, time is a warp, an intangible. I did not realise until decades later that, at ten and eleven years of age, I was handing out those 'mock asparagus' sandwiches to men who only ten years earlier had been killing other men in places like New Guinea and Guam and Guadalcanal. Men in their early thirties who had seen so much death. Had seen their mates' guts spilled in remote jungle places like the Kokoda trail.

One of my dad's mates had lost a leg and had a primitive, creaking artificial replacement. Another had lost an eye and others had mental scars you couldn't see. Maybe that is why I call my old man every Anzac Day to tell him that I love him. They were a generation that, like their fathers in World War I, paid a price we who followed can never repay.

I remember that annual ritual from the time I was about nine until I left home at seventeen and still feel anger when younger Australians claim, erroneously, that Anzac Day glorifies war. It doesn't. It glorifies peace.

The night before every Anzac Day Mum would get out and press the suit that my dad only wore to weddings, funerals, visits to the bank manager – and Anzac Day. The lapels were too wide and the suit jacket too tight. Each year I would take a piece of cardboard, cut slots in it and feed my father's war medals through it so that the cardboard would protect his campaign ribbons when I attacked the medals with Brasso. I would smother them with cleaner until they went dull and chalky and then buff and burnish them with zeal until they sparkled under the kitchen light. It was an annual job I cherished. They were exotic medals to be handled in awe. Heavy and mysterious from a world a ten-year-old could not know about and a world a father would not talk about. The medal ribbons were sewn on to a piece of wire so that they sat flat like a row of soldiers. I remember they were heavier, felt more precious, than any coin I had ever known. To a kid in New Zealand they were an awesome, magical, sort of currency. I could not know how much blood had been spilled, how much hurt and pain, had gone into their creation. You didn't know how many people died for your father's right to wear them. In those days you didn't ask 'What did you do in the war, Daddy?' And, anyway, he wouldn't have told you.

Looking back with the blood of Korea, Vietnam and the Gulf War behind us I can now, sort of, comprehend the faraway look in a Digger's eye. Can understand and empathise with the frenetic, desperate, pace of the Anzac Day drinking from the first nip of rum at the dawn services.

By the time I became a teenager the annual Anzac night medal-polishing ritual expanded to include my own bits and pieces of military brass. I had become the lead drummer in the local high school band in which we wore abrasive, neck-chafing, khaki serge uniforms and Glengarry caps. The night before Anzac Day I would still drag out the Brasso to burnish my father's medals but I would also attack my own brass buttons and cap badge from the New Plymouth Boys' High School cadet battalion.

Every year, as the lead drummer in the school battalion, I would march to places like the town cenotaph and the local cemetery's war memorial. Resplendent in khaki uniform, corporal and then sergeant's stripes, and white gloves with huge starched cuffs, I would pound a constant roll on the side-drum while the bugler blew the goosebump-producing mournful notes of 'The Last Post' followed by the full-of-hope, revivalist 'Reveille'. The plinth of the cenotaph was festooned with wreaths and the nearby church had a sloping lawn that was covered in row after heart-breaking row of white, wooden crosses. Each had the name of a dead soldier on it. Each had a red poppy pinned to it. It looked like a miniature Flanders field. And years later you realise they were all so young. So tragically young.

At the cenotaph, an ominous dark grey heap of stone, we would regroup as a military band and the drummers – buttons and badges gleaming – would posture with chests like pouter pidgeons as we played staccato marching music, 'street beats', as the Diggers marched past.

On such a day a wink from your own dad, as he marched past, was like being given a gold sovereign.

Later, after the parade, the kids would laugh about old so-and-so, the town soak, who, obviously, had had more than a nip of rum at the Dawn Service. But we were too young and too innocent – and life was too sweet – for us to wonder about or question what he may have gone through, or what sacrifice he may have made, or what he may have seen in the slaughterhouses of the Somme or Gallipoli.

Men like him risked their lives, and some of his mates lost their lives, so that their wives and kids (and their sons' wives and kids) could live a life and a lifestyle that the jackboot and the samurai tried so ruthlessly to eliminate.

World War I of course was even more selfless, more

extraordinary, for Australians. This raw-boned, awkward, naive and tentative country at the arse-end of the world was only (post-Federation) fourteen years old. People still thought of themselves as Victorians first, or New South Welshman first, and Australians second. (In Queensland they still feel that way but that is a different story for a different time).

Three hundred thousand of Australia's best and brightest, and certainly our most scarce, volunteered to fight a war 12,000 miles away. They volunteered. It is true that many, especially country boys, saw it as a great adventure. 'Come on mate, you gotta be in it.' And 60,000 of them died in some of the dirtiest, bloodiest slaughter this century, or any century, has ever seen.

They came from small towns, with often unpronouncable names, from all over Australia and New Zealand. They signed up, volunteered, 'to kill Fritz'. They were indeed 'wild colonial boys' and they won a reputation for guts and bravery that stunned the enemy and impressed their allies. Fathers, brothers, fiancés. Hardly a family got through without being touched. If you think back to childhood days we all knew of the 'widow Smith' whose husband didn't come back from the war. (In those days it was a scandal to even think of marrying again.) Or Jimmy the garbage collector who talked to himself because he went strange in the Army, or the old man who spoke funny because of something called mustard gas. And there was always old Charlie with the gammy leg. It was selfless courage that, truthfully, in this increasingly 'I'm all right, Jack' cynical world, I wonder if we will ever see again. Next time, like in the Gulf War, the killers on both sides will increasingly become anonymous, button-pushing vaporisers.

We haven't done our returned servicemen justice. Diggers in Repat hospitals are treated like shit. It is not a shame it is a national scandal. Victims of the *Voyager* disaster have gone decades without compensation from successive Liberal and Labor governments. Agent Orange victims from Vietnam have been treated like lepers. These days, as the memories of the Anzacs and their heroics fade, the word 'poppy' is more synonymous with opium and mind-bending heroin than with the gallant, but horrific, price so many Aussies paid.

Even on Remembrance Day, November 11, things have changed. The one or two minutes silence at 11 a.m. on the 'eleventh of the eleventh' is now ignored by many. Some radio stations don't even observe what used to be a sacred, emotional, national moment.

Now, November 11 (apart from Ned Kelly's hanging) is remembered as the day that the 'tippler in the top hat', that snide and secretive assassin, John Kerr, did his dastardly work on an elected Prime Minister, Gough Whitlam. And even that is a mere memory, a footnote in history, to a lot of Australians.

Paul Keating, years later, presciently talked about the risks, the real chance, of Australia becoming a 'banana republic' unless we lifted our game. I thought we became one on November 11, 1975 when a silver-haired snake, using alleged powers that the Queen could not even invoke, sacked a democratically-elected government. I have never felt the same about this place since.

Once a year, the memories of those mashed green pea and Vegemite sandwiches bring it all back.

Suffer Little Children

The following wire service report from Australian Associated Press churned out of the fax machine in my Hawaiian holiday house in December, 1991:

> HINCH CAMPAIGN UNDERMINED GLENNON
>
> A Catholic priest has been cleared of child sex charges after an appeal court found it had been impossible for him to get a fair trial because of a media campaign by broadcaster Derryn Hinch.
>
> The Full Supreme Court today freed 47-year-old Father Michael Glennon from a nine year and one month jail term imposed after his conviction for sexually assaulting children at a youth camp.
>
> In its ruling the Full Court effectively blamed Hinch for undermining the criminal justice system, and said his campaign was responsible for possible sex offences going unpunished.

> Hinch went to jail for 12 days in 1987 and paid a $15,000 fine after being found guilty of contempt of court for prejudicing Father Glennon's trial. Outside court today, Father Glennon said he had forgiven Hinch and that he prayed for him.
>
> Father Glennon had pleaded not guilty to three counts of indecently assaulting children under 16 years, one count of attempted buggery with a boy under 14 years and one count of buggery with violence.

I read it and variously felt nauseated and angry. When that news came through it was undoubtedly one of the low points of my life. Lower even than the day I went to jail over the very same Michael Glennon.

Suddenly Hinch had become the villain not the convicted priest. The ultimate betrayer. There was a rush of television, radio and newspaper requests for comment and I lashed out. At that stage I had not seen the sanctimonious pictures of Father Glennon clutching a cross and supposedly praying for my soul.

Ironically, on that very day in Hawaii when the news came through, I had spent several hours trying to help a brave American woman in her campaign to have her ex-husband charged – on overwhelming video and medical evidence – with the rape of their young son. Also advising her on a book she was writing for abused kids.

As she correctly pointed out there are now, finally, lots of books about child abuse written by adults about their childhood traumas. Horror stories about teenage girls, even much younger girls, being robbed of their innocence, their precious childhood, by a father, a stepfather, a grandfather, uncle, cousin or family 'friend'. But there are few, if any, books written for children when they are children. Books designed to show them that they are worthwhile, that they can still have self-esteem and, most importantly, that 'it was not their fault.' That they could still, as she put it, 'create their own dream castle' and put the nightmare behind them.

At the other end of a fax machine in Hawaii I did not know, for some time, the vehemence of the 2–1 Supreme Court judgment. But I did know that suddenly I was being front-paged as the guilty party, not a Catholic priest with a prior jail sentence for sex crimes against children and now freed on what I will always maintain was a technicality.

I also did not know that I was being trashed in some wildly inaccurate newspaper editorials – especially one which appeared in the Sydney *Telegraph Mirror* under the headline 'Hinch must elevate his ethics'. It said things like 'True to form, the star of the hour will tell us the court's decision makes his flesh crawl, or some such, and will eschew responsibility for a blue which lowers the standing of his profession. But that's Derryn Hinch. That's life. And that stinks!'

In another, inaccurate, swipe the unsigned editorial also said, 'It would take a cynic indeed to suggest that TV ratings motivated Mr Hinch's dramatic revelations of the priest's previous conviction for assault while the trial was still in progress.'

A cynic indeed. The crime for which I went to jail occurred in 1985–86. I was convicted of contempt of court in 1986 and did not start on television until 1988.

Not only was Glennon's trial not in progress, it was years away from starting.

On that personal Black Friday I read the AAP story a number of times, did some radio and television interviews and challenged Glennon to sue me as I continued to call him a convicted child molester and disgraced priest. Then I sat down while the facts and the emotions were still fresh in my mind and wrote this. One irony not lost on me was the fact that a full, three-man, Supreme Court appeal in Victoria had voted 2–1 to release Glennon from jail. Back in 1986 the Appeal Court's vote that ultimately sent me to jail was 2–1 against me. In 1992, in a 4–3 judgment the High Court overturned the Supreme Court appeal verdict and sent Glennon back to jail to serve his sentence. (The High Court also instructed the Victorian Supreme Court to hear, and rule on, another welter of Glennon appeals. In August 1992 that court rejected all of Glennon's remaining appeals. After nearly six years of tension (plus jail) for me, and after nearly a dozen court appearances by the ultimately discredited priest, it was over. I was vindicated. He was back in jail to serve the custodial sentence he so richly deserved.)

If anything, the Glennon news renewed my commitment to a cause and a slogan for which I have been sometimes lampooned: 'Who's looking after the children?' Over the years I have had the proof driven home to me time and time again that obviously the states, the courts, the churches are not.

To be honest I had almost convinced myself (or to be more honest almost been convinced by others) that I had become obsessed by, and obsessive about, paedophiles. Probably because I had been molested as a child.

I didn't believe it and still don't believe it. If that experience – my penis naively coaxed into the mouth of a family friend's brother visiting New Zealand from Australia – had been such a searing, lasting scar surely I would have written about the issue, campaigned on the issue much earlier in my thirty-odd years of journalism. (And, truly, this is not a case of 'he protesteth too much.')

As editor of the *Sun* newspaper in Sydney in the mid-1970s I didn't crusade, stridently, blindly, passionately in that newspaper's pages on the issue of child abuse. It is true I ran a few stories about light sentences for repeat offenders but in no different fashion to the way my newspaper handled stories on light sentences, slap on the wrist sentences, for rapists, drunk drivers and recidivists. One topic I recall that we did campaign on was the carnage on our roads especially when culpable drivers, who had spread the limbs and brains of totally innocent people over our roads and highways, were not even getting charged with manslaughter.

Without apology, I ran graphic, even horrific pictures of road crashes in centrespread features on the Friday before a long weekend as part of a generally futile campaign to shock people into driving more carefully and not driving if they drank.

There was one case around Christmas 1976 when I targeted a deviate known as 'Mr Magic' on the front page of the *Sun*. From memory he was a former New Zealand dentist with a scungy criminal record in that country and a habit of hypnotising his female patients in the dentist's chair. His unsavoury background was obviously why he washed up in Sydney like a lot of New Zealand crims.

I decided to run Mr Magic's criminal record on page one with the headline 'Why isn't this man in jail?' after he virtually walked free from yet another charge after being caught peering in an eight-year-old girl's bedroom window late at night.

'Mr Magic' led to MY first personal experience of the long (political) arm of the law.

On Christmas Eve I received an apparently friendly call from the New South Wales Attorney General, Frank Walker. He invited me to visit his office. It was Christmas Eve and I was more keen to spend ten minutes with colleagues or family rather than an hour with a politician and, I guess, intimated as much. I declined. His voice got cold. 'This call is from the Attorney General to the editor of the *Sun* newspaper. It would be in your best interests to get here within the hour.'

I went. He was serious. He came on like a friend, then a headmaster and told me how he could and probably should send me to jail for contempt and insisted on a letter guaranteeing that the *Sun* would never again print somebody's criminal record.

I gave no commitment, walked free from his office, enjoyed my Christmas break, talked to my lawyers, and no letter was ever forthcoming. Ten years later I would do time for contempt of court over some other deviate's actions involving children.

As I tensed for the phone calls following the news report of Glennon's release, it suddenly seemed the whole, sordid saga was all my fault. Obviously I hadn't allowed for the hypocrisy. The courts. The Department of Public Prosecutions. In retrospect I believe they should all jostle for position to shoulder the blame. I don't use the word hypocrisy lightly, loosely, or recklessly. I don't believe, generally, in conspiracies (here or abroad) and I have gone on record as saying that although I lost 5–0 in the High Court hearing that ultimately put me behind bars I felt, quite honestly, at least in that court, I had had a fair and full hearing. I didn't like the result but an appearance before the High Court, even the granting of 'special leave' to garner an appearance, is an earned privilege not a right.

But when it comes to blame – and when it is being publicly sheeted home to me because a priest convicted of sexually abusing children is walking free – I believe some things have to be clarified.

Years ago I instructed my skilled, conservative barrister, John Winneke, to make an appeal to the court on Day One of my trial, to the presiding judge, Mr Justice Peter Murphy, for an adjournment of my case. I instructed him to (in legal terms) 'strenuously' ask the trial judge for an adjournment of my case until after the Glennon case had been aired in court.

I am not brilliant in law, but I have spent a lot of time in courts, have been around lawyers and courts for many years, and thought I was stating the obvious.

It seemed obvious to me that if I was being paraded on a contempt of court charge which, in my head, amounts to a perversion of justice charge, then morally, we should do what ever we could to make things as straight and as legal as possible. To try not to taint, in any way, the Glennon trial.

It was a genuine, honest, moral and (I thought) legal stance that the judge and the prosecutors would jump at. After all, their whole *raison d'être* for going after me appeared to be a desire to protect the legal status quo and the rights of a defendant. And shut me down. As a layman, it seemed to me that if I had in fact committed an offence, a contempt of court that could poison Glennon's trial, then surely my trial should be postponed, leap-frogged, until after his trial in case the publicity surrounding a Hinch legal circus tainted Glennon's legal status.

My lawers legitimately feared that publicity surrounding my contempt trial – which ended up making page one headlines in newspapers around the country – could compound the contempt. They honestly feared that court reports of the Hinch case could, in fact, prejudice Glennon's chance of getting a fair trial. It was not a ploy by us to avoid my own day of judgement. It was not an attempt to avoid the unavoidable or the inevitable. It was a genuine attempt to match, or touch, the courts in their legal heart. It was a genuine attempt to legally alert the court to a possible (even probable) problem. Those problems I tried to flag in court back in 1986, came back to bite my reputation and ethics right on the balls in 1991.

We tried so hard to 'park' my trial behind Glennon's. My journalistic nose smelled the headlines and the legal problems if we went ahead first.

With no disrespect for Mr Justice Murphy, and remember I was there, he seemed to give it scant consideration. Both judge and prosecutor appeared keen, to use the vernacular, to 'get it on'. And maybe Justice Murphy was right. Maybe he believed that the Glennon trial was eons away. As it turned out it was more than four years down the track.

Frankly, I believe the decision to uphold Glennon's appeal and let him out of jail was an insult to the intelligence of the jurors who originally, and diligently, found him guilty.

Supposedly they were tainted by my actions, by my comments, all those years before. Two appeal judges found that – one did not. To me it is ludicrous. Think about it. Supposedly a jury was so tainted by my behaviour all those years ago that they were mentally manipulated and brought down a verdict that wrongfully put a man behind bars. Their minds poisoned by something said five years before. And yet jurors can be told, by a judge, to ignore something prejudicial they heard in court five SECONDS earlier let alone five days, five weeks or five years.

I actually, quite fervently, believe that jurors take their commitment seriously and do their jobs earnestly. That old classic movie *Twelve Angry Men* wasn't too far off the real-life mark. A good example in Australia was the jury that had to sit on the court case following the savage slaying of two Victorian policemen in Walsh Street, South Yarra. The case got huge publicity. Understandably massive, sustained, mega-publicity. The newspapers, magazines and TV news services were filled with lurid, gory details. Two fresh-faced young cops were dead. Gunned down in the dawn hours in an ambush in a fashionable Melbourne suburb. If you didn't cry when you saw their funerals on TV then you would have to have ice in your veins.

Despite all that powerful, emotional, pre-trial publicity the Walsh Street jury brought in verdicts of not guilty beyond reasonable doubt. Not guilty 'beyond reasonable doubt' on the evidence put before them. They did not, necessarily, find anyone innocent of the crimes. They found them not guilty beyond reasonable doubt. And that is the way our legal system is set to work.

The other canard about prejudicing a trial is that I, supposedly, committed some heinous crime by revealing Michael Glennon's prior convictions. And, it is true, I did reveal them.

I know of some veteran lawyers who almost clutched their hearts in shock and some judges in the Melbourne Club gloated and slapped each other's backs when I finally went to jail for my sins. A man is innocent until proven guilty . . . you cannot undermine the system . . . the law is the law is the law . . . etc. We must preserve and maintain the probity and the sanctity of the courts . . . etc. You must not reveal a defendant's history, his prior record, etc.

And yet every two-bit court reporter, not to mention every magistrate, every lawyer and every judge, knows that prosecutors, especially police prosecutors in Magistrate's Court, reveal priors almost on a daily basis. In bail application after bail application the police opposing the granting of bail say things like, 'Your honour, this man has 27 prior convictions for car theft and a history of jumping bail. We oppose the granting of bail in this case.'

Those details can be, and are, reported in the daily newspapers. In fact, in Glennon's own case his prior record, including the fact that he had spent time in jail for child molesting, was introduced into open court three months before I said anything about him on radio.

In general I do not believe in conspiracy theories. They are usually merely stuff-ups. But I had been warned that some people in the Department of Public Prosecution were out to get me. Around the courts I was being painted as a lawyer-hating 'cowboy' and 'Hinch must be stopped' was a prevalent slogan at the DPP. I was accused of thumbing my nose at the courts and that was just not true.

I recall one night at a function at Parliament House in Spring Street, Melbourne, an Australia Day function to which I had been invited wearing my other hat as Jacki Weaver's husband (my wife being on the committee that voted on who would be Australian of the Year.)

In the middle of some light-hearted cocktail party banter I was suddenly confronted by one John Cain, Premier of Victoria. That creased-faced, outwardly friendly, avuncular, 'premier of all the people', earnest, plodding and (as it eventually turned out) economically discredited state leader. Everybody's uncle, who was in fact a jugular-seeking street-fighter, suddenly turned on me between trays of canapés and said: 'You are going to jail.'

Before I could try to get odds or find out how he was so sure Premier Cain spat 'Remember your priors! Remember your priors!' His opinion was right. I did go to jail. But as I write this, within hours of Michael Glennon slipping through a clever legal loophole my anger is not with a premier but with a system that lets a man go free who cruelly, cynically, despicably, used children – little kids – for his own sexual gratification, while masquerading as a compassionate, caring man of the cloth. The only, scant, consolation, is that according to the early wire service reports Glennon said that he would never again work with children. As I said in several radio interviews I hope somebody got that in writing.

On radio and in print, after his freedom, I again called Glennon an evil man. A user and abuser of children. The ultimate 'poacher in the sanctuary'. I can still see the letter from a former Glennon altar boy. It was a suicide note. Before he killed himself he wrote a last note in which he named Michael Glennon and said that the priest would be pleased by the news of his death. It was a letter I had in my possession but could not use, publish or publicise, until after Glennon's conviction. A letter that the jurors never, ever, heard about or read in court or during their sequestered deliberations.

I thought of that letter as I sat in the courtroom for Glennon's sentencing and listened as an old, perspiring, well-meaning but misguided Irish priest twisted and squirmed as he gave 'character' evidence for a fellow man of the cloth. Twisted and squirmed because he was defending a man who had already spent time in jail for molesting children. The priest's defence made a mockery of Jesus Christ's quote: Suffer little children.

Some of them certainly suffered under the mental pressure and the physical body weight of Michael Glennon. Keep in mind that Glennon's batch of charges – on which a jury convicted him but an appeals court freed him – included allegations of sexual offences against children that reportedly occurred less than a month after he was released from jail the first time!

It points to the inevitable fact that I will (again) be vindicated over the poisonous priest. Sadly, inevitably, he'll offend again. Some other young boy or girl will suffer. What hope is there for a man who re-offends against kids less than a month after being released from jail?

And another child's innocence will have been stolen. A letter that also sticks in my mind was from the father of one of his alleged victims – a little boy in Adelaide. He was flown to Melbourne to give evidence in yet another Glennon child-sex trial. In that case Glennon, accused of rape, was acquitted. The young boy got so agitated in the witness box he broke down, sobbed, and was unable to continue with his evidence. In the court corridor, with the police prosecutor almost in tears, the terrified boy vomited.

I have said ad nauseum on radio and television and in newspaper columns that the way our laws are structured in this country if you are a paedophile, the younger your victim the less chance of being caught, and if caught the less chance of going to trial, and if charged the less chance of being convicted. Our courts do not accept the uncorroborated evidence of witnesses under fourteen years of age. Most courts still have a ban on video evidence, painfully recounted by young victims. Most courts now insist on evidence that gives the exact date and time of an alleged offence – even if an incest offender has raped his daughter or son fifty times over a couple of years.

It sounds brutal but what the courts are in fact saying to child molesters is: get them young and get them often. If caught, a molester's victim may not be allowed to testify against him. And if called, his (or her) evidence may be rejected on the grounds that they are too young or that their evidence is uncorroborated. And if you assault them often enough they won't be able to remember the exact dates or times and their evidence will be discounted.

And then, I guess, if all else fails and you do get

caught, and tried, and convicted and jailed for nine years – you hope that some radio commentator has made the mistake of going public in a last, desperate attempt to stop you. That's justice.

The news of Glennon's freedom had a profound effect on me. Rather than bruising me it built me. Rather than staining me it sustained me. Sitting there, safe and comfy in a Hawaiian country club, I decided to become really personally committed to the cause of molested children. Really committed. For years I have been a member of the greatest children's charity in the world, the Variety Club, and am a former divisional president but the Glennon news hit me and bit me hard. Until that wire service story came through I cared but I wasn't really a committed crusader for kids. I tried to be. Now it is passionate. Now, since Glennon, it is MY cause. I am proud of the slogan, for which I am sometimes mocked, 'Who's looking after the children?' I'll admit that for a while there it was a catch-cry that had me mocked and scoffed at. It almost had me apologising for my so-called 'obsession'. Well from now on it will be a proud obsession. As an adult with no biological children of my own I can think of no more noble a cause. None.

By the time this book is published I will have launched a new, national, child protection society. It will be called PEACH – an acronym for Protect Every Australian Child Here. Our motto: So precious, so easily bruised.

One of our early aims will be to have uniform laws in every state to protect victims of child crime. I know it sounds fascist but I want a national register of convicted child molesters so that they don't, (as they have) get jobs in government departments like Community Services. And, most importantly, the Education Department.

I remember one rockspider, a school principal I exposed on radio. The Education Department seemed more concerned about preserving its reputation than flushing out a child molester. Almost like the Catholic Church's policy of moving a problem rather than confronting it. Forget, or ignore, the physical or mental wounds of the victim.

This school principal boasted at a paedophiles meeting (that was bravely, and secretly, bugged) that the best way to meet potential child victims was to get a job as a weekend taxi driver. As people like me highlighted the problems facing families with predators stalking their kids more and more parents were reluctant to let their children use public transport. 'They send their kids to and from parties by taxi.' Perfect. Especially at weekends. Especially on Saturday nights. That was the night that this school principal and charged child molester – his name was Bussey – worked as a driver for Silver Top cabs in Melbourne.

When I found that out I went on air on 3AW in Melbourne and announced a one-man boycott of Silver Top. I said as long as that man drove a cab for Silver Top I would not ride in one of their taxis. Would not hail one, would not flag one, would not phone and book one. And I recommended that other people do the same. The boss of Silver Top finally called me and said I was being unfair. It was out of his control. He could not sack or suspend a driver. It was all up to the taxi bureau etcetera. I said I didn't care. As long as he had a man working for him who boasted he worked as a taxi driver mainly as a way to meet and molest kids he would not have my custom. Or, I hoped, my radio station listeners' patronage. After 48 hours Silver Top suspended their predatory driver.

Bussey was, in fact, a classic case of the 'poacher in the sanctuary'. He was a high school principal who targeted and then zeroed in on the young teenage sons of troubled women. Divorced or struggling, separated women. As school principal he would tell the already emotionally (and often financially) stressed mother that he understood. That their sons needed a 'father figure', needed a 'male anchor'. He would glibly convince the vulnerable mother that, maybe, she needed a day to herself, needed a break from the pressures of being a single mother trying to bring up teenage fatherless boys. He would even – nudge, nudge, wink, wink – offer the plausible theory that maybe she should have a couple of days away from the kids and maybe go out on a date or at least spend some time in other adults' company.

Bussey would offer to take the young boys off their mother's hands for a weekend. A couple of days away camping with their school principal. What could be more noble. More innocent. A mother, overwhelmed by such a caring attitude from a teacher, wouldn't think twice about it.

Once away, Bussey would do such cunning and deviate things as deliberately pour water on a boy's sleeping bag and then insist that the youngster should discard his sopping bag and spend the night in the principal's sleeping bag.

Another potential victim under threat.

Suffer little children.

After I submitted the manuscript for this book I had lunch at a Japanese restaurant with several clever and articulate executives from Penguin Books. The lunch turned into a spirited discussion about violence – spurred by my essay on boxing. Two, sophisticated, professional women could not understand how I could publicly abhor violence and yet write a sort of paeon to punching. How I could admit to going to, and enjoying, heavyweight boxing matches. From that frank discussion (which I think I lost) we drifted into yarns about life overseas, my time as a foreign correspondent covering tumultuous events in often exotic places and then they sort of edged towards a discussion on some of the things I had said (and hadn't said) about personally being the victim of a child molester.

In the debate on adult violence they came out with guns blazing. On the personal issue of child violence, sexual violence, they used velvet gloves. Beneath the velvet there was a need for answers to a lot of questions. Not only what really happened to me, when molested by a man as a child, but how it affected me, and why I had glossed over it in my manuscript.

Was I reluctant to talk about it? Was I scared? Embarrassed? Scarred? My only fear about talking about a mercifully brief childhood betrayal is that I will be misconstrued. That my genuine concern for the victims who face lifelong shadows from their forced experiences will be taken out of context when I say, yet again, that 'Yes, I was molested but, no, it didn't affect me.' That somehow it will give some bizarre support to the predators who claim 'child-love' is not unhealthy if I commit to print that an adult male acquaintance of my parents once pounced on me, put my penis in his mouth, and I suffered no apparent lasting trauma or damage.

Still, if it adds something to the debate – but more importantly if it helps one other kid caught in the same situation – then I am prepared to describe what happened to me as a child and how people reacted.

In the early 1950s, with not much money about and with a World War less than a decade behind them, my parents and their friends looked forward to simple 'at home' Saturday night parties. On a 'big night' they would go to the local aero club for a few flat beers and 'coloured drinks for the girls'. But most Saturday nights one couple in the group would put on a BYO party at their home. One Saturday night, when I was about ten years old, Mum and Dad hosted a party for ten or fifteen people. I loved it when the parties were at our house. The women moved in a world of powder and taffeta. When my mum was getting all gussied up I would perch on the end of her bed and watch the make-up ritual, the laying on of the sparkling jewellery (which, years later, I realised was imitation) and the smell of 'Evening in Paris' perfume which was squirted out of a tiny green bottle with a lace-encased rubber vapouriser bulb. Talk about life in the fast lane. The kids were allowed to stay up until the adults arrived and then were sent to bed. The game was to see how many times you could ignore the go-to-bed instruction and, saucer-eyed, listen to the grown-up conversation.

One of the single males at the party was the brother of a local who owned the Citroen car yard licence and, I guess, played golf with my father. The ritzy car yard man (we were obsessed by cars in those days) had asked my dad if he could bring his brother who had just arrived from Australia. He was a great party trick. He even talked funny. It seems out of context but it is important to record that around that time, to commemorate the Coronation of the new Queen Elizabeth, the New Zealand Mint struck a wondrous new coin – a heavy, silver crown. (We had shillings and sixpences, and half-crowns but never a Crown). It was magic. An opulent, glinting coin that would never become legal tender. It sat encased in a black and clear plastic box. I was given two of them and it was like owning the Crown Jewels in the Tower of London.

The night of my parents' party my first conversation with 'the alien', the Australian visitor, was about the Queen's coin. The visitor first chatted to my brother and offered to buy his commemorative crown. Des refused. Not then, or now, a party person he retreated to his bedroom. My dad's friend's brother then offered me 'a quid' for one of my coins. A whole pound. To a kid who never saw folding money and whose parents didn't see much of it either, it was a dream. I had two of the silver crowns, in their jazzy plastic boxes, given to me by my dad's bus-driving mates when I used to hang around his garage. To sell one for a pound was a dream. About two years pocket money. The deal was done. I cringe now over not only how naive I was but how my parents and friends billed and cooed. Then I went to bed.

Somehow the man found a reason to come and talk to me again. He latched on to my most cherished possession – an HMV wind-up gramophone that played, one at a time, 78 rpm records. The stylus was a brass pin and the heavy playing head bobbed around as it chewed its path through Teresa Brewer and 'Doggie in the

Window'. The visitor was mesmerised by the machine. Sat next to me, close to me, asked questions about my prize possession. His voice was soft and friendly and confident. Looking back his voice was probably soft because my teenage brother was asleep in bed in the same room.

Suddenly, and how does a kid know how it happens or when it is going to happen, he had his hand inside the opening of my pyjama pants. The innocent opening that all kids had in their flannel jarmies in those days. Within seconds he was on his knees. I was standing and sort of pushed up against the bedroom wall. And I was frozen with fear. I doubt a scream could have passed through my throat. I was bewildered because this was a person in authority doing this to me. An adult, a grown-up. Then he had my penis in his mouth and my childhood fear was joined by embarrassment as I felt the boyish tinglings, the dirty bits that I had never talked to anybody about, start to grow in my pyjamas. I was mortified. Petrified. I knew it was dirty. I knew it was wrong. It wasn't my fault but I was there. Somehow I pulled away from him. The whole thing was fleeting but, looking back it seemed to take forever, it seemed to be happening in slow motion.

I slammed the leather lid on the gramophone and edged along the wall towards my bed. I remember saying, 'No, stop it' more loudly. My brother, in his bed across the room, turned on his mattress and made a waking-up noise. My attacker fled. All the time the noise of the party bled through the walls.

In the so-called safety of my bed I lay rigid with fear. I was scared but also angry. Suddenly, in the darkened bedroom we shared, my brother said, 'Are you OK?'

'Yeah,' I answered too quickly, 'why?'

My voice was tiny and very high, even for a kid whose balls had not yet dropped.

'What happened before?' he asked.

'When?'

'Before!'

'Nothing . . . nothing.'

I could not tell my brother. Couldn't tell anybody. My chest was so tight and I didn't have the words. I was mortified. I knew what had happened was wrong and dirty but how does a kid who has never in his life heard the word 'penis' explain to an older brother that a grown man had not only 'touched your doodle' (or whatever we called it) but had put it in his mouth.

I cracked and said, 'I want Mum.' And then I started to cry.

When my mother came in, in her taffeta gown and her 'Evening in Paris' exotic scent, I couldn't tell her the truth. I hedged. I said I'd changed my mind – I wanted my Queen Elizabeth coin back. I didn't want his money.

My mum started to give me a lecture about fairness and commitment and responsibility. Earlier she had asked me if I really wanted to sell the coin. Had warned me not to be avaricious. Then she went to tuck me in and said, 'Go to sleep.' I couldn't tell her what had happened. I was too ashamed. Mum was about to leave when my usually shy and reticent brother said, 'Mum, that man did something to Derryn.'

'What man? Did what?'

'That Australian. He tried it first with me in a way and I pushed him away.'

My mum screamed for my father. The rest is a blur.

I know it was very late at night. The party had stopped, the lights were very bright and I was in the kitchen (way past my bedtime) being comforted by my unofficial, but favourite, aunt, Auntie Freda, my mum's best friend. She was also comforting my tearful mother. I was sheltered from what else was going on but I did realise that all the men were missing – they were all outside.

I learned, years later, that when my mother called for my father's help after she realised I had been molested, the visitor quickly left our house. He was found standing outside and denied everything. He was vehement until he saw three men holding back my father, a raging bull with hands the size of plates of meat, with the party beer making him even more threatening, more physical, as he shouted, 'Let me at the bastard. He's been at my son. I'll kill him.' The molester's brother, apologising profusely got the offender out of there within minutes and out of town within hours.

It wasn't mentioned for years and years. A decade, maybe two decades later, I asked my parents why they hadn't called the police, why they hadn't had the man charged. I said he had probably been in New Plymouth that night because he had fled Australia and a similar crime. And having been sprung in our town had probably gone to somebody else's. Their best answer on advice from friends (especially the molester's embarrassed brother) was to let the matter rest, keep it quiet, the man had gone, and wouldn't be back, it would be 'too traumatic' to subject the boy to an appearance in court and there had been 'no real harm done'.

Of course not. Surprisingly perhaps, I agree. No lasting harm was done. And that, in itself, is probably remarkable After all, here's a kid still too young to have been aware of the facts of life (in that era), too young to contemplate or visualise what intercourse is, too young to know anything about the warmth or affection or healthy side of sex. At his age it is all ignorantly dirty. And suddenly he has to describe to his mother how a man at her party put his penis in his mouth.

(Despite my genuine belief that the incident left no lasting scar on me how come I suddenly started to cry when I wrote about my dad fighting three of his mates so he could get at the man who had interfered with me?)

I never blamed my parents for not prosecuting my attacker, although I have long wished they had. And I have sometimes wondered where that man has gone and what other minds and bodies he has tried to attack.

After I mentioned my own experience on 3AW I was inundated with stories, horror stories, from people (especially women) who had kept their own secrets about violation for 10, 20 even 70 years. One woman, from Geelong, Victoria, told me she was 44 years old, had been an incest victim and had never told a soul. She had had a dreadful, guilt-ridden, tortured life, had had virtually no sex life with her husband apart from two children and she had never told him why the barriers were there.

The story that sticks in my mind, from those radio days, is the young mother who was suddenly tongue-kissed by her three-year-old daughter. The mother told me she froze and then asked her child, 'Who taught you that?' The bubbly answer, 'Granny did.'

When the mother was a child her mother had molested her. Now another generation was under attack. And people try not to talk about it. Even when little kids don't want to go to Grandma's for the school holidays because Grandpa makes them sit on his supposedly senile knee.

Sounds sick. It happens.

Who is looking after the children? Sometimes you are tempted to say: nobody! But despite the flood of paedophilia cases, despite the scandals involving churches when they transfer molesting priests rather than confronting the problems, and despite the putrid worldwide trade in child pornography, there is hope, there is real hope, for kids as we head into the twenty-first century. Groups like VOCAL and other protection organisations are helping. The use of video evidence in courts to reduce the traumas for child witnesses. Better sex education, Stranger Danger programmes, Safe House systems for school kids, they are all helping. And kids, our most precious commodity, are getting smarter.

A Captive Audience

There is a cigarette lighter on the desk in my study overlooking the Yarra River as I write this. It has been there for more than four years. Will be there for the next thirty, I hope – and I don't smoke. The lighter is one of those cheap, disposable ones but it is in fact priceless. At least to me. One of my most treasured possessions. It doesn't look like a disposable because somebody has laboriously 'customised' it. It has had slivers of matchsticks glued all over it which have been carefully sanded down so there are no edges or ridges. Then it has been painted black and varnished. There are two bits of artwork in gold paint. On one side of the lighter is a closed padlock, on the other side a pair of handcuffs plus the words 'Morwell River'.

It was a gift from a fellow-prisoner when I was in jail.

His present meant a lot because of all the crims I met in two prisons – the armed robbers, the standover men, the white collar crims, the double-murderers – he stands out in my mind all these years later as the one who should never have been there. I didn't think I should be there either but I knew what I was doing and knew what the ultimate penalty could be. I expected, eventually, to go to jail.

The young prisoner who gave me the streamlined cigarette lighter in Morwell Prison in 1987 was a classic victim of our legal system gone haywire. That's why the lighter stays on my desk as a reminder. His was a tragedy of Greek proportion and it was an obscenity that he spent a night, let alone six months, in jail. In the lead-up to his imprisonment he lost his wife, his little son lost his mother and the man responsible did not spend one night behind bars.

I can't tell you the young prisoner's name. I don't remember it but I'll call him John. In jail you don't ask too many questions and you don't ask why a person is in there unless they volunteer it. I think I met him as we went through the nightly ritual of queueing to use the one coin-operated public phone in the 'main street' of the prison camp. (I nicknamed it Broadway after the main thoroughfare in New York's Attica prison where I once covered a jail riot in which 43 people, including ten hostages, were killed by their 'rescuers'.)

We were 'sitting on the stoop', as they would say in New York, and the conversation turned to the jailing of drunk drivers. The story John told me was a Hitchcock nightmare. I was sceptical of most sob-stories in jail. I was livid about this one.

'I'm in jail because of drunk driving,' he said, slowly, cautiously. Jail conversations are like that.

'What? You drank and drove?'

'No. A drunk driver killed my wife.'

'So what are you doing here?'

And then he told me and I knew, yet again, that justice is not only not seen to be done in this country, it is often, patently, NOT done in this country.

John, was a country boy: mid-twenties, knockabout Mr Fixit. He and his wife lived a secluded life high in the highlands of country Victoria. They had a young son they both loved. One day John and his wife were walking along a country road – well off the road in the starving grass that abuts the roadside gravel. They were walking hand in hand. Suddenly John's wife was literally torn from his grip, wrenched out of his hand and then mangled by a fast-moving car. He saw her die before his eyes. And then had to go home to explain to his young son that mummy wouldn't be coming home anymore.

The wheels of 'justice' churned on, churned excruciatingly slowly. The Melbourne motorist, who ripped John's wife out of his hand and ripped her life out of her, appeared in court and got off with a bond. Sometime later, to assuage his own guilt, for killing a woman with his car and his carelessness, the motorist returned to the scene of the crime. He asked people at the local pub where John lived. Somebody told him. And he drove there – to a well-hidden mountain-top hideaway where John was trying to cope with the ache and the agony of losing his companion and trying to raise a motherless son.

John did not react well when the uninvited visitor, the killer of his young wife, appeared on the doorstep. He asked him to leave. The man protested, spoke words of 'healing' and 'understanding', but then left. A few minutes later he returned, determined to, at least, get the monkey off his own back. With his young wife dead, his son grieving and bewildered, John exploded. He (as he put it to me in prison) gave the guy a hiding. An out-of-control beating fuelled by all that pent-up anger, and pain, and hurt, and frustration. The 'victim' complained to the police and John was charged with assault. For some reason – make your own 'smart lawyer' assumption here – the case was transferred from the country to Melbourne, to a court in a wealthy suburb near where the 'victim' lived. John, probably foolishly and certainly naively, couldn't afford and so did not get, counsel. He thought he'd just tell the truth. Admit what he had done in a moment of blood-coursing anger. Surely the court would understand and he would be home by night-time.

He got his dad to babysit his son and turned up in court in a posh Melbourne suburb wearing country trousers and a short-sleeved jumper. He was a country hick in the cross-hairs of 'justice'. And they got him. The man whose selfish, dangerous, reckless actions killed a young mother did not spend one night in jail. On the other hand John did not get home to see his son that night. He spent it in jail . . . the first night of nearly two hundred nights he would spend behind bars for assault. Six months jail for thumping the man who had made his son motherless and who had then had the gall to, uninvited, track down a grieving father to try to cleanse his own guilt.

That story affected me more than any other in my time in Pentridge and Morwell. It was a classic case of justice just not being done. Apart from anything else a little kid who had lost his mother in tragic circumstances had then lost his father for six months. John was such an innocent, so convinced the law would do the right thing, that he didn't even reassure his son that he may not be back when he left him with his grandfather and trudged off to court. John was behind bars within an hour. He did not, could not, speak to his son for days.

That is why a battered, supposedly cheap, cigarette lighter has pride of place on my desk in my study. I will never forget a young man brutalised by the roads and then brutalised by the courts.

Jails, notoriously, are full of men proclaiming their innocence. At one stage, in Morwell Prison, I thought I should contact the *Guinness Book of Records*: I appeared to be the only guilty person in there. One killer who befriended me was an old sideshow boxer called Robbo. As I gained his trust 'inside' he started hauling out reams of paper – letters he hoped would finally convince the parole board to give him a chance again on the outside. Robbo had been in jail for around twenty years. His voice sounded even worse than mine after so many years of being punched in the larynx in sideshow tents. He kept saying to me in that rasping voice, 'It was a miscarriage of justice. It was a miscarriage of justice.' Finally I asked him a prison 'no-no' question: 'Yes, but Robbo, did you do it?'

His answer: 'That's not the point. It was a miscarriage of justice.' I used to tell that story as a joke until the James Finch 'Whiskey a Go Go' saga came to a climax. Finch proclaimed his innocence all those years. Even cut off part of one finger as a protest. He was finally released from jail in Queensland, was deported (still proclaiming his innocence) but once safely back in London admitted his guilt. When he heard rumours he might be brought back to Australia to serve the remainder of his sentence for the deaths of all those innocent nightclub patrons, Finch had a memory lapse, or a feigned breakdown, on national television and again proclaimed his innocence. There is no doubt that Finch was involved in the Whiskey a Go Go carnage but his original conviction WAS a miscarriage of justice. In the belief that the ends justify the means the Queensland Police 'verballed' Finch. Concocted a confession to make sure they got a quick conviction. They got the right man but they stained our system of justice in getting him.

These memories stem from the twelve days I spent in jail in October 1987. It was a time that, despite the emotion and the trauma (and the personal deprivation), I have not really dwelt on since. Ever. I can remember my convict number, and sometimes use it in Tattslotto: 44146. And I have a copy of my mug shot, pot-bellied and holding a sign that says:

Name: Hinch D
D.O.B: 9 2 44
No: 44146

But I had never opened the scrapbooks about my incarceration until now. And had never re-read the detailed diary I wrote every day that I was behind bars. I also hadn't gone back to some of the support (and some of the vitriol) in Australian newspapers at the time. Like the *Daily Advertiser* in Wagga, NSW, running an editorial under the headline NO TEARS SHOULD BE SHED FOR HINCH which said, virtually, that

I had betrayed my colleagues, neglected my responsibilities, and 'deserves no sympathy. His incarceration is fair.'

The nicest thing written about me at the time of my jailing, and I include it in this book, is a column by a man, a colleague, who has never been a friend but whose craft I have admired: Peter Smark. I read his column again today for the first time in nearly five years and it brought tears to my eyes.

So did some of the cartoons. Men with bags of lollies saying things like: 'Hey kids, wanna come and watch Derryn Hinch being put in jail.' Or George Haddon's cartoon in the Melbourne *Herald* which summed up my frustration being sentenced to more time behind bars than some of the child molesters I tried to curtail. He sent me the original. It hangs in my study. It shows two emaciated, scruffy, prisoners, in chains, hanging on a wall, 'Wizard of Id' style. One says: '. . . Two and a half years for interfering with little kids, what did you get?' And the other man hanging on the wall, in chains and with a distinctive Hinch beard and a rose in his lapel says 'Six weeks for trying to stop you.'

What follows are the original diaries of my days in jail. As an author and a former newspaper editor I have been tempted, but have resisted the temptation, to change them. They are Hinch in the raw. They are the thoughts I committed to paper at the time I had them. Not rewritten, not edited – even though I have a strong urge to 'clean them up' now.

It all started on Thursday, October 15, 1987 in a Chinese restaurant in Melbourne. Actually it started at 10.17 a.m. in my studio at 3AW in Melbourne's LaTrobe Street when the word came through from

Canberra that the High Court had voted 5–0 to reject my appeal and send me to jail for 28 days – the first Australian journalist ever to be incarcerated for contempt of court.

Jail Diaries

Thursday, October 15, 1987

At the Flower Drum restaurant in Melbourne's Chinatown the waiting was the worst part. Like the waiting had been the worst part on air when I had kept doing my 3AW radio programme like an automaton waiting for the news to come through from the High Court in Canberra. News that could have me in jail by the end of the day. Actually there had been months and months of waiting. Most of it caused by me and my radio station as we worked through the expensive appeals maze. First the Victorian Supreme Court (we lost) and then an application for the right to a High Court review (we won) and then the High Court case itself (we lost). I was convicted in May 1986 and eventually jailed in October 1987. As I waited in my crowded studio on that Thursday, I had an incongruous mental flash of the old line from the siege of Khe Sanh in Vietnam: The waiting is the worst part. I got the bad news while on air and broadcast it. I interrupted a phone interview with headkicker Wilson Tuckey to tell my listeners that the case was lost, my appeal had been dismissed and I was waiting to be taken to jail. The authorities, through my conduit lawyer, suggested I could surrender myself at a certain time at a certain place. I told my trusty, and trusted, lawyer John De Kohning, 'I'm not surrendering anywhere. They convicted me. They jailed me. They can come and get me.' I told him the restaurant I would be in which started a round of bad jokes about 'the hearty man ate a condemned meal'.

At the Flower Drum, surrounded by friends and family, it really started to sink in that the vote against me had been so overwhelming. A vote of 5–0. Wipeout. At least in the Victorian State Supreme Court it had been 2–1. One more vote there and I would have been totally vindicated and would have missed (or avoided) a stint in jail. I did not know then, and could not know then, that although all five High Court judges gave me the thumbs down there were actually some positive attitudes expressed by some of the top flight legal eagles on that exalted bench when the printed judgment was released.

The next few hours, after my rejection by the High Court, were a blur of radio, newspaper and television interviews. And time was running out.

I kept trying to remember to get the salient points across. After all, the actual broadcasts were more than two years old and the original court case, and original jail sentence, were eighteen months behind me. I knew it was going to be hard, and it was hard, to dispel the image that it was all just a case of 'Hinch thumbing his nose at the courts'. The cowboy versus the courts. It wasn't. It was Hinch, a radio journalist with a large audience, trying to alert parents about the Glennon camps.

Jacki was there through it all. Even in the radio studio, with her hand on my back as I tried to fulfil a promise that I had made to myself: no matter what the decision by the High Court in Canberra I would finish that day's programme, and finish it with some style.

Apart from about twenty minutes out of the studio to huddle with lawyers and 3AW management and to explain to my wife and my stepson, Dylan, what it all meant, I finished the shift. I had also taken time to phone my parents in New Zealand to make sure they heard the news first from me and not from some enterprising reporter – as happened when I was sentenced to jail. Talking to my mum and dad, and hearing them both cry made me feel helpless, put a lump in my throat and made my eyes smart. They didn't, couldn't, know from a distance what it was all about but they were close enough to know a son was scared. Actually I knew it was going to be a tough and emotional day when, at five to nine on 3AW, I played the Dionne Warwick/Stevie Wonder/Elton John song: 'That's what Friends are For.' I had played it on radio after some public and loyal friends wrote or turned up at court to give character references for me: a priest, Archbishop David Penman, a former leader of the Federal Opposition, Andrew Peacock, a former Lord Mayor, Ron Walker and a former top cop, Deputy Police Commissioner, Phil Bennett.

It is funny how, in those emotional times, emotions change. The word was coming to me from several sources on the day of the High Court guillotine that there was no way I would be arrested that day. 'Could be tomorrow . . . could be Monday . . . could even be a week. They don't know what to do with you.' All I asked of my legal team was that they were to ask for no favours. That everything had to follow usual procedures.

'There are no "usual procedures",' my frustrated, but hard-working lawyer told me. 'You are the first journalist in history to be jailed for contempt of court.' (Despite the alleged ego it did not make me feel good. There are firsts you do not need.)

Within hours of being ordered to jail I knew my mood, despite the public face, was wobbling, oscillating. Despite the calm the tension became raw when I was interviewed by a former colleague, Elissa O'Neill, from Channel Ten. The interview seemed to go well. We finished it. And Jacki was in post-interview gossip when the cameraman said quite nonchalantly that we would have to do it all over again because of extraneous sound bleeding through the camera mike. Something he hadn't picked up on because he had not switched some gizmo over. I unleashed a tetchy four-letter word flurry. 'Fucking amateurs.' It should have told me that I was not taking all of this as calmly as I hoped it appeared to people on the outside.

To be honest, when people – lawyers, journalists, executives – started talking about it maybe a week before the Sheriff's office moved against me I felt strange. I had got out of bed the final day braced for the worst. Prepared to be handcuffed and taken to jail within hours of arriving at the studio. I had been geared for the worst and started that day, tense and dry of mouth, ready to be grabbed anytime.

For several days there had been conflicting, confusing reports. It won't be Thursday, if they find against you, it can't be. High Court papers have to be physically sent to Melbourne from Canberra, then the Supreme Court has to issue an arrest warrant, then the Sheriff has to come and get you. It won't happen.

After hours of confusion and misinformation it seemed that things had changed within the arresting ranks. By 2 p.m. it was obvious that somebody (the courts? the Sheriff? the Attorney-General?) wanted me in the slammer that day. In a strange way so did I. If I wasn't arrested that day I could visualise the headlines – like the one I had written about somebody else more than ten years earlier: Why isn't this man in jail?

I know it is not over until the fat lady sings and I was impatient for the fat lady's appearance. Get it over with! I didn't want to be emotionally stretched through a Thursday night and then a Friday and maybe a whole weekend. Even though I would be missing the long-awaited combined 40th birthday parties of America's Cup hero, John Bertrand and his wife, Rasa. It was to be a come-as-you-like fantasy party. Be whomever you would like to be. I had planned to go as myself. When the word finally came through that I would be arrested in an hour I felt a real shiver go through me but I also felt a weird relief. The denouement was upon me after more than eighteen months.

At the Flower Drum we sit, speaking in bursts followed by longer bursts of emotional silence. Friends and staff straggle in and extra chairs are added to a large lunch table. A bit robot-like I start explaining how you should take the partly-steamed, partly-fried Szechuan dumplings and dip them in a bowl of sauce made from red vinegar with some soy sauce and slivers of hot pepper, ginger, and chilli paste to spice it up and to cut the grease.

The word comes in mid-dumpling: 'They'll be here around four.' It's followed by some gallows humour about, 'Tell the sheriff I've left without him.' When I leave the table to go to the lavatory, Peter Steedman, the maverick federal politician, the leftie 'bodgie in aspic' arrives and relates some convoluted and extraneous story about how, somehow, one of the McGaurins (one of the pretend Kennedys) has ended up as a passenger in Steedman's huge, lairy, bright red Cadillac or Fairlane convertible – his tribute to the days when the air was clean and sex was dirty.

Jacki, who has been holding up fantastically well – except for a couple of short weeps – finds the anger guard is no longer strong enough and really cries.

'Don't let it change you in there.'

The Sheriff and a couple of escorts arrive around 4.20. Habits your parents taught you die hard. I shake the Sheriff's hand and almost thank him for coming. He gives me a couple of discreet minutes to say goodbye to family and friends, including the bearded man who will replace me on air for up to a month, the former editor of the Melbourne *Herald*, Neil Mitchell.

A few minutes earlier he had been shaking his head in disbelief . . . the old print journo in him wondering about the news judgement of the new-look, revamped *Herald* and its editor Eric 'Baron Zamedi' Beecher who argues with other *Herald* executives that the jailing of the first journalist ever for contempt of court is not a real news story.

Minutes before the Sheriff arrives the credit cards are emptied out of the pockets and handed to Jacki along with Kerry Packer's gold cufflinks – the ones he gave to all the male guests at the joint party for his daughter Gretel's 21st and his own 25th wedding anniversary. He didn't give them to me. I wasn't invited to the party. One of Kerry's guests sold them to an antique jeweller in Toorak and Jacki bought them. It was around sharemarket crash time.

A strange, straggly, emotional procession heads down the stairs and out into the cobbled lanes of Chinatown. Another blur of cameras and boom mikes and reporters. A journalistic amoeba. A public and emotional farewell to Jacki and Dylan and to longtime colleagues Mike Frazer and Pamela Graham. Into the Sheriff's car. The last thing I see, through a parting in the throng, is Mike Frazer consoling Jacki. I ache for what she has gone through and will go through. She has to appear on stage tonight in a gruelling role as the mother of a severely handicapped child in the play *A Day in the Death of Joe Egg*.

A sense of unreality. It is nearly peak hour. People are going about their daily business. Getting ready to go from their work to their homes. In an unmarked car four men are heading for Coburg and Pentridge Prison. Adding to the detached mood is the instant replay of what has just happened coming through the car radio: Murray Nichol's drivetime programme on 3AW. The trip to Pentridge seems surprisingly quick. We go in the back way, past high wire mesh walls, topped with the notorious razor wire. Actually we wait for several minutes before a huge metal gate is raised and we are inside. I am thinking I must relax. Must take it all in. Must let the journalist take over.

Remember you are not the first person to come in here and you certainly won't be the last. You'll be out in a month . . . maybe less. (The rumour that I will be sent to Morwell prison farm within days, maybe even hours, is comforting.) Inside the jail it is an easier admission track than I had expected. Maybe that's the reason for the timing.

They swing me straight into 'D' block – the block that holds a lot of prisoners on remand. I later discover its nickname: Collins Street. It is the top end of prison living in Pentridge . . . such as it is. The timing is in my favour again. It is around half past five. The rest of the prisoners have been locked in their cells since four o'clock. I am guided straight into a small office and asked for contents of pockets: money, business cards, messages, keys. Then my watch. My belt. Then I am asked (ordered?) to strip. First the R.M. Williams boots come off and the heels are banged on the table in case they are hollow and hide something. Next jacket pockets are checked, jacket lining, trouser pockets. Then drop the underpants. I am grateful there was no internal search. No warder's finger up the anus. It is the first of two strip searches I will endure in twelve hours. Personal toiletries are confiscated: toothpaste, razor, shampoo. It sounds unfair at first until it is explained to me how a syringe can be hidden in a tube of shampoo or a shaving cream cannister. As a man who rarely carries any cash I have, for some reason, a few hundred dollars this day. There are some Fort Knox jokes as my strip-searchers count it and give me a receipt for it. Silly thing to bring but it relaxes a few people – including me. The seriousness of the strip-search comes home when they insist on taking my belt, in case I try to hang myself. Luckily, the jeans stay up.

My first Pentridge meal is served about an hour and a half later after my being grabbed by the Sheriff at the Flower Drum. An instinct tells me that, despite my recent restaurant meal, in jail you eat anything and everything whenever it is put in front of you. I eat alone at one of the long wooden tables, lined with benches, that run all the way down the middle of Collins Street. The three-storeyed stone building has something else in common with Collins Street, I haven't seen architecture like this – with the domed roof and narrow walkways – since a visit to Melbourne's Menzies at the Rialto. Hardly the same decor, I'll admit: yellow with brown trim everywhere. Hardly the same food either: a heap of grey/green boiled cabbage, some grey 'roast' meat and potatoes. Followed by an apple and a carton of warm milk. Then into a very primitive two-man cell. I find out later that I am in fact in the best part of D Block, the top end of Collins Street, I'm told I could have copped a dormitory bed and I wonder, if this is the best what on earth is the worst like.

The 'two-man' cell is actually a single cell converted with bunks into a two-prisoner unit during the overcrowded jail crisis, and funding crisis, of the late 1980s. Also a spin-off from the closure of the huge F-Division dormitories. If the BLF's occasional inmate Norm Gallagher, and John Cummins (himself a frequent Pentridge occupant these days) ever permit the completion of the new remand centre in LaTrobe Street, the D-Block doublers will, theoretically revert to single accommodation.

My cell is so small (for two people) that my cellmate, an old lag called Popeye, spends most of his lock-up time sitting on the stainless steel, seat-less, lavatory. Not because of any bowel problems but because it is the most comfortable, accessible, and most convenient place to watch his black and white television.

Popeye has been in and out of jails for nearly thirty years. He has the knack of being able to talk incessantly and smoke constantly at the same time. And he does. My first night behind bars I watch the newscasts on his old black and white TV. I feel sorry that my wife is carrying the can outside and also having to appear that night on stage. I watch some of the ABC's timely special 'Out of Sight, Out of Mind' which is one of the main topics of conversation over the next few days both in Pentridge and at Morwell. I don't watch it all. After an emotionally gruelling day I fall into a fractured sleep. Throughout my first night in jail, Popeye seems to wake up on the hour, every hour, for another cigarette. In the almost airless small cell, with chipped stone walls painted pink and an old-fashioned white domed ceiling, the air is choking.

I decide to uncharacteristically hold my tongue and not to launch into any anti-smoking lectures. Instead, as the smoke wafts up to my top bunk I bury my head in my mouldy pillow and try to use it as a filter. Throughout the night I somehow acquire through the food hatch in my cell door a doughnut and a bologna, tomato and cheese toasted sandwich. They come at the strangest times. Still working on the basis that whenever anybody in prison offers you food you take it, I eat it. And have the first of a thousand cups of tea or coffee.

Friday, October 16, 1987

Popeye is an early riser for kitchen duty. I hardly seem to have been asleep at all before his alarm goes off at 4.15 a.m. I can't complain because I am grateful that somehow he has a clock in our cell. My watch has been confiscated and as a journalist I feel castrated without a timepiece. Totally stranded. Popeye lights yet another gasper, another coffin nail (as my mum used to call them) and heads for the prison kitchen to prepare the morning sludge. With the cell to myself I selfconsciously move my bowels, have a crap, for the first time since entering prison twelve hours earlier. I couldn't do it, although I wanted to, while in an enclosed space with a stranger. The icy cold stainless steel, seat-less dunny rim is a great waker-upper. I clamber back up and stretch out again on the top bunk with a cup of tea and the light on. For the first time I examine the cell in detail. A kettle, a small water-marked mirror, a battered wooden cabinet. No wardrobe, no coat-hanger, no place to hang clothes. My jeans, blue shirt and Yves St. Laurent jacket are piled in a heap on the only chair in the cell. I notice that at least they've given me my boots back.

The high, narrow walls below the domed roof have one recessed window. It is glassed in and locked or else I would have opened it to let the foetid smoke out and some fresh air in. Behind the window, as the dawn comes up, I can see the previously hidden thick metal bars. For about fifteen minutes I watch the travels and the travails of a moth – back and forth across the wall.

It gives me a clue as to why the Birdman of Alcatraz got so involved with birds and why some long-termers in Pentridge have laboriously trained mice. And, shit, I haven't even been here for twenty-four hours yet.

I think back to some of my cellmate Popeye's advice while sitting on the rim of the cold, metal dunny the night before. A simple message from a man who had spent decades behind bars: 'Don't trust anyone.' On that first morning in Pentridge I feel a strange mix of emotions, a mixture of curiosity, alienation and caution. I decided before I stepped inside Pentridge that I would not ask anybody what they were in for. Would ask 'how long?' but figured the rest had to be volunteered. I'll admit to an understandable outside feeling of 'Am I talking to a rapist, a double-murderer or a white collar thief?' (In fact I later discovered that one of the first conversations of more than ten words that I had with anybody in Pentridge was with an alleged child molester awaiting trial.) On my first morning in Pentridge I ask a fellow inmate at breakfast what all the shouting and aggro and cell-door rattling had been about the night before. He pours a cup of tea and says, 'You.' The bursts of garbled obscenities were aimed at me. I get the feeling I am being orchestrated through a prison. I'm not getting it easy but I am not seeing the REAL prison. For example, my block, D Block, houses about 200 prisoners but in one afternoon, one night, and one early morning somehow I only see about ten of them. And all of those, including my cell-mate, my chain-smoking trustee Popeye, all seem to be on kitchen or table-cleaning duties. The few prisoners I do get to talk to in Pentridge seem obsessed by one thing apart from how many days, months or years before they will get out. They are obsessed by drugs, by drug abuse by prisoners and by guards who trade in drugs. Within hours of being locked up in Pentridge I am told in intricate detail how to make a syringe out of a cheap ballpoint pen. Another junkie inmate tells me how heroin addicts, in jail, seem to have no fear of AIDS and syringes get passed from junkie to junkie. I doubt the Grim Reaper TV commercials got much response in Pentridge. Several prisoners tell me about drug-related stabbings and attempted suicides that do not make the papers. Even allowing for the usual embellishments, exaggerations, and misinterpretations that flourish in jail a lot of it must be true. One young prisoner told me he had seen between twenty and thirty stabbings in two prisons in Victoria. 'I just stick to meself and mind me own business,' he tells me.

It has been decided by the powers-that-be that I should be moved, very early in the morning, to Morwell. Before most of the other prisoners are up. I have a welcome, luxurious (?) hot shower at 5.45 a.m. The same luxury does not await prisoners who shower later in the day. Breakfast is a heap of dry toast. I think, I guess, that this is prison style. A kind kitchen trustie finds me some tinfoil pats of butter. By this time, less than 12 hours after being locked up, the journalist in me is taking over. I think of jobs that have been even less comfortable. Even more threatening. I think of people I have seen in India, in the poverty-stricken villages of Gujurat. Think of seeing people dying, not in their hundreds, but in their thousands in Ethiopia. Think of confronting the guns of soldiers outside Addis Ababa and in the desert sands outside Khartoum. I think of sleeping in a rusted corrugated iron frame of a bed under mosquito netting in a cholera ward in a refugee camp in the middle of the pus-bowl of Africa. Put the fact that you are here in jail by court order and not by choice into the background. Observe. Chronicle. Treat it like an assignment.

Suddenly I know I am going to make it. Nothing will break me.

I am also buoyed by the number of prison officers who – sometimes out of the corner of their mouths – tell me, 'A lot of us don't think you should be here. Especially with all these other bastards getting bonds.' I'm not so sure about the term 'OTHER bastards' but I acknowledge the sentiment.

At 6.45 a.m. on Friday, an hour after I get up, there comes the shout 'Wakey, wakey, everybody awake.' A chant followed by a cacaphonous ringing of bells which reverberates throughout the cell block. Rolling through the three floors and bouncing off the ceiling.

I say goodbye to Cell 59 in D Block (for, I hope, the last time) and am led through a maze of pathways and steps to the administration block for more processing and paper-signing. The other prisoners, I am told later, were not let out of their cells until after I had gone. On the way through I stand in the infamous exercise yards. There are still three of these yards of shame in Pentridge. They are an abomination when empty. God knows what they are like full. If the RSPCA or the pound kept dogs in them for a day, let alone months and even years, they'd quite rightly have animal rights groups up in arms.

The yards are narrow, almost pie-shaped, bare concrete strips with high stone walls. Some of the 'facilities' must date back to when Pentridge was first opened in the 1850s. There are a couple of shithouses. You can't call them toilets or even lavatories. They are exposed shithouses. In recent years, following decades of protest, the state government has taken dramatic, decisive action. They have placed a couple of two-foot high screens in front of the open-to-the-elements dunnies. The yard does not have seats for all the seventy men who use the yards all day. Just a bare, dirty, concrete floor, stone walls, and seventy men, most of them – supposedly all of them – innocent men because they are awaiting trial and have not yet been found guilty. Some are there for days, some for months and some for more than a year. They are locked in the yard, locked in the kennel run, after breakfast and stay there until lunch. Then they are locked in the yards again until dinner (which is served around 3.30 p.m.!) and then they are taken out of the yard and locked in their cells from around 4.30 p.m. until the following morning.

There is one shower for seventy men. Two toilet bowls. There are old crims and young kids and tax avoiders and drunk drivers all lumped together. The boredom is excruciating. The weather, even in March sometimes, is so cold that the men sometimes take up to three showers a day to get warm. If they can get to the shower.

These are facts. Not the whingeing words of a do-gooder. And most of these men, in three similar yards, are not convicted but are awaiting trial.

Luckily for me – but perhaps deliberately 'lucky' for the authorities not looking forward to my post-jail diary – my early bird departure from Pentridge means I avoid the remand yards and all those seething prisoners. I am taken to the office of the Assistant Commissioner, a Mr Payne. I am photographed (yet again, two photo sessions in fact) holding a board with my name and date of birth written on it in yellow chalk. I am searched again. Asked to strip again. During my verbal assessment to see if I am in fact a low-risk prisoner eligible for transfer I am asked all sorts of questions, some of which are offensive and would be banned under most anti-discrimination and equality laws.

'Are you aboriginal?'

'Do you have an aboriginal wife?'

Why does my family's ethnic background matter?

Eventually I sign for my belongings which are returned to me in a big, brown, paper bag – except for the money which has been converted into a cheque.

I am to travel to the Morwell River prison farm locked in the back of a police divvy van with a young prisoner who has been in Ararat Prison and Pentridge for nine months. He has eight months to go. I find out later he is in for culpable driving. Killed a man, a mate, when he was drunk behind the wheel. It is going to be a long, cramped ride. I carry a cardboard carton of his belongings to the van.

The divvy van is small, low-ceilinged and a spare tyre takes up much of the room plus two boxes of the other prisoner's belongings. There are heavy wire screens on the windows and the roof is so low that the best, and most comfortable position is almost lying down. We are late leaving. It feels incongruous being locked in the back of a police wagon and still being able to see Melbourne morning peak hour traffic heading off to work and catching snatches of my replacement, Neil Mitchell, on 3AW as he talks about tying yellow ribbons 'round old oak trees' as a gesture of support. When he plays my theme song and Sinatra sings about having been 'up and down and over and out' I feel some pangs.

One newscast on one station follows the *Australian's* erroneous punt and says I'll be out by Monday. 'Hardly worth sending you,' says my fellow passenger. I still feel it will be the full 28 days. Especially after the Morwell prison officers, Mr Taylor and Mr Bailey (you are instructed to address them that way at all times) raise the question at Pentridge about my eligibility for any remissions at all for good behaviour on a contempt of court charge. Since Thursday I have resigned myself to serving the full 28-day term and have told my lawyers not to request any deductions even if they are available.

An estimated time of less than two hours turns out to be a near three hour bum-numbing, back-thumping journey. Halfway down we stop for petrol. No leg-stretching opportunity but the side windows are opened a bit to let in some welcome fresh air. Mr Taylor buys me a couple of newspapers. I have no money to reimburse him. Funny reading about yourself in the back of a paddy wagon. It is not only a new mode of transport for me but a new part of Victoria. I peer out of the tiny, barred window as we drive through some of the greenest, most beautiful, country in the world. Around Leongatha there are rolling farm hills and bucolic scenes with cows and calves. All the other young prisoner is interested in is spotting girls.

At Mirboo North and District Hospital there's a stop for a medical examination and compulsory blood tests. They were meant to be done before we left Pentridge but the powers-that-be were keen for us to get on the road. I heard one Pentridge officer say to Mr Taylor,

'Would you get on your way and get him out of here. I've got 500 still locked up over there until he's gone.'

Marching into a country hospital flanked by two large uniformed officers feels a little strange. Mirboo North isn't far from the prison and nurses and patients (including a group of elderly patients playing some sort of blackboard game with a nurse's aide) take it in their stride. I leave one person happy. A slightly embarrassed nursing sister, says, 'Kate, the cook, thinks you are marvellous but she's too shy to ask for an autograph.' Standing in a hospital corridor flanked by uniforms and signing 'Best wishes Kate' on a piece of paper when you are on your way from one jail to the next is Monty Pythonish.

Next a stuff-up. Neither the doctor nor the pathologist are on deck at Mirboo North to process me. Escorted outside, climb back into the divvy van, locked in again. Go to a doctor's surgery, I presume, in the main street. A charming, even if a little flustered, middle-aged female doctor runs through all the obligatory medical history questions and, after requesting a urine sample, takes me through a series of corridors and doors to her lavatory. Left alone in a room for the first time since showering at home the previous morning I let a mischievous thought surface: What if I just turned left instead of right when I leave this loo and keep going? I pass the thought on to Mr Taylor and Mr Bailey when I return, clutching my warm bottle of urine.

'If we thought there was a chance of that you wouldn't be coming to Morwell in the first place,' said Mr Taylor.

'How fast can you run?' said Mr Bailey.

Still fantasising I thought I could easily outrun Mr Taylor, a corpulent but very decent bloke. I'm glad I didn't try to outrun Mr Bailey. (In prison a few hours later I saw him bathed in sweat but hardly puffing as he returned from a training run in the Strzelecki Ranges.)

Back in the van, locked in again, and off for a blood test. And then the final, winding run through the high country. The van twists and jolts along the High Ridge Road with steep drops on the right before sweeping down on to the prison camp along the banks of the Morwell River. We accelerate fast past the TV crews and reporters and it is processing time Take Two. Heading down the hill it looks like a logging camp or a gold mining camp. Forty, outwardly-identical, two-man huts, each the size of a small gardening shed. Each has a steep V-shaped roof and a jutting V-shaped verandah roof. All identically grey with pale green eaves. A huge hill, denuded of trees as a firebreak, rears behind the camp and is topped with masssive pine trees. Broad gravel paths separate the rows of huts.

People call it a farm, a summer camp, a Boy Scout camp, or – as I am told a number of times – a 'Clayton's prison'. But the camp governor, Ken Small, a tall, barrel-chested man who looks tough but fair (and turns out that way) stresses in my arrival interview that it is still a prison. The best, the most humane, prison with the most freedom of any Victorian jail, and the best food. But still, as he put it, 'one of H.M's prisons'. If I need any proof it is provided a minute later when I line up against the wall to be photographed again holding a sign which says HINCH, DERRYN 44-146. The moment really hits that I am a prisoner. I look at the Polaroid picture: name, prison number, mug shot. I think about the times since my days as a young police rounds reporter being handed similar photos by police when writing stories about prison escapees.

The governor is friendly but his power is palpable. 'If anybody doesn't behave here my answer is simple: back to Pentridge,' he says. Then out of the blue, 'How long have you had the beard?'

It took me aback. 'Um, nearly thirty years.'

'Want to keep it?'

'Yeah . . . yes, I do.'

'Okay, you can.' The governor had established his territory and his power in the fiefdom.

The first item on the agenda after the meeting with the governor is lunch. Lunch is usually served about 11.30 a.m. (why is everything so early?) I am too late but I am given a plate of spaghetti bolognaise in the kitchen where prisoners assigned to kitchen duty are cleaning up. In a room full of strangers, old and young, with one having already served 22 years in jail, I feel a bit awkward. Even feel as if I am imposing. Everybody, I can sense, knows I'm only a short-timer. A 'show pony' prisoner. A few, I later realise, resent the fact (understandably) that they have spent months, even years, at places like Pentridge, Ararat and Sale, waiting to get to Morwell. And I have, virtually, come straight in. Forget the extent or the enormity of the crime there is a pecking order and, I also realise later, a sort of resentment from some of the lifers that prison has changed. There are now accountants and lawyers and tax-cheating executives in the slammer. Even some of the prison officers yearn for the 'good old days' when life was more simple. When an errant crim or a troublesome lag merely copped a biffing to pull him into line. Or, as I heard one veteran prison guard say, quite seriously, 'The biggest mistake they ever made in the prisons was when they gave you guys sheets.' And he meant it.

In the kitchen the ice is broken by one long-timer who has spent thirteen years in jail, this time for murder.

'I know you,' he says. 'We met in Pentridge.'

I quickly remembered the other time – the only other time – I had been in Pentridge and plucked out a year.

'1978?'

'Yep. You got it.'

I remembered having gone out to the tough H division in Pentridge to give a speech and answer questions from some tough lifers when I was working for Melbourne's 3XY.

In the kitchen for my first meal the conversation rapidly goes to the issue of how long everybody has yet to serve. Today's bitching is about the new sentencing structure. How it is unfair for a man to have done 22 years for a crime when other people are now getting maximums of 12 to 15 years for similar crimes – and then being released from jail in six or eight years.

Next stop is the clothing and supplies store. Again off come all the clothes except the jocks and socks. I'm supplied two t-shirts, a green tracksuit, green work trousers, two shirts, a parka and shoes. Some mirth over the shoes.

'What size?'

'9½ or 10. Wide if possible.' I say and grimace when they guffaw and toss a pair of tan, one-width-fits-all slip-ons in front of me. I feel like I am in the army – but there is no weekend leave.

I haul it all off to Hut 38 and meet my cellmate Bob. He's a big, affable man who, thankfully, doesn't smoke unlike my last cellmate, but whose snoring makes mine sound like Tinkerbell's laughter. Next it is back for bedding. A thin foam mattress that does not disguise the hardness of a board bed that I discover was built for me the day before I arrived. Blankets, rough calico sheets, a pillow case. Then back for the daily ration of milk and fruit. Then a trip to fill a water bottle from a rainwater tank. Each trip means a trek past the long lenses of the media cameras at the prison gates. I am forbidden to go over to them, but, hell, they are just doing their jobs, so I give a wave and a thumbs up.

I'd heard on the radio news in the divvy van on the way from Pentridge that Jacki was going to drive to Morwell with my radio programme's investigative reporter Pamela Graham and my assistant Mandy Muschamp to try to deliver a typewriter, some books, a TV set and notepaper. When they arrive they also have some Reeboks and a windcheater. The windcheater is confiscated, jail rules, because it is not plain and has a logo on it. For some reason they also confiscate my Berocca vitamin B tablets. At first it seems strange and arbitrary but then I try to think of it their way. Drugs do stream into prisons. Especially Pentridge . . . even Morwell. Heroin or cocaine could easily come in disguised as harmless vitamins. Everything, on arrival, has to be examined, accepted or rejected, by prison officials. Everything again is catalogued.

A late afternoon surprise: my name is called over the prison loudspeaker in a camp that I keep thinking reminds me, for a number of reasons, of something out of *M*A*S*H* (maybe because of the Army type huts, the white t-shirts, jungle greens, and hard-edged, cynical, sometimes bitter, humour). At the Administration block I am permitted a short meeting with my wife. It is strangely awkward although for a minute Jacki sits on my lap. Too quickly there is a gruff, 'Time's up.' Jacki, Pamela and Mandy are all wearing yellow ribbons. There are piles of telegrams and one note from one family on a ribbon about ten metres long. I'm knocked out. Although it doesn't really sink in until I see it on the late night news. (We can't watch the six o'clock main news because we are mustering for roll-call and dinner at that time.)

I spend a few dollars out of the six dollars I am permitted for a week's 'canteen'. I buy cordial and coffee. Some Earl Grey tea has arrived with my books. I am told that next week, when I am working either in the bush or cleaning or in the kitchen I will have earned about $12 for the canteen. From a week's work. In the low security prison I am allowed to keep my watch. You can't lose track of time here anyway because the muster siren goes nine times a day and each time you have to drop whatever you are doing and line up to be counted. And counted. And counted. First one early in the morning. Last one, after which you have to be in your cabin for the night, at 9.30 p.m.

Mr Bailey takes me and my van mate David for a tour of the boundaries. He reads us all the rules and regulations. I retreat to my hut. Somebody whistles conspiritorially through my window – a fast talker who, I am later told, could 'sell feathers to chickens'. He invites me to a certain hut for a cup of tea. In the hut three or four men introduce themselves to me and one explains that there was some resentment towards me by some 'so-called heavies' in the camp. Later I find out that four or five prisoners have been called into the Governor's office for 'a little chat' about behaving themselves while I am there.

By the end of Day Two in prison, Day One in Morwell, I have drunk tea and chatted in three or four huts with probably fifteen or twenty prisoners. I feel a bit like a novelty, an oddity, but I have been warmly accepted . . . at least by some.

Dinner muster at six. 'Present sir.' By twelve minutes past six we are not only eating dinner – we have finished it. As one of the world's slowest eaters, a dinner dawdler, I am lucky to get a mouthful. Bob, my cellmate, takes one look at my full plate of fish, chips, coleslaw, onion and tomatoes (plus slices of bread and a plate of fruit salad and ice-cream) and advises speed. Most other plates and tables are already empty. I learn to inhale my food like a vacuum cleaner. Pre-jail philosophical thoughts about lingering over a leisurely meal, no matter how bad the food, just to fill in some night hours, are privately laughed at. In jail, eating is a habit. Something to get out of the way. The wolf-it-down syndrome is exacerbated by the kitchen staff who just want to get out of there. Tables are virtually wiped, and swiped, in front of you. Some of the diners in jail can demolish huge plates of food in five minutes or less. Not uncommon to see a man devour eight or ten pieces of bread in the time I would eat two spoons of mashed potato.

I quickly start to pick up on some of the unwritten, but unbreakable, prison laws. Nobody tells you anything. You just live on your wits and your 'street smarts'. To make phone calls at Morwell (reverse charge calls only, no incoming calls) you must stand outside Hut 32 and wait your turn. One call only at a time. Ten minutes and the natives get restless. You learn you must go past a certain point when entering the mess hall. Laundry goes in once a week – but no socks or underpants. Those you do yourself. In the shower block you must yell out, 'Watch backs' whenever you turn the shower taps on or off in case a surge of water scalds or freezes a neighbour. In your cell you must shout, 'Jug's up' when switching on the kettle for a cup of tea or coffee because if a few jugs are gurgling at the same time it can knock all the electricity out. You learn to head quickly to the roll-call centre whenever the muster siren goes – and it goes at least nine times a day. You don't cross the bridge over the river to the well-trimmed ferny garden on the other side because that is the Officers' Quarters and out of bounds. Don't ask visitors to bring soft drinks or cordial. All liquids are banned from visitors' hampers because a soft-drink bottle could contain vodka or whisky.

The first night in jail at Morwell, at the so-called 'holiday camp', I stretch out on the rock hard bed, with the thin blankets and coarse sheets, and watch the Fenech fight and the news and then go to sleep. Around 11.30 p.m, just after I drift off, a light flashes in my eyes. An officer 'just checking'. Another torch beams into the hut around 2.30 a.m. It may well be a 'Clayton's prison' but it is a prison nonetheless.

Saturday, October 17, 1987

A Saturday morning without a post-Friday night blowout hangover. A Saturday morning without feeling tired. No post Golden Gate Hotel dehydration. Up at

5.30 a.m. (who could believe it!) and out, alone, into the early morning mist to explore the prison camp. Nobody around except the prison officer in the duty hut in the middle of 'Main Street'.

On arrival yesterday the camp seemed huge and sprawling (after Pentridge) but a few dawn laps of the perimeter with Out of Bounds signs popping up with increasing regularity and you realise that the capacious size is an illusion. How small must it seem to men who have been here for four or five years and for whom at least some of the cramped memories of Pentridge have started to fade. Not all fade. Some bad memories are etched forever.

Even the privileges. Like permission to make reverse charge phone calls to Melbourne most of the day and early into the night, bring back memories to inmates like one I talk with several times. It is not that long ago when any phone calls were forbidden in many prisons. In Pentridge, not that long ago, you were allowed to send and receive one letter a month. Later it was eased to one letter a fortnight. Incoming letters, even from your wife or your fiancée, were only allowed to stay in your possession for 24 hours and then they had to be returned to the censor. Why? Those were the rules.

Magazines, like *Women's Weekly* and *Woman's Day* were censored. They had all the female underwear advertisements cut out of them in case they made the male prisoners frustrated. Frankly, it would seem to me that it would frustrate them more by cutting the lingerie ads out rather than leaving them in. Being caught with a copy of *Australasian Post* could be worth a week in solitary confinement. A copy of the salacious

Truth newspaper could be worth two weeks in solitary. (The latter presumably would be for having no taste.)

My first full day at Morwell and pretty aware of the surroundings, I start to put together some of the psychologies of the place. Your life is run by sirens. Wake up siren (I've actually had my constitutional walk and shower by then). Then the get up siren. The breakfast siren. Breakfast is bacon and eggs, sorry, egg. Bacon and a boiled egg and baked beans and toast. Breakfast lasts six minutes. I'd love to have the Alka-Seltzer or Pepto-Bismol concession in this place.

More of the sixty or seventy inches of rain a year drop out of the sky. Some prisoners, on their day off, attempt a game of cricket but it is washed out. Very few take advantage of the library. Several though are attempting to master the one typewriter in the place. A couple of white collar inmates are trying to show a couple of other prisoners how to use a computer. It's a jazzy PC owned by one of the inmates. I spend most of the day (in between the klaxon horn of the muster just to remind us that we are really just prisoners with numbers) hunched over my typewriter. Writing this. It is partly to pass the time, partly to compile a journal of my time in jail – even though I don't know if I will ever publish it – and partly a stream of consciousness thing, to see, when I look back, if my attitudes have changed. To see if I have changed. To see if, even in a short time, being denied your freedom does anything to you.

I spend some time reading in my hut. Heaps of newspapers I have arranged to have delivered daily but in here I am already skimming over some of the world news stories and can understand why, perhaps, some of the people who have spent five or ten years in jail have absolutely no interest in reading the news headlines. To them they are totally irrelevant. In most cells though, the television set rarely goes off even if the sound is turned down. The ultimate time filler.

Lunch is two meat pies. Dinner a piece of chicken and a heaped plate of overcooked vegetables.

Throughout the day, whenever more than two prisoners are talking, the conversation inevitably turns to 'how long to go'. They talk in a mathematical formulae all their own: '9 and 6, 5 and 2 plus the third remission etc.' It is all about maximum sentences and minimum sentences, non-parole periods, pre-release deductions. It is a consuming conversation. I tell the prison governor I would be a hypocrite if I took early-release or remission. He says I have no choice and cannot refuse the one-third off for good behaviour and some other reductions even if I want to. I tell him I want to. A vision crosses the mind of them throwing me out one day and me trying to get back in to keep my principles intact. In the end the governor says I do not have to take some days off that I would be entitled to under the 'pre-release' formula. That means instead of being released on a Friday I can stay in until the following Monday. I tell him that is what I want to do. As always, that debate quickly gets around the jail camp. Two wags ask me if I won't take the bonus days of freedom then can they have them.

Saturday night I think of the party I could be at in Melbourne. The 'come as your favourite fantasy' party. Carol Smith goes in white overalls and racing emblems. Her fantasy is to be Paul Newman's pit manager. My sidekick Pamela Graham goes as – I'm told when I manage to get a reverse charge phone call through – an extraordinary tizzy-haired Tina Turner. The simplest and funniest is the guy who goes as a tablecloth because 'they get laid three times a day'. I hear all this and feel lonely. Birthday girl Rasa Bertrand tells me her dad lived in this very camp at Morwell in the 1940s when it was a displaced persons migrant camp. Her father planted some of those soaring ridge-top pines that I admire on my morning walks.

On the phone I tell Rasa that although I have been 'unavoidably detained' and cannot be there I am in fact in fancy dress – green prison uniform. I try to crack jokes. Rasa cries.

Later that night I listen to some horror stories from first-timers on their initiation to Pentridge and 'the yards'. Some stayed there a few days. Some a few weeks. Lawyers and accountants, they were taken to prison on remand and dropped in their pin-striped suits in the yard. They were immediately suspected of being 'jacks'. Several did not even know what 'jacks' were. They didn't even call policemen 'cops'. They told me about the boredom. The cold. The averting of the eyes so as not to attract an accusing, 'What are you staring at?' which could easily trigger a fight. Stories of sleeping in the rank dormitories. The farting, the fighting, the open dunnies located directly under the television sets at one end of the dorm.

The little things that outside you wouldn't think of. For example: there is Vegemite on the tables at Morwell. There is no Vegemite on the tables at Pentridge. Not just a reward for men in a low-security prison. In Pentridge some drug addicts try to inject Vegemite into their veins. There is salt in shakers on the table at Morwell. It is in open trays or troughs at Pentridge. After meals it is left in those open troughs on a shelf and when the floors are swept, two and three floors up, the dust and the dirt drifts down and turns the salt troughs a speckled brown. Serves them right some of you will say. But surely that went out with scurvy and the convict ships.

Am I getting soft I think? Have I already, so soon, heard so many, too many, hard-luck jail stories? Are we all too far removed from the real world? My last conversation for the day is with a group of other prisoners. None of us is sure whether daylight saving comes in tomorrow or not. At three o'clock in the morning (DST or not) I wake up in my cell and, after gallons of tea before bedtime, resign myself to the inevitable need for a trek through the rain and the cold to the lavatory block.

As I crunch across the gravel in the wet, with a full bladder and teeth chattering, I wonder what the hell I am doing here.

Sunday, October 18, 1987

I realise I must already be losing track of time and dates and days. I've headed yesterday's journal entry October 16. Also, almost missed breakfast muster because, for some reason, I was an hour out of my timing calculations. If I can do this after a few days in jail what is it like after months . . . years? Sunday is one day though where, I soon discover, you start to count every hour and almost every minute. Sunday is Visitors' Day.

I keep telling myself that it is only a couple of days since I saw my wife. Some of these men have not seen their families for months. Visiting hours are 10 a.m.

until 4 p.m. You start to get some idea about how long some of these men have been in here when you overhear a conversation that goes like this: 'My daughter was five when I came in here. Now she's got three kids.' Emotive stuff, but you have to keep remembering what one veteran prison officer told me, 'If you can't do the time, don't do the crime.' A line I have used many times since. I also start to wonder if I knew the gory details about what some of these men were in here for, would I feel so sympathetic?

Back to Visit Day. Prisoners who didn't shave yesterday, shave today. Some who didn't shower yesterday, or the day before, shower today. Most of the men expecting visits, and some who are not but keep hoping, are showered, dressed, ready and waiting by 9 a.m. By this time large areas marked 'No Visitors' have been roped off. At 10 o'clock the *M*A*S*H* loudspeaker starts its (this time welcome) staccato 'Smith – visit. Jones, go to the gatehouse – visit.' Name after name rattles off. Men waiting for wives, lovers, parents, children, to arrive, mill in groups outside their huts. Those with no visitors are not permitted in the visiting area.

By noon, two precious hours into visiting, some show obvious anxieties. 'Will she come?' must be in the forefront of many minds. 'She didn't come last week, will she come today?' 'I said things I shouldn't have said last week . . . will she come today?' You wonder about the young prisoner who says 'I told my visitors to stop coming.'

'When?'

'Two years ago.'

Some prisoners, sweating on an arrival, wonder if

there has been an accident. High Ridge Road with its sheer drops on a twisting dirt road is hardly a casual drive through the suburbs. I must admit I'm getting excited and wishing Jacki would hurry up. Almost forgetting I told her not to rush. Almost forgetting I had said, 'It's a hellishly long ride . . . come around noon or one o'clock. It'll be fine. It'll be fine. Don't rush.' By noon, two hours into the official visiting hours, I am thinking, 'Please hurry.'

There are bittersweet feelings watching families arrive. Food baskets are first inspected for booze and drugs by prison officers in a walk-through guard-house. Any food left over after lunch is also inspected and given a green or red light before a prisoner is permitted to take it back to his hut.

I watch the kids, the wives and the lovers. The tears and the touching. Several couples manage to find a doorway . . . their bodies glued together. Jacki arrives with friends who are also colleagues: Suzy Jaeger, my personal assistant; Pamela Graham – she was in on the Glennon case from the start and I know feels guilty that I'm in here and she's not; Mike Frazer, a professional and personal mate. Stepson Dylan isn't with them. I asked him not to come the first time. Didn't know what to expect or what I would be exposing him to. Some awkward moments. Where to set up 'camp'. The outside spots are claimed by long-timers. We get a big table in a new, almost finished, prefabricated prison hall. I sense Jacki and my mates – a long way from Flower Drum feasts or caviar at Gowing's – find it funny seeing me in prison greens and, incongruously, wearing yellow gumboots. Conversation, at times, surprisingly strained. Like around hospital beds. Much of it about the case and the radio reaction. The cordial is warm and there's far too much food. None of us are really hungry. Already I think, 'I hope they'll let me keep some of this.'

The visiting hours pass so fast. Suddenly the announcement for all visitors to leave. That moment underscores the prison adage that the wives and families on the outside do it harder than those on the inside. On the outside it is the not knowing about what is going on on the inside that hurts. The hardships, the loneliness, the stigma at times and the responsibilities of trying to raise a fatherless family alone. Inside, although the separation hurts, there are hundreds of other men in close proximity in the same boat, the same predicament.

At Morwell, eighty men, after Visit Day, go back to their huts with cryptic conversations: 'Good visit?' 'Yep, good visit.' Their families, by car and bus and train, go back to empty, struggling homes. I know you should think about the weight on the family and the pain for the family before you do the crime but from this side – from the inside – there are still some poignant, emotional scenes. Especially the late afternoon tears of the little kids who can't comprehend why Daddy isn't coming home too.

I get the news Sunday about my first job in prison. Starting tomorrow I'm joining Norm Gallagher's mob as a brickie's labourer. At least it will pass the time.

Monday, October 19, 1987

The fifth day in custody if you count the Thursday when I was arrested and I certainly do. And the day when I have changed a bit. Or, should I say, changed back a bit.

On my now habitual morning walk around familiar boundaries, this time in a fine drizzle, I get thinking again about some of the conversations in recent days. I feel I have been wooed into a sort of false world perhaps because, unlike in Queensland's prisons, a person's crimes are not printed on a card on the cell door. Working with men whose crimes are not known to you and when they appear to be, on the surface, ordinary, courteous, rule-abiding people, albeit in a prison camp atmosphere, can be beguiling. But then thoughts of the victims and the victims' families come, increasingly, to the surface. As they should. Sure, as I said yesterday, it is hard for the families. Families on the outside do it as hard, if not harder, than their husbands, or boyfriends, or sons on the inside. But it is also tough and heart-breaking for the victims and the families of victims. I mentioned a prisoner who said his daughter was five when he entered prison and now she had three kids. There are women out there whose daughters were five when their fathers were murdered by men in this prison. Their dad did not live long enough to see his daughter grow to womanhood.

Still in that mood, trudging round the camp boundary with the Out of Bounds signs every twenty yards as a reminder of where I am, I think of a policeman crippled with a bullet in his spine from a gun fired by a man now in Morwell with me. And I feel increasingly angry about the repeated jail use of the innocuous-sounding word 'knock' for killing someone. A bland, non-deadly word that doesn't conjure up visions of a woman raped and maybe stabbed, or a person bludgeoned to death with an axe. Or a crippled policeman. Or somebody's brains on a footpath. It doesn't make me a 'lock 'em up and throw away the key' sort of vigilante but it is a warning to me – and I hope it warns me for the rest of the time that I am in here – not to generalise and not to get sucked in by every story.

I believe there are some innocent people in Morwell, or at least people who should not be in jail (and I am leaving myself out of this). I believe there are some people in jail, be it Morwell or Pentridge, who are not serving the community or being properly punished by being there. I also believe that there are some people in jail – not necessarily this one – who should be entitled to get out on the early-release system.

Breakfast today: toast and/or porridge. I give the porridge a miss. Even the guy dishing it out says I should come back after breakfast with a wheelbarrow and use it as mortar on my first day as a brickie's labourer. After breakfast it is work time. Doing a BLF man's job without a ticket. Suffice to say we work at BLF pace. Not exactly the fastest diggers, shovellers or wheelbarrow pushers in jail. Still, a bit of manual work won't hurt me and after four days without a beer or a glass of wine I am feeling pretty good. Pretty healthy. And not missing it. We are preparing to build a new prisoners' hut. The 'Hinch memorial hut', it has already been dubbed. There is a lot of Monday morning activity in the camp. The three bush crews, totalling around thirty men, have already gone out and, as usual, when they return they will talk about leeches and snakes, including tiger snakes up to five and six feet long. (Later in the day when I go up river I have to flick the slimy, wriggling, clinging leeches off my arms and hands. I hate them.) I'm glad I have copped a work detail inside the camp although one member of our gang gets a fat, blood-filled tick on his neck.

There's some excitement in the prison with the news that singer/dancer/actor David Atkins and the cast of his new hit show *Dancin' Man* plan a surprise visit. They are coming by bus on Wednesday to put on a mini-version of the show for the prisoners. A big gesture: three hours up by bus, some song and dance routines, another three hours back by bus and then on stage that night – in Melbourne for their regular performance. They offered to do it for me – partly because I had organised a team of investors, 'theatre angels', to bankroll the Melbourne season after David 'the human dynamo' Atkins' original backers had suddenly dropped out. Their gesture overwhelms me. Like the show business friends who assembled last night at Metropolis studio in South Melbourne to record a song of support for me. All of that plus letters and telegrams daily from friends and strangers: from Victoria, from Sydney, from Perth. I wonder how I can thank people, and express what it all means to me in these crucial days, when I get out. *When* I am getting out increasingly consumes my thoughts and conversations in Morwell. Unless things go wrong it now looks like I'll be sent out early next week.

All the mail isn't wonderful, isn't supportive. I sit on my bed in Hut 38 late one afternoon reading the day's mail. It has already been opened by the prison staff. One of the first letters, signed by a Pentridge prisoner, says things like:

> 'I can assure you that you would not be put in our unit as the screws know we would never allow

you to leave the unit alive. You would not just cop a kicking or a few slashes with a Stanley blade. You, fatboy, would be given the full treatment and that thing you married would be living it up on your life insurance. You would be our plaything, you weak, slimy maggot.

'Hopefully you'll run into some crim whose got a bit of go and you'll find a piece of metal hanging out of your fat gut. Anyway critter, you never know your luck. See ya fatboy. Jim Loughnan.'

(Editor's note: Loughnan was one of the men who several years later deliberately set alight to his cell block in Jika Jika and accidentally killed himself).

Not only because of the threats in Loughnan's vile note which I take seriously, I decide to eat my evening meal in my hut. One of the other reasons? There is one thing I cannot get in jail, not in this jail, and I don't mean my wife's affection, or wine, or friends, or good food. The one thing I cannot get is solitude. The longer I am here the harder it is to find time to type up my journal. I know people talk about boredom in jail – and it is there. For some, for long termers. But suddenly a barrier seems to have been totally broken here. The way to express friendliness in Morwell is to invite somebody into your hut for a cup of coffee or tea. I am drowning in the stuff. It is as if suddenly I don't have two heads and have been accepted. My hut mate Bob says we should hang out a shingle. He says he's practising a secretarial manner for 'Mr Hinch will see you now.'

After risking being considered anti-social and taking my evening meal back to the hut to eat I am tracked down by an 'official visitor' (a layman or woman who acts as a sort of mini-ombudsman and reports on prison conditions, welfare and any problems, to the Attorney-General's department). She has a couple of prisoners lined up for me to have a meaningful chat to that night. Like right now. I am talked out with prisoners' problems. I tell her no offence but I'll talk to them in my time and in my own way. After all, there's plenty of time and I'm not exactly going anywhere.

My negative, almost brusque reaction to her request surprises me a little. Maybe it is because I am subconsciously on guard about something. Maybe it is because I am trying to get through it all without making waves. Maybe I am getting tired of trying so hard to fit in so well. I just know I desperately want some time alone. I am sick of lining up nine times a day. Sick of it!

Sick of five minute breakfasts and ten minute dinners. Sick of shouting 'watch your back', to other naked men showering every time you turn the water on or off, to ensure nobody gets scalded. Sick of sharing a room with a stranger . . . even though he was here first and has been courteous and good company.

I remember the words of the prison governor the day I came in here and had my official admission chat. He said everybody's attitude changes in here eventually . . . even after a week.

Tomorrow is Day Six.

Tuesday, October 20, 1987

Thoughts of food this morning during a shortened morning walk in the drizzle. Not dreams of food. No longings for Gilbert Lau's Peking duck or Dennis Gowing's beluga caviar. That hasn't happened. I anything, I have eaten too much in here. A lot of it clag . . . and I have even skipped some meals. I remember stories written as a young police reporter, around Christmas and even Easter, about prison meals in Australia and many people (me included) have thought 'If things are that good in jail why aren't we eating in there?' The stories describe Christmas on the inside: 'traditional turkey, cranberry sauce, Christmas pudding, ice cream.' Sounds great. Scrumptious. But if you have ever been in the army then you know that really bad food can sound really good on paper. Last night for example, in Morwell Prison we had (on paper) tender roast lamb, mint sauce, roast vegetables. It was so bad, the vegetables overcooked and strangely oily, the lamb so overcooked and leathery that I ditched it all except for one slab of meat which I brought back to my hut and turned into a sandwich. Lunch yesterday was bangers and mash. Breakfast today: porridge and toast. And before you start thinking that it sounds better than a lot of people eat – especially pensioners – let me point out that the budget for feeding an adult prisoner in Victorian jails is $3.20 per man. Not per meal. That's $3.20 per day. The dessert factor in that $3.20 per day works out at just under 20 cents per man, per day. No wonder rejected cans of fruit find their way into prisons.

One of the great kitchen scandals running for the past few days concerns the Case of the Missing Corn Flakes. The storeroom refuses to release another case of cereal to the kitchen because, they claim, the quota has been reached. The kitchen claims it was a bookkeeping error and one case of cereal is still owing. It has caused a lot of snap and crackle. So far the storeroom is winning. We haven't had corn flakes since I've been here. They're still serving up dollops of putrid porridge that wouldn't fall out of the huge pot if you turned it upside down.

Today's lunch is ambitiously called chow mein. Possibly Armenian chow mein. Virtually inedible. I flee to the hut for some cheese, biscuits and fruit I have squirrelled away after the Sunday visit by friends and family. The squirrel mentality catches on quickly in jail. It gets me thinking of a way to cut taxpayers' costs and cut waste in prison kitchens. Permit prisoners – at their own or their family's expense – to install small refrigerators and microwave ovens in their huts or cells. Not as a luxury but as a practicality. Once a week on visiting day wives, parents, children, could bring in food (inspected at the gate) that could virtually last a prisoner all week. It could be kept in the fridge and heated in a microwave or mini-oven. A man who could cook a few fresh eggs of his own for breakfast is going to spurn the scrambled, rubbery slops floating in water without salt or any other condiment in the mess hall. The prison's egg bill would drop dramatically.

It may sound naive, yet again, but on Sunday and Monday nights after the family visits you see prisoners generously sharing food from the outside with other inmates in an environment where selfishness is usually the password.

For part of today, in between the rain, I work on the wooden boxing for tomorrow's concrete floor. Also shovel a lot of sand.

Daily I hear hardluck prison stories, 'the judge was a dickhead' stories. Some are bizarre. Unintentiona black comedy. Lines like, 'I should have been out on parole eighteen months ago they tell me.'

'Why aren't you?'

'I have to serve extra time for breaking an earlier parole. The system stinks.'

Another one delivered without a hint of remorse, 'I copped seven months including one month for being lousy .09. If it had happened in South Australia I would've got off.'

'What was the other six months for?'

'Driving while disqualified.'

'First time?'

'No me ninth. I copped ten years for driving while disqualified back in 1980 or '81 and that was about me third or fourth time. It's bloody unfair. I never hit anybody or anything.'

The young offender can't be any older than 26 or 27.

'I've been disqualified for a total of 29 years but luckily they are all concurrent.' He can't understand it when I tell him that people with his sort of road record, his illegal driving record, should be banned for life.

I hear some real gallows-humour stories from young prisoners who have brought additional jail sentences on their shoulders after clashing with the enemy – the judges.

Example One: 'How do you plead?'

Defendant: 'Unlucky.'

He copped an additional one month in jail for contempt of court for those two words. Why did he say it? 'I was unlucky to get caught. It was the truth.'

Example Two: A maintenance case. The defendant was prepared to pay for the food and clothing and care for his young daughter but he told me he was adamant he would not pay a cent to 'the bitch of a mother' who had walked out on him for another man. A 'mate'. After hearing the evidence the judge said: 'I intend to give her $30 a week.'

The young defendant replied: 'If that's the case I'll toss in a couple of dollars meself.' That cost him an extra two days in the court cells for contempt.

Feeling a bit edgy and a bit bored today. Maybe because I have finally got the word that I'll be getting out at 8 a.m. next Monday. Maybe I'm starting to think like a prisoner. For example I get some glee out of the fact that in a small way I've beaten the system. I'm not due out until 8 o'clock Monday morning. But daylight savings comes in on Sunday. Under normal conditions it would still only be 7 a.m. I've 'stolen' an hour from them. Prison think.

I have not allowed myself to feel down since I have been in here. Phone calls to my family and to friends have helped. Mail from around the country has really helped. Editorials in the *Sun* and the *Herald* were good for the backbone. Although the *Herald* calling me a clown did hurt. To all those safe, cossetted, ivory tower editors, and judges and lawyers, who say I could have done it some other way . . . to all of them I say: Name One. We tried everything else.

Wednesday, October 21, 1987

Shovelling gravel and sand into a concrete mixer for most of the morning is interesting after reading in the *Sun* about all the 'special treatment' I am getting in

Morwell and the 'special treatment' I got at Pentridge before that. I am making concrete for the floor of a new prisoners' hut and am actually getting paid for it. True, it is less than $15 a week. Not per hour, not per day, but per week. And of that I am told I can spend $12.38 per week through my canteen slip. $12.38! Let's have a party! I can spend it on cigarettes or soap or shaving cream or toothpaste or talcum powder or cordial or chocolate bars. The order must go in by 7.30 on a Sunday night and the canteen goodies are available for pickup late Tuesday.

I suppose tonight on the news they'll be saying I'm getting more special treatment because the prison authorities have given permission for the cast of *Dancin' Man* to appear at the prison and to give a mid-afternoon concert for inmates and staff.

The troupe arrives amidst much excitement in the camp. It has given people something to look forward to for days. Some oldtimers who have been here for up to five years say they have never seen a live, professional show here. Ever. The anticipation fills in some hours, relieves some of the pressure from the boredom and sameness of prison life. For some reason I feel nervous. Hoping it will go well. Not knowing how these strangers, some long-isolated strangers, will react.

The reaction from the 'captive audience' is fantastic. Tremendous. They love it. The troupe really seem to enjoy what they are giving too. Apparently some TV news services make it sound like there is a special performance in jail for Hinch and 'other inmates are allowed to watch too.' An unselfish gesture from some great people has the shine taken off it.

All I want to do now is get out – doesn't everybody?

I notice some newspaper stories saying I will probably serve 'only' 11 or 12 days. 'Only'. Some people 'only' get 11 or 12 days for their annual holidays. I'm touchy but I have survived a week in prison and, I feel, survived it well. I have been helped by the letters and the telegrams and the cards and all that yellow ribbon. Today I hear, for the first time, the song recorded at the weekend by friends and supporters in Melbourne. It starts to feel like it is happening to somebody else – and maybe that's good.

It's funny how quickly you adapt to situations. Example: At milk call this afternoon I am also given a pear. On the way back to Hut 38 I almost, absent-mindedly, go to bite it. The prison mind says 'save it for breakfast' and it is squirrelled away. This, after seven days. How would I be after seven months? Or seven years?

Tonight I received a certificate from a prisoner nicknamed 'Bubble' because of his considerable girth. He has spent a lifetime in the building trade and is a member of the BLF. We have been working together on the hut project. The certificate says:

'I karnt do maffs but I kan lift hevy fings. This certifies that Derryn Hinch has completed his builders' labourers apprenticeship.'

Thursday, October 22, 1987

More dirt digging, boxing and sand spreading ready for more concreting. Must be honest and admit that already I can sympathise with some of the prisoners who go to all sorts of lengths and use all sorts of subterfuge to get out of doing much work. After months or years of it some of the jobs must pale. And there is a niggling feeling of 'Hey, they locked me up. I'm a prisoner not a cheap gravel shoveller.' On the one hand it is something to do to pass the time but sometimes there's a feeling that things are just being found to be done.

I'm still, increasingly, yearning for some solitude which I know sounds strange from somebody in a prison. My early morning misty walks are now a combination of a walk and a sit on a river bank to watch the dawn antics of the ducks. I watch them and think of the sitting duck . . . the young man I have written about who should never have spent a night in jail. He leaves tomorrow. He confides in me that even though he has spent most of his six months at the Morwell Prison Farm and not in Pentridge he has never, as an ingrained country boy, ever got used to so many people in one place. Eighty of us plus the officers.

On a lighter note – no breakthrough yet in the Great Corn Flakes Mystery. A porridge poultice again for breakfast this morning . . . if you are game. One food mystery is solved though. Yesterday's lunch was officially called fried rice. It made the traditional Chinese dish of sticky rice look positively runny. I now know why. Yesterday's rice was cooked for one and a half hours!

Much trepidation and tension in the camp today. The Classifications Board is coming. Tomorrow it is the Parole Board. Men lining up to see if their chances of parole are better than last time or to see if their classification has improved or regressed. Much rumbling about the few minutes that are spent with each prisoner. The board chairman later tells me, when I am summonsed to the governor's office to meet him and other board members (how often does that happen?)

that most of the paper work and case reviews have been done before the short, personal interviews. One board member, a prison governor from elsewhere, seems bewildered by the fact that my jailing, and continuing incarceration, is considered 'news' by TV stations and newspapers.

Modesty aside I gently remind him that being the first Australian journalist ever jailed for contempt of court might be considered newsworthy but even more importantly I point out (hoping he will include himself in the net I throw) too many courts and politicians have not yet come to fully realise the epidemic of concern, fear, even rage amongst ordinary mothers and fathers in this country over the risks to their children. He does at least nod sagely when I point out that many people now believe that interfering with a person's car attracts a bigger and more severe penalty than for a person who interferes with your children.

Tonight, in bed, I read a news story about a father in England who molested his two teenage daughters for years and caused them to get pregnant a total of nine times. You wonder where will it all end? Imagine the scar tissue – mental and physical for those young girls.

Maybe it is because around this time last week I first entered the bluestoned walls of Pentridge that I am now counting the days more than ever. I've had it. I want out. I stop myself from thinking that I don't deserve to be here. I am also increasingly niggled by the reports that I am getting special treatment inside. Although I certainly got it today.

Late this afternoon about eight or ten prisoners were about to go for a jog along bush tracks outside the prison. Accompanied of course by a prison officer.

Keeps them fit. Tones them up for bush work, for tree-planting, and path-clearing. For the first time in a week I decide to go with them. I pull on my track suit and sneakers and we all head for the gate. A more senior officer calls me back, he has to check with the chief honchos by phone. 'Sorry, you can't go. You're grounded.' I think he said my file was marked 'R.I.' which means remain inside. My late afternoon burst of physical fitness is reduced to a few turns around the prison boundary from the inside. They obviously didn't want any TV cameramen or press photographers getting shots of Hinch doing it hard – outside Morwell. I guess it's another example of the special treatment I'm getting.

Friday, October 23, 1987

For this jail journal I have diligently been putting the date at the top of each day's first page. But to be honest after a few days in a cell I have to look at the previous day's newspapers (they arrive a day late) to find out what it is. My second Friday in jail. Feelings a mite different. On the one hand the second Friday in Morwell makes the sentence feel somehow longer. But that competes with the stronger feeling that, come Monday, I'll be out. Free of the guards, free of their rules, free of the endless roll-calls. Free of it all. It gives me a lift. As always I am cognisant of the fact that my incarceration is a mere smidgeon compared to most – but it is a forced separation, a legally ordered separation from my family, from my friends and from my job. It is time to think of some of the things I have learned, good and bad, while in prison.

I have learned how to make a syringe out of a

ballpoint pen. I have learned that drugs are rife. There must be some marijuana in Morwell, especially with all those surrounding forests, but I don't see any. Beer also, obviously, gets in here. I don't see any beer or hard liquor but I have seen a few empty cans under the huts. I've learned that Ararat is called the 'junkies' jail'. I've learned that drugs are almost epidemic in Pentridge. I've learned that TV sets, clothes, radios, watches, are traded for drugs. And I've learned that some prison officers must be dealing in drugs. Must be, at times, dealers. It isn't all coming in from visitors.

I know that senior prison officials, the ones actually working in the prisons, no longer think it is preposterous that hyperdermic needles may eventually be provided free for addict prisoners. Even though that is an admission that the authorities are losing the war against drugs on both sides of the wall. I have learned just how reckless and how irresponsible governments are being about AIDS in prisons. They might as well call some of our jails 'AIDS incubators'.

I have learned that I can buy a new driver's licence under a false name for $50 or $60 and if I am in real trouble there are some government employees who will sell me one for $500. Think I'm exaggerating, try this one.

In Morwell prisoners can train for and, legitimately get, driver's licences, especially heavy equipment licences. One candidate asked in all sincerity, when I was there, whether or not he could use one of the four names he'd been using on other licences. Or would he have to come up with a fifth one! The attitude is so cynical that a typical inside joke goes like this: 'I have not had one traffic conviction, not one endorsement, since I bought this licence.'

I have learned that cliques form inside prisons the way that society fragments on the outside. The lifers and the long-termers form a prison core (usually in the kitchen) and there is a tangible, palpable, resentment of the 'new crims'. Life was more simple in the old days when the people behind bars were killers and biffers and bank robbers and standover men. Some of them, even in Morwell, resent the changes from the days when a crim was a crim. It was a black and white 'them against us' society. A prisoner wouldn't talk to a screw or he would cop a thumping. Any prisoner seen talking to a screw would have to be 'giving somebody up'. One prisoner who has spent more than ten years in jail tells me he preferred the old days when you knew where you stood, when there weren't 'assessment committees' and 'attendance sentences'. He yearns for the days of 'black gold' and 'white sand'. Rare commodities in jail, known on the outside as tea and sugar.

Months, years, in jail were a series of tactical battles between the inmates and the authorities. He tells me, as we sit on the verandah step outside his hut, that he misses the old traditions, things like somebody copping the 'blanket treatment'. That's when a prisoner was punished by other prisoners by having a big, grey prison blanket dropped over his head and then pinned to his sides. He would then suffer an anonymous but thorough (and excruciatingly painful) kicking from four or five other prisoners. The same punishment was sometimes handed out to bully-boy officers. That was a time when crims never, ever, gave up another prisoner. Now, says the old lag, because of drugs in prison 'they'll shop their own mother for a fix.'

I have also learned, or at least had reconfirmed, in

this pressure-cooker time in jail, that at times our courts are woefully inconsistent and the punishments do not always fit the crime. It has not changed my mind that punishments are too light. It has not changed my mind that the early-release system and time-off permutations are wrong. And I say that not as a released-early hypocrite but as a person who could have legally chosen to be out of this jail right now. Could have opted for a 'pre-release' formula which could have seen me now spending this weekend with my wife and family.

And I have learned not to be sharp or sarcastic when well-meaning people tell me or write to me 'at least you are having a rest.' If lining up nine times a day, losing all your privacy by showering every morning with at least a dozen strangers, sharing a tiny hut every night with a stranger, and eating meals that are budgeted at $3.38 per day, per man (I was wrong it wasn't $3.20), if all that is having a rest then give me the worst package tour ever invented. And remember I haven't mentioned the flashlight in the eyes at 11.30 every night and 2.30 every morning.

Jail is a four-letter word that means loss of freedom. Loss of privacy. And, if you let it, loss of pride and motivation.

Saturday, October 24, 1987

In the thousands of words I have written in this prison journal I don't think I can be accused of being bitter. I haven't shouted 'unfair'. Haven't said 'Why me?' Haven't said 'What about the real criminals who often go free?' I haven't even canvassed an issue I intend to take up when I get out of here about a person, up on a contempt of court charge, being heard and adjudicated on by a jury of his peers. Not the judge whose court he was supposedly in contempt of. I am confident – I'll be so rash to say from behind bars – that I am sure no jury would have convicted me on the charges I was sent here for.

I have been buoyed while in jail by two things: by my own, unswerving, belief that I did the right thing, and near the end of this jail sentence I still feel the same way. And by letters from all over Australia. Many of encouragement and support. Great letters. Inspiring letters. I have been sent bibles and prayer books even though I am not a religious man. Yellow ribbons, cards, wonderful letters in crayon from little kids whose parents have obviously interpreted for them what they have seen on the TV news. Plus letters from victims of child abuse and incest. Not last month or last year . . . some of them go back thirty and forty tortured years.

One letter from Canberra from a woman who wrote: 'There is something else those who criticise you don't understand or don't want to understand. They don't understand what it is like to be one of the children. Perhaps I am being hard on them, perhaps it is impossible to comprehend unless you have lived through it.' When this woman was a little girl she was terrorised by a trusted man 'for the most important years of my growing up'. His actions 'laid my life waste in ways I could not even begin to describe'.

She then wrote to me: '. . . I worked in a hospital for several years. The children seemed to form a line with no beginning and, sadly, no end. I saw baby girls of only six months who were so dreadfully injured that they will never be able to have babies of their own.

There are no words to describe the anguish of their mothers.

'I know of teenage girls who, through sheer good luck, were found by someone they could trust before they finished sharpening the carving knife with which they intended to really punish the man who put them through years of hell.

'I know of scores of young women who – to the horror of their boyfriends, fiancés or husbands – become utterly hysterical because a kiss became too passionate or a touch too intimate. Having lived through the last myself I know how terrible it is and I begin to understand how difficult it must be for even the most patient and gentle of men to face such unreasoning terror and habitual lack of trust.'

That's what the child molesters do. Not only the physical things. They also steal trust and destroy innocence. Their victims' suffering may go on physically for one, two or five years. Their mental suffering can go on for decades. That is why, in jail today – for trying to warn parents about child molesting and especially about 'poachers in the sanctuary' – I have no sympathy, only anger and frustration when I open a letter from a South Australian address. Out falls a newspaper clipping from the *Adelaide Advertiser* with the headline 'No Jail For man in Incest Case'. The court report says that a man, aged 79, convicted of incest with his nine-year-old granddaughter has had a jail sentence suspended because of his age, ill-health and 'previous good character'.

Why? To hell with his age, health and character. What about her age? She was nine years old for Christ's sake! What about her health? This man, who can hide behind a wall of secrecy because to identify him would identify the poor girl, penetrated a nine-year-old kid. A little girl. A little girl who trusted her grandfather. His lawyer called his foul actions 'recent aberrations'. They occurred over a nine-month period. The judge calls the molester's actions 'abhorrent sexual molestation' and yet that man does 12 days less jail than I'm doing and pays $15,000 less in fines.

And if that isn't enough to stir me there is another report in today's news about a man – another man whose identity must be hidden to protect the identity of his victim – who avoids being sent to jail even though he indecently assaulted his grandchildren, not grandchild, grandchildren, over a nine-year period. He did get a $5000 fine and 300 hours of community service after pleading guilty to eleven counts of indecent assault. That bastard's attacks on his own family included sexual assaults on one who was only three years old. The assaults on that poor child continued until the child was eight. One was seven years old when the attacks started. One was nine. And the seven-year-old had the nightmare all over again when assaulted between the ages of 15 and 17. The attacker did not go to jail.

I tell you, as I sit here in my prison greens for my tenth night behind bars, I wonder what the hell is going on in this country.

But one thing that makes me know things are changing in Australia despite cases like those I mention above, and despite the way the courts seem to play down the attacks on our most precious commodity, the kids. Parents ARE increasingly aware. Parents ARE increasingly suspicious. And parents, and the community at large, are increasingly angry at the way some of our judges seem to hold the theft of a car more heinous a crime than the theft of a child's innocence and childhood.

Sunday, October 25, 1987

Last day in jail!

Tomorrow morning I will be out and, I hope, quickly back on air on 3AW. On this morning's walk – even earlier it seems because of daylight saving – I discover that my morning trek around the perimeter of the prison farm totals 595 steps per lap. I counted them in the dawn mist. Am I really down to such trivialities after such a short time?

I find myself looking even more closely at the people around me. It can't only be the journalist in me that wants to know what everybody is in for, that searches faces of convicted killers looking for signs and not really knowing what signs I am looking for. I keep reminding myself that these men killed – some more than once – and that an overcrowded prison system, in an increasingly broke state, is trying to push them back out into the community. Some could be absorbed back into the community and never offend again, let alone kill again, but some, well, I'm not so sure. Do we, as a community, really believe in rehabilitation? Or do we believe in locking people up and throwing away the key? Would a man who killed in passion at the age of 18 or 22, kill again if released from jail 20 years later? Most wouldn't. But if that is the case then is the community prepared to take the risk on the unknown future of the few?

The answer to that I believe is 'yes, with trepidation.'

And if the answer is 'no' then you are going to have to lock people up for the term of their natural life, dehumanising both prisoner and guard.

Speaking of guards, I haven't actually talked about them much in this jail journal, even though they play such an obviously oppressive role in anybody's life in jail. I don't know how many mentions they have warranted because, deliberately, I have not gone back and edited these raw thoughts, raw pages. What is written here is a stream of consciousness in diary form. An instant journal. It is what fills the mind at the time when you are in the slammer. Somebody told me the other night that there are some prisoners who would make good guards and some guards who would make good prisoners. A few guards, it seems, have gone into the prison security field as a career – especially some of the governors. Most of the screws seem to me to have gone into the job for the money. It certainly can't be the conditions. Even allowing for nine days on, five days off, and a chance for double-shift overtime. For many guards, especially at places like Pentridge, it is like being a prisoner in a way. And they resent it. Their daily view, day after day, night after night, consists of gates and bars and people who despise them. Prisoners who spit on them, try to play mind games with them, try to demoralise and defeat them.

A few guards must be sadists. Some do get an extra swagger with an extra pip on the shoulder. At the relentless muster calls at Morwell some were fair, human, amenable. A couple thought it was Alcatraz and for one, counting heads from one to eighty seemed an insurmountable hurdle.

But, as I said, they remain in their own sort of prison. In Morwell there are those well-tended officer's quarters across the duck-filled river but it is hardly a haven. They eat together and must get as fed up with the musters and the nocturnal torch-flashing checks as the prisoners do.

One pessimistic, disillusioned guard at Pentridge complained to me about the stress, the dirt, the grot, the excrement that some prisoners spread around, the spittle, and in tougher sections of the jail, the risk of being jumped or stabbed. He said, 'After the prisoners, we are the lowest of the low or we wouldn't be in this job.' Hardly a slogan for job satisfaction.

Day and night they hear the prisoners' anthem: How many days, weeks, months, years, before I get out of here on pre-release, attendance centre, good behaviour, remission time etc. Behind the door of the Officers' Mess they too must discuss how long until retirement, superannuation and a pension. On both sides, it seems to me, they know the system is sort of working. At least it is holding together.

Admittedly it is rank that people get different sentences for virtually identical crimes. Some people getting revolving door remissions from dangerously overcrowded prisons while others spend more than 20 years in the slammer for similar crimes. Those let out, pushed out, are being regurgitated rather than rehabilitated. Politicians on both sides know there are no votes in prison reform.

On this Sunday afternoon in country Victoria with a massive backdrop of ranges and pine trees I watch as the curtain comes down on another Visit Day. Watch my wife, looking so small with mental lead weights on her shoulders, trudge out of the jail, past the gatehouse, and into the car for the long, tiring and tortuous ride home. As I head back up Main Street in a place I have described as a cross between *M*A*S*H* and *Catch-22* I feel just one thing: I want to go home.

Monday, October 26, 1987

Day 12. Free!

I'm coming home. I've done my time. One last mist-morning solo trudge around the prison's parameters or perimeters. I'm up early, dressed in civvies, ready to go. The system prevails, I must attend breakfast muster. But when the duty officer reaches me after dozens of 'present', 'present', 'present sir' I can't resist it. What can they do to me after lining up more than 100 times. I am five minutes away from freedom. When the screw (and I think of him that way) asks me if I am present, I say 'Just.'

Within minutes my battered cartons of belongings are loaded into a limo outside the prison gate. I meet my wife, run a media gauntlet, am driven to a helicopter pad near Austin's radio tower and am out of there. The chopper pilot, at my request, and like a scene from a bad *M*A*S*H* script does a run down Main Street over the prison. I recognise my hut and feel no pangs. Somebody put a bottle of good French champagne in an ice bucket in the helicopter. Nobody opens it. It's not really something to celebrate. From chopper to limo to LaTrobe Street and within hours of clicking heels to a man in uniform at Morwell Prison in country Victoria I am back on air in Melbourne using the corny, but appropriate line,

'As I was saying before I was so rudely interrupted.'

My lasting memory: that sea of yellow ribbons and yellow roses in my office, my studio, the 3AW foyer. Even on cars in the cobble-stoned car park. They brought a knot to the stomach and a tear to the eye.

I'd made it.

My Peers React

The cartoonists had a field day with my jailing. Most of them sympathetic. Plus a few pompous, anonymous, tub-thumping anti-Hinch editorials.

Martin Flanagan, in the *Age* made note of the fact that in the tense and emotional minutes when we were all waiting for the news to come through from the High Court in Canberra, I was playing a Billy Fields record, 'Bad Habits'. In his day-after report he quoted the words. '*Well, I'm in a mess, because I can't repress, all of these bad habits.*'

He likened me to a combat pilot, tense and hunched over the microphone with my bulbous headphones, awaiting the verdict. And when the thumbs down came through at 10.17 a.m. he wrote: 'And that was how they captured him, the wild colonial boy'.

Through all the bumpf and all the bullshit that I read in jail one column got to me and made me cry. It was written by a journalist, a craftsman, whom I have met but do not know. A writer, whom I suspect, does not know, respect or even like me, Peter Smark.

I read his comments for the first time in nearly five years the other night and they made my eyes smart.

On Friday, October 16, 1987, in the now defunct Melbourne *Herald* under the headline 'Victory for the law, but dignity rests with the convicted Hinch', he wrote:

> The High Court has found that Derryn Hinch was wrong to use illegal means to achieve what was, in the words of Mr Justice Toohey, an entirely legitimate purpose.
>
> In other words, he has been Jesuitical, not diabolical. Yet Lucifer's lot is his now, cast away from his fellows for the sin of pride.
>
> There was never really any question of his guilt on the contempt of court charge. His defence was gossamer thin, that the contempt laws in Victoria were archaic and therefore it was permissable to defy them.
>
> Station 3AW spent most of last year's profit and a good part of this year's in a quixotic attempt to make wrong seem right, but never really had a chance of success.
>
> The question here is: for what crime is Hinch being punished? Is it the crime of contempt? Or is it a crime that did not appear on the charge sheet? That's the crime of hubris, the overwhelming arrogance the ancient Greeks believed so offensive to the Gods.
>
> If hubris has indeed been judged to be his sin,

and I believe it is, a sad case has become a tragedy.

The media ranks are filled with odd people. So many are ego-driven, living nerve-edged, that the bar-room cackle at the anguish of a superstar can be a substitute for thought. There have been cackles enough amid our kind at Derryn's torture.

This time he had gone too far, finally he had been put in his place. What was he but a manipulative motor-mouth anyway and couldn't they all do better, given the chance? It's the way of our world.

And there have been, and are, no few legal and political guffaws at his discomforture. Old scores evened now, look, look at the TV news. He's trying to grin but wincing inside. And look at his wife, that so familiar face a mask of pain. That'll teach them.

Teach them what? That crime and punishment are often ill-related? It's hard to avoid the belief that in this case Hinch is being punished savagely not for what a broadcaster undoubtedly was wrong to do, but because of who this broadcaster is and what he has done before.

Fair enough, you may say. A housebreaker with a string of convictions draws a heavier sentence than a first-timer, what's wrong with that? I would say what's wrong is that in this case, Derryn's own childhood so marked him that he was gripped by irresistible impulse to speak out.

He knew he was in contempt. He is not only

a vastly experienced journalist but a former editor of the Sydney *Sun*. And despite the bravado of his pose since, he was trying at the time to pay a mite more respect to thc rulcs than he had on previous occasions.

But this case bore so agonisingly on the scar tissue of his soul that he was compelled to speak. I'm tempted to say more in justification on the specifics of the case, but I cannot. I cannot because I am acting as a prudent journalist but am none too happy about myself as a man in holding back.

Derryn acted improperly as a journalist but well as a man.

Yes, he is a skilled controversialist, a stirrer, an egotist, a gadfly. And yes, he has been guilty of hubris on occasion. And yes, his self-righteousness at times can be painful and his anger mere petulance.

And everything I have written here is a job description of what he does. Goad and guardian, without fear or favour. Sometimes, principle can be melded cunningly to pragmatism, but it often remains principle nonetheless.

He is for disclosure over secrecy, for democracy over oligarchy, more often than most of his fellows for the battlers over the almighty. And he has done a lot more good than harm in this town over the years he has served it and, yes I do mean it, he has served it.

Derryn Hinch is a man ruled more by emotion than by logic. That can lead him into trouble, and has. There is also enough of the hungry Kiwi kid who kicked his way up in the piranha pool of the Sydney newspaper world to have kept him sharply aware of the self-promotional value of clashes with authority. He has used that well.

And I still say that in this specific case, none of the streetwise tactics mattered. He was driven, he was forced to speak because of what had happened to a young New Zealand boy all those years ago.

That is why, in the same circumstances, he would do the same thing again, defying professional training and the law. Wrong? Of course. Criminal? No.

So what earthly use is served by a jail sentence for such a man? I could not write as I have here about at least one of his previous broadcasting sins. I would not have.

But in this matter, he now serves as a prisoner of conscience. I cannot laugh at that, or chuckle or sneer.

They are having their vengeance, and vengeance it is. Let them degrade him if they must, but keep him safe. Every minute he stays they are shamed.

Yesterday, there was victory for the Law and the State against Hinch. But all the dignity rests with the convicted.

I first read that column in jail. And have read it several times since. Each time it made me cry.

Keys to a Future

At 8.25 p.m. on a Friday night in New Plymouth in January 1960 I made an expensive decision that changed and shaped my life. Five minutes before the end of late night shopping at Medley's typewriter and adding machine shop in Egmont Street I bought my first typewriter. I was fifteen years old, had been working for a week and it cost £33. I was earning £2 a week ($4) plus overtime. We got an extra pound for working Saturday nights on the *Taranaki Herald*'s sports edition.

In my first days in the smoke-filled, ramshackle, paper-strewn newsroom at the *Herald* I had looked in awe at the Olivettis, the Smith-Coronas, the Olympias, the Regals, that chain-smoking journos with loosened ties would flail at, fingers flying across the keys. Until the day I walked through the newspaper's front door I had never seen a typewriter.

I had been a 'reporter' for five days when my Dad

and I went to Medley's. I looked at all the lightweight (for then) portables and kept being drawn back to a sleek, gun-metal-grey, heavy but streamlined Remington. Top of the range. I couldn't afford it but I bought it anyway. Thirty-three quid, plus interest, and I paid it off at 15 shillings a week for most of the next year.

My most precious possession. It smelled like a Singer sewing machine or one of those old, well-oiled, portable record players. I sat it on my parents' formica-topped kitchen table and thought 'I have just signed my life away for a machine I cannot use.' In those days £33 to a fifteen-year-old cadet reporter was like a married couple buying a house.

I took it out of the case, read the instruction book (the first and last instruction book I ever read), coaxed some paper into the platen – that's the roller – and, with two clumsy forefingers, typed something deep and meaningful like 'xmxmxmxrgrgrgrcbcbcbjdfjdjdj.' It was called a Remington 'Silentwriter' which meant it didn't sound quite as loud as the upright, tank-sized cast iron office Remingtons I would use. Cumbersome, slow machines I would bash out hundreds of thousands, probably millions, of words on them over the decades. Draught horse typewriters. My first Remington portable in its speckled grey and green case travelled the world with me. That machine became a growth on my arm. I never went anywhere without it. It weighed more than thirty pounds. I used to joke it was a 'Volkswagen with a handle'. In those days airline people were zealots about excess baggage and I couldn't afford to pay extra. Every time I checked in (when I was paying for my own ticket) I would hide the beast in or behind a pot plant. When I couldn't, I would nonchalantly swing it from my middle finger even though the weight was killing me.

I pounded its keys in New Zealand, Australia, Canada, the United States, Mexico, Jamaica, Singapore (we both stayed at Raffles), England, Brazil, France, Germany, Italy, Switzerland, Austria, Lichtenstein, Holland, Haiti, Grenada, Bermuda, the Bahamas, the Virgin Islands, St. Lucia. Belted the bejeesus out of it on moon shots, at race riots, and presidential conventions. It suffered its first physical abuse when a panicking colleague threw it over a wall as we all scarpered from the Oxford Hotel on the banks of the Avon River in Christchurch, New Zealand. It was nine o'clock at night at a time of six o'clock closing and the legal drinking age was 21. I was 17.

I loved that typewriter. Still do. Still own it. More than thirty years later. Over the years and through the continents it has become more of a reminder than my passport as to where I have been and when. It is plastered with stickers: Apollo 7, Apollo 10, Apollo 11 (the manned moon shot), Apollo 13 (the lump in the throat near-disaster), Apollo-Soyuz (the American-Soviet space link-up that, when you think of it, foreshadowed glasnost and perestroika). There are even older, fading stickers like the cabin baggage one from the Hang Fung Line in February, 1963, when me and my typewriter settled down on the *MV Wanganella* for a gut-churning three-and-a-half day trip from New Zealand to Sydney. In steerage, sharing a cabin with a stranger, it cost a mind-blowing £22 (around $40) one way. That was back when the New Zealand pound was worth twenty-five per cent more than the Australian pound. I arrived in Sydney with a duffel bag, about £20 to my name, and the typewriter.

The machine was still with me in the early 1970s when there was a recession in the United States and of course we all know that when Wall Street sneezes the world catches cold. It was a recession that, in retrospect, was a mere hiccup compared with the Wall Street crash of October 1987 and the grinding, debilitating, worldwide recession of the late 1980s and early 1990s.

In bad times, I noticed that 'how to' books clawed their way onto bestseller lists. I was living in New York during the '72 recession and the fact was not lost on a young, keen-to-succeed (read that as desperate) money-hungry journo that strange things work in tough times. These were the days of pet rocks and a best-selling New York yuppie book (before yuppies were identified) called *How to Care For Your Pet Avocado*. There was even a book on how to train your pet rock. It gave some sense to the fact that during the Great Depression people still went to the movies. Escapism lives.

So I wrote *The Scrabble Book*. It became an American Book of the Month Club selection. A Pan paperback edition still sells nearly twenty years later. I shouldn't complain, I still get royalty cheques for £50 from a literary agent called Abner Stein in London every six months, even though Abner has since died.

(An Australian policeman who was seconded to the Sultan of Brunei for eighteen months to work on a huge fraud case approached me at a charity dinner in 1992. He said something like, 'I know this is silly but I've just spent eighteen months in Brunei where there is not much to do. And one day at the market, when I was wandering around, bored shitless, I saw a dozen copies of a Scrabble book by Derryn Hinch. Is that you?' I told him it was although I haven't got any royalties from Brunei sales yet.)

The man who invented Scrabble using blueprint paper, 3-ply wood and a fretsaw was architect Alfred Moshe Butts. He said of my book (published in America in 1976 and Britain in 1977), 'Derryn Hinch's book is delightful. It's the best, most complete book ever about my game.'

I played Alfred Butts at Scrabble in his house in New York and beat him. But that's nothing to boast about. The inventor of the game told me that he had never, ever, challenged an opponent's word in his life. 'I trust people,' he said. When it came to the chapter in the book on cheating he said, 'Derryn, you have ruined my game.'

I mention all this here because it gets back to typewriters in a funny way. I wrote the Scrabble book on an old, heavy, Remington. The text ran about 60,000 or 70,000 words and, as a young print journalist, I figured I had to submit a 'clean' manuscript. And I did. I couldn't afford to pay a typist so I would go home every night to my apartment in a New Jersey skyscraper on the banks of the Hudson River (with a breathtaking view of Manhattan and the Statue of Liberty) and I would type. And type. Hunched over the old Remington I would type, word perfect, with fingers and sinews tensed like claws. Seventy thousand words. I had hand problems so bad, my knuckles so inflamed, so sensitive I could not make a pinch between my thumb and forefinger to grab a sheet. I couldn't play tennis because my inflamed fingers could not grip a racquet. Day and night it felt like I had burning sand under my skin, i my finger joints. I would crook a finger and angry red shards would show up around my knuckles. I would knead them for hours trying for some sort of relief. Probably why I still fidget with a handful of metallic balls like a modern day Captain Queeg in the *Caine Mutiny*. And every night, foolishly oblivious to what was causing the problem, I would hunch over the typewriter, tense the claws and type the night away.

Eventually I went to a doctor in uptown New York. An expert at Mt. Sinai hospital. The medico and his team did some tests then sat me down and told me that the news wasn't good. In fact it was bad. Shithouse. I had rheumatoid arthritis, and would end up as a cripple in a wheelchair. It was all said, dispassionately, in a couple of minutes.

In a mental fog I walked out of the hospital on one of those autumn New York days when it is finally cold enough for you not to smell the dog shit on the streets – that's when you know summer is over – and tried not to look too long or too hard at the row of wheelchairs clustered outside the hospital entrance. I remember getting back to my office in Times Square and staring out the window at the business, the busyness, of Broadway. And I thought I am going to be a cripple. I am going to spend the rest of my life in a wheelchair. I gave no hint to my staff that anything was remotely amiss until the classic Jewish mother, my company bookkeeper, Ilya Olshever poked her head in the door.

'Are you okay?'

'Sure. Fine.'

'Really sure?'

I couldn't lie to her. I broke down and cried. Told

her I was going to be a cripple. A wheelchair-ridden, gnarled, twisted arthritic invalid. She held my hand and dried my tears. She didn't say much, just reassured me that it was not the end of the world. It was good to have her there. Ironically, Ilya Olshever (an amazing New Yorker who, out of the blue, would give me a genuine page of a newspaper dated 1711 or a precious Minton tile) became a New York victim in the 1980s. An anonymous, reckless, hit-run cyclist bowled her over on a city street and crippled her. Physically flawed a gem.

As it turned out I had RSI years before it became such a publicly debated illness. When I stopped pounding an upright beast of a typewriter it improved. I could not only pinch a thumb and forefinger together and pick up the edge of a bedsheet but I could even once again grip a tennis racquet handle.

Back to typewriters. I collect them. Have for more than twenty-five years. Some of them are more than 100 years old. We are talking about museum items here: computers have made the Remington a dinosaur and computer screens have made the old, feed-it-in and rip-it-out typing machines archaic. But I have a passion for them, maybe an obsession.

I am not obsessed by sport – by playing it or watching it, not obsessed by gambling on the horses (I only bet on Melbourne Cup day) and gave up on a weekly poker game more than ten years ago. I'm not one to 'shop till you drop'. Shopping not only bores me . . . it often makes me perspire. I don't go to the movies any more. Don't rent videos. Shit. What do I do apart from work?

But my eyes do light up when I see old typewriters Metal machines more than one hundred years old.

probably have the best private collection of pre-1900 typewriters in this country. And that makes me feel good because, as somebody once said, the typewriter was something that 'somebody had to invent'.

Robert Graves once wrote: 'A veteran typewriter of which you have grown fond seems to reciprocate your feelings, and even encourage the flow of thought. Though at first a lifeless assemblance of parts, it eventually comes alive.'

No wonder nobody ever throws a typewriter away. It makes it tough for serious collectors.

In his book *Century of the Typewriter* Wilfred Beeching, director of the British Typewriter Museum, made the point that the typewriter played a leading part in the emancipation of women. And that is true. But the origins of the typing machine go even deeper into the history of man (and woman).

> 'It would be impossible to write the history of the typewriter from it's actual inception, for there was no true beginning. In order to view things in perspective we have to look at the original efforts of man to communicate.
>
> Throughout the ages, men have had the urge to convey their thoughts, ideas, and hopes, and to record them for those who came after.'

(Is that the driving force behind people who write books? An urge to leave something behind?)

Wilfred Beeching also wrote:

> 'To this end men have scratched, drawn, painted, chiselled, written, engraved, printed and finally typed their way through history. We can begin our

story in the Stone Age, when men left their record on the rocks in the form of drawings and paintings. For millions of years before man appeared on this planet, wasps made paper from wood pulp which they used in the construction of their nests. The Egyptians were the first to use it as a writing surface in the form of "papyrus" from which our English word "paper" is derived.'

During the following 2000 years everybody got into the writing act: the Assyrians, the Babylonians, the Sumerians, the Akkadians, the Chaldeans, the Nine-vites, the Hittites. About 1000 B.C. the Phoenicians came up with a complete alphabet plus numerals. The Chinese were expert printers as long ago as the Sixth Century but it took nearly another thousand years before their wood block expertise reached the west. The Gutenberg Bible didn't emerge in Germany until 1455 and William Caxton's press didn't surface in Westminster Abbey until 1476.

Jump ahead to the 17th century. In 1647, one of Samuel Pepys mates, William Petty, invented a machine that, I guess, was the forerunner of the typewriter. The patent for the gadget sounds more like a typewriter than it really was: '(a machine) of great advantage to lawyers, scriveners, merchants, scholars, registrars, clerks, etcetera; it saving the labour of examination, discovering or preventing falsification, and performing the business of writing – as with ease and speed – so with privacy.'

Sounds great. Sounds like a typewriter. It was actully a device that permitted a person to write with more than one pen at a time. President Jefferson used a similar gadget to sign letters. The forerunner of the typewriter was a machine concocted by James Ranson in 1711. It had keys on spinets and harpsichords, long steel rods and an inked ribbon. It apparently 'amazed all beholders'.

In 1714, in the last months of her reign as England's monarch, Queen Anne, issued Patent Number 385 to Henry Mill. Apart from inventing waterworks and being a whiz at mathematics Mill invented a printing machine. The patent of January 7, 1714, proclaimed that he, 'by his great study, paines and expense, lately invented and brought to perfection an artificial machine or method for the impressing or transcribing of letters, singly or progressively one after the other, as in writing, whereby all writings whatsoever may be engrossed on paper or parchment so neat and exact as not to be distinguished from print . . . the impression being more deeper and more lasting than any other writing, and not to be erased or counterfeited without manifest discovery.'

It sounds like a typewriter but, in fact, Mill was closer to inventing Braille with his 'deep impression' machine.

Then came typing machine heroes like Switzerland's Pierre Jaquet-Droz. Hungary's Wolfgang Kempelen, Italy's Pietro Conti – and I am playing a little fast and loose with the calendar here. In 1823 Conti claimed to have invented a machine that 'wrote fast and clear enough for anyone, even those with poor sight' and in 1830 an Italian artist called Galli was reported as having devised a 'mechanical potenografo' with keys and a paper drum. It impressed a reviewer in *The Times* of London in June, 1831. Six years later Queen Victoria ascended to the throne. By the end of her reign she had been given a gold-plated typewriter for her personal use.

In 1830 American William Austin Burt produced a machine that actually typed one letter after the other and in Europe, especially in Italy, similar work was going on. Burt called his machine a 'typographer'. He actually typed a letter to his wife on March 13, 1830 in which he said: 'Dear companion, I have but just got my second machine into operation and this is the first specimen I send you . . .' Burt also invented a solar compass which survived as standard equipment for about 75 years and the equatorial sextant which he patented in 1856.

In 1874 Mark Twain wrote his first letter on a typewriter, an epistle to his brother. He said things like 'Dear brother, I am trying to get the hang of this new fangled writing machine, but am not making a s-ining (sic) success of it. However this is the first attempt I have ever made & yet I perceive that I shall soon & easily acquire a fine facility in its use.' The letter was written in Hartford and signed 'Sam'.

I am, obviously, besotted with the tools of my trade. In my first novel, *Death At Newport* I used the main character Hunter's passion for antique typewriters to engineer a meeting between him and Dee Dee Marsh (multi-millionaire Penelope Pike personal assistant).

Hence, this exchange with journalist Jonathan Hunter caught by Marsh while snooping in the library of the Pike Newport mansion.

> 'An old typewriter on an ornate, leather-topped desk caught Hunter's eye. It looked as if it were made of wrought iron. He pushed down one of the keys and watched the precise, kneejerk

reaction as that key activated a tiny arm which, in turn, touched a third metal prong which then pushed a long, slim, metal bar forward and punched it through a narrow slot in front of the machine's platen.

From behind him a half-accusing, a half-mocking female voice asked: "Looking for something?"

With the old typewriter still in his hands he turned towards the voice. "I was just thinking how I could get out of here with this under my jacket."

"Do you realise how valuable that is?"

"I do, actually. This is a Ford, made in New York in 1895 or 1896. They were sold in France as the Hurtu and in Germany as the Knoch. Henry Ford, incidentally, had nothing to do with them."'

That was pure Hinchspeak.

When you think of it the typewriter was one of the greatest inventions in history. In his book Wilfred Beeching claims that printing has 'probably had a greater impact on human progress than any other single achievement since the discovery of fire'. And he is probably right. He is certainly right when he ties it in to the emancipation of women. The 'typing machine' got millions of women into the workforce and paved the way for their independence and freedom. But it took a long, long time getting there.

The Remington 'Silentwriter' – the typewriter I nicknamed my 'tripewriter' all those years ago – remains a dear friend. It has been, for thirty years in the business, my ticket to ride.

Shedding a Load

In 1991 I wrote a diet book surprisingly called *The Derryn Hinch Diet*. The cover blurb said I was a 'toothman, a trencherman, a legend in his own lunch-time.' I have to admit it felt strange, after decades of over eating and drinking and marathon lunches and dinners around the globe, to suddenly emerge as the author of a bestselling diet book.

I had written about Scrabble, had killed people off and done other terrible things to them in two novels (*Death at Newport* and *Death in Paradise*) and had also written about the real-life horrors of a worldwide epidemic in a book about AIDS.

But, as a notoriously big luncher, and night-time haunter of restaurants, it was strange for a fattie who rarely removed the nosebag to have a book about food and diet on the bestseller list. A book that by now has probably sold more copies than both of my novels.

In the weeks and months following publication it was fascinating to gauge the reaction of people: on planes, in restaurants, and especially at literary lunches, I could suddenly feel people's eyes on me and on my fork and plate. Watching every mouthful. Was I 'breaking the diet'? Those three feared words for any dieter. Was I CHEATING! At a charity luncheon in Adelaide I walked into a packed room at the Hyatt and immediately reached for a cold beer and a bread roll. I heard a chubby woman in a tight, expensive dress at the next table tell her companion in a stage whisper, 'That can't *possibly* be on ANY diet.' I turned to her and said, 'It's on mine.'

Strangers would stop at my table in restaurants, point accusingly at my schnitzel and say things like, 'Aha! Caught you. Where's the soup?'

In hindsight I should never have, flippantly, called it the 'soup and white wine diet' or made jokes about, 'This isn't the Fit for Life diet . . . this is the Pissed For Life diet.' Or the 'Fit For Nothing' diet. That only happened because I never intended to write a book about it. The diet was something that my producer, Dermot O'Brien, and I just did. And, as it worked, and as I shrank, the diet was featured in a few newspaper articles. Unfortunately the image spread: Sure Derryn Hinch is losing weight, who wouldn't on his diet? All he does is drink wine all day, drink soup at every meal and eat a few bread rolls.

At a barbecue one of O'Brien's overweight friends patted his girth and said he would love to find a diet that he could stick to but he couldn't live on soup and white wine. My driver, John Perry, confessed one night that he had tried the diet for a few days but had then given it away. Why? Because the white wine was giving him heartburn and acid attacks.

I asked him if he was drinking a different brand than he usually drank and he admitted that he never drank white wine. Hated it. Preferred red. I told him to have soup and bread and RED wine at night. He then sheepishly admitted that, despite the dyspepsia, he had stuck to the white wine because he thought there had to be some magical, chemical, organic connection between the three diet ingredients: white wine, soup and bread.

He was quite relieved when I told him that was bullshit. Even more relieved when I explained that Brian Wentzel, the actor who plays the cop in 'A Country Practice', was allergic to wine but had lost more than two stone (around 13 kilos) on a personally adapted night-time fare of bread, soup and scotch. Brian actually went on the diet a year before the book came out when I described it to him at a Perth telethon. His weight loss was so dramatic and so obvious that 'A Country Practice' scriptwriters were told to delete any fat cop jokes. Wandin Valley's walloper, wasn't a whale anymore.

Throughout all this dietary attention and culinary conversation I have to admit that I felt like a bit of a fraud because, for me, it had been relatively easy to lose weight. At no time had it felt like a REAL diet. Diets are meant to hurt, right? Maybe that is why my homemade diet worked. The Hinch diet did not have complicated calorie charts, food groupings, extensive no-no lists, special, expensive food packages that had to be bought through one of those heavily-televised weight-loss programmes. My diet also made no mention of dietary milk-shakes, pills, powders, exotic fluids or other concoctions like those little dry fibre tablets that were supposed to blow up and fill your stomach like a sea sponge suddenly immersed in water. Many of them were advertised and relentlessly pushed as expensive, but vital, diet weapons that had to be used or you fell into a vat of fat from which your body could never be rescued.

In all the travels, public appearances and interviews about my diet, one person still sticks in my mind. She was a secretary, around 23 years old, and she was fat. In the old days I would have callously joked that she was a 'venetian blind with the cord broke'. She approached me at a lunch-time book-signing in the Melbourne Central shopping complex and asked, in a tentative voice – a voice stripped of all confidence – 'Will this work for me?' I told her I honestly did not know. I told her it had worked for me.

'Well,' she said with a huge sigh, 'I might as well buy it because I have tried everything else. And nothing really works.' She was an earnest, understandably perturbed, young woman with a hint of a pretty face but obviously, hugely, overweight. Several times she told me she was 'just a secretary' or 'only a secretary' who had spent $1100 she really could not afford on special food from one of those televised, gee whiz, miracle diet transformations that leap out of our TV sets every night with magical 'before and after' pictures of happy (now) dieters. An incessant bombardment of diet commercials that make failed fatties feel like even bigger failures.

'I couldn't afford to buy the food any more. I stopped the diet . . . and I put it all back on and more,' she said.

For a change I ignored her self-deprecation about being just a secretary or only a secretary, although those descriptions were telling clues to her lack of self-esteem and lack of confidence which undoubtedly had a link to her weight problem.

This young woman was walking, desperate, proof that no matter what diet you go on you are going to stack it all back on again, maybe in spades, once you stop, unless you change your lifestyle. Permanently. And it doesn't just happen to secretaries. The most publicly dramatic weight losers in recent years have been Elizabeth Taylor, Dolly Parton and TV's Oprah Winfrey. Taylor and Parton have yo-yoed amazingly. Oprah Winfrey was the size of Ella Fitzgerald one year, Twiggy the next, and now she is chubby again. Closer to home TV's Bert Newton and Melbourne radio's Craig Willis both commercially endorsed Jenny Craig's weight-loss programmes. Both lost weight, stopped the regimen, and moved back into the Billy Bunter league.

Once my diet book was published it was fascinating to get feedback from all over the country from some of the 35,000 people who bought the book and (I hope) started to diet before Christmas 1991. People in their letters, and in their comments to me, shared such personal things. It was unreal, as a male, to get so many letters and so many personal comments from women, miserable women, painfully unhappy women – especially in their forties and early fifties – who were fighting the battle of the bulge. I never have, and never will, call myself an expert but when you touch a nerve with people who have been part of the flab battle it makes you feel better than all the experts.

People like Lynda Slade from Wollongong – and unlike some so-called diet gurus I won't edit her written testimonial to make it sound better than it is. She wrote to me and said, 'I have been on your diet for 14 weeks now. I have lost 14 kilograms and I am enjoying eating raw fruit and salad. I used to take a size 18 in a dress and now I take a size 12. This diet is the best thing I have done in a long time. This book is the best thing I have done in a long time.' At the risk of sounding like one of those 'read these remarkable endorsements' advertisements I want to pass on two more: one complimentary, one savaging me unmercifully.

Joanne Foster of Devon Meadows, Victoria, said, in part, 'I've been on hundreds of diets and diet classes and never been able to stick to them as I don't seem to have the willpower or something. But your diet seems to make a great deal of sense to me. So, here I go. I'm on it. It's only early days but I have not mucked up yet and I promise myself to get there. I've got 30kg to lose so it is not going to be easy. In 12 months I will write to you again and tell you how I am going.'

I liked the letter. I liked her attitude. I felt she would make it.

But then came a zinger, a bitter diatribe, from a 'slightly overweight' mother of teenage children in Sydney. Christine Nash, of Mosman, didn't like my book. Liked me and my lifestyle even less. She wrote, 'Dear Mr Hinch, Diets that don't take the real world into consideration are diets that are doomed. You are absolutely right, and your *Derryn Hinch Diet* falls directly into that category!

'The real world isn't made up of people who eat their lunches in restaurants and spend half their lives in hotels. Take a slice of our real world. We're 45–50, slightly overweight, working parents of teenage schoolchildren. Our day starts with one of the kids rowing at 5.45 a.m. and finishes after our working day and their flute/basketball/debating/hockey homework etc., etc. In between all this, the wardrobe supervisor in our home (me) not only supervises, but DOES the wardrobe, cleans the set and so on.

'As school canteens and our offices don't provide Thai, Indian, Hungarian or any meal during the day, it is totally unrealistic to expect a main meal then, particularly as lunch frequently has to be taken on the trot. It goes without saying that restaurants don't fit the budget. The chef (whoever is available) in our family canteen has enough trouble coping with different sittings and appetites without providing separate menus, so a bowl of soup for dinner after a sandwich for lunch is not going to suit these REAL people at all. About the only thing we agree with you on, is that we're ready for a glass of wine.

'I am really, really angry that I have wasted my money buying a book that supports the lifestyle of a pampered, unrealistic, out of touch egomaniac, and I would like a refund.'

I resisted the chance to take a cheap shot. I resisted the chance to point out that the one million unemployed people in Australia and the sloggers in Sydney's western suburbs might not embrace Christine Nash as the epitome of the 'real people' when her major gripe is about taking the kids to rowing and then trying to juggle 'flute/basketball/debating/hockey/homework etc.'

Instead I replied thus:

'If you had spent as much time and enthusiasm on

the "attitude" section of my book as you did on thinking up adjectives to describe me you would have realised that for this (or any) diet to work you have to find ways to DO IT – rather than hunt for excuses to avoid it. P.S. Here's your $10 back.'

Funny, the refund was never acknowledged. Too busy with the flute/basketball/debating et al.

For every sour letter there were heaps of sweet ones. I loved one from Moya Dyer of Mortdale, NSW. It said, in part, 'I am impressed with your diet for several reasons including its practicality and ability to fit into my particular lifestyle. I would however like to enquire about the amount of wine you can consume and why.

'As an experienced "dietician's victim" I have been programmed to avoid ALL alcohol completely while trying to lose weight. I do enjoy a glass of wine at night and both my husband and I would like to begin your diet (we both have about 5kg to lose) once you cast some light on my doubts.'

I hope I did.

Joy Kneale of Ferntree Gully, Victoria, loved the book, started the diet, but had some questions:

'1. Can nuts be eaten at lunch-time, e.g., almonds, cashews? If I am not that hungry would a bread roll be sufficient?

2. Re the dinner-soup meal. Can I have too much soup? For instance I was quite hungry tonight and had two full bowls of vegie soup. Was that too much?'

Answers:

1. Of course nuts can be eaten at lunch-time. Anything can. But if you have heaps of french fries and other fatty foods at lunch (your main meal) your weight loss will be slower than if you don't. As the diet months

go by you will find that twenty nuts turn into five . . . twenty chips turn into two. A bread roll is NOT sufficient for lunch. The whole premise, the whole structure of the diet, is that the main meal (no matter how much or how little you eat) must be the mid-day meal. I know I was quoted, when I first started the HINCH programme on television, echoing the quote from Michael Douglas in his Gordon Gekko role in the Oliver Stone movie *Wall Street*: 'Lunch is for wimps!' I said it. I was wrong. Unhealthily wrong. In fact, medically dangerously wrong.

2. You can't have too much soup . . . because you won't. In the first weeks you'll probably have two bowls every night, or every second night. The same way you will have two bread rolls on some of those early, craving nights. But, within weeks, you will find yourself, voluntarily, cutting back from two bowls of soup, to one bowl of soup, to one cup of soup. And cutting back from two huge herb or cheese or onion rolls to one bagel.'

Probably the best letter I received about my diet book in the first months after it came out was from 71-year-old Joyce Cooper. I single her out because SHE singles out and cuts through this, often shameless, exploitative, diet industry that threatens to engulf us. And I say that as a person who has made money out of a diet book.

Joyce summed it all up when she said:

'I don't want to go to the expense of Weight Watchers, or any of these places, as being a pensioner I couldn't afford it for very long. A couple of times but that would be it. But to lose weight naturally would be much better and healthier for me. I am 71 years old. I am overweight and I feel uncomfortable.

'Tablets are not the answer. You say you have soup every night. Good. I would like that. But I only like vegetable and pea soup. Chicken is not on my menu at any time.'

I pointed out to Joyce Cooper that her soups sounded fine – and that neither chicken nor wine were compulsory.

In the diet book mail I also got an inspirational letter from a 19-yer-old New South Wales teenager, Janise Ellen Burke. She was NOT on my diet but she saw me on Steve Vizard's *Tonight Live* programme talking about the book. And she wrote, 'I had the urge to write to you and congratulate you on your weight loss. I used to weigh 26½ stone until I had gastric bonding and have now lost 11 stone in weight in just over a year.

'Before I lost my weight I was very depressed. I could not walk down the street without someone saying disgusting and distressing things.'

Then Janise touched on an issue, touched a nerve, that affects thousands of teenage girls in this country. She gave me a glimpse of the key that explains things like anorexia nervosa, the so-called 'slimmer's disease'.

She wrote, 'I left school despite high grades because of constant teasing. I thought of suicide many times which is very distressing to think of at only 18 years old. With the love of my family I have had success at last at losing weight and am now looking forward to a brighter future.'

With an attitude like that Janise will make it.

As a male writer of a diet book it was also interesting to meet so many fat women who were trying to lose weight. As a novice in this, increasingly commercial weight-loss world, it seemed to me that they were

TRYING to lose weight but not necessarily WANTING to lose weight. And that is a brick wall. I'm not trying to give a huge plug to my own diet, or to any diet, but one fat fact stands out like the proverbials: if you are going to lose wight, and lose weight that does not come back in a few weeks or a few months, then you must honestly, sincerely WANT to lose weight. You have to want to . . . really want to. Not feel forced to but want to.

It is like you have to WANT to stop smoking. You have to WANT to stop drinking. Until that genuine mental commitment is there, there will be no permanent solution, the weight-shedding days, the alcohol-free days, the nicotine-free days, will be temporary. They will happen. But they won't hold. You are almost under command to go back to big eating, more smoking and/or drinking because at the start you were in a forced situation, an unnatural (for you) environment when you stopped. You may have cut your calories, reduced your alcohol intake and backed off the cigarettes but if it has been done by forcing yourself, or if it has been accompanied by artificial props, then forget it. You will fall by the temptation wayside in no time.

Once you stop the trendy 'cream and carrot juice' breakfast milkshake diet, or stop chewing nicotine-flavoured gum, or stop squirting bitters in your lime juice, the old habits will rear their ugly heads again. And often people feel so disgusted with themselves for falling, for seemingly failing, they won't try again under the 'what's the use' excuse.

I can only quote my own book, because I guess that's what I know best, and although I am not into 'psychobabble' and sports-psych jargon I do like Ron Barassi's burst of two-letter inspiration. 'If it is to be, it is up to me.' I am also not into the ra-ra American psych cycle called 'affirmations'. Cards that people pin on their fridge doors or bathroom mirrors with slogans like: 'My body is lean and toned and in perfect proportion' (even if you look like a suet pudding). Or 'I see myself thinner and more beautiful than ever.' Which is fine if you actually do something to make yourself 'thinner and more beautiful than ever'. I bought one of these stick-on-your-mirror affirmations in the United States as a joke. At the risk of adding to the ego, mine read: 'I am powerful, beautiful and creative and I can handle it.' Well, everybody else lies.

Having derided cutesy slogans and 'affirmations' I'll confess that when a friend was consumed by family troubles in America, when a justifiable hangup was ordering her life, my advice was: 'Be progressive, not obsessive.' I could have got a job in an affirmation card factory. Although, seriously, what I was trying to say, in an outwardly glib slogan, was that you shouldn't ignore a problem. Shouldn't bury it. You should front it but don't let it totally consume you. Don't inhale it, eat it, gnaw at it or let it gnaw at you like a cancer through every one of your waking hours. And, when you are in bed, everybody knows that things look their blackest, their most bleak, if you happen to wake up at four o'clock in the morning and start churning things over in your mind in those cold, dark pre-dawn hours. Even, maybe especially, for struggling, wavering dieters.

The diet actually surprised me for several reasons and on several levels. Personally it was good to feel physically better even though I wasn't really exercising: shirt collars no longer strangled me, trousers didn't strain over the thighs. The belly didn't bulge over the belt and the buttocks no longer looked like a couple of wombats were fighting in there as I walked. And, like Paul Keating, the jackets to my Italian suits (made out of great Tasmanian wool) looked like they were draped over a contoured coat hanger rather than on a barbed wire fence.

All of this happened as I nudged towards 50 and slipped closer and closer to the edge of being a permanently fat and bloated person. Heart-attack-on-a-plate material. My father, from his thirties, was a short, barrel-chested fat man. My grandfather was a stocky, short and tubby patriarch with the same body shape. They both kept their hair past seventy but they showed signs around the girth that they had also kept everything else. That sort of background gives you the greatest excuse not to do anything about your own expanding profile.

It is so easy as you reach for another pie or another slice of pizza, to hark back to the hereditary factors. Our family was supposedly big-boned. Our men were all barrel-chested. I used those 'facts' for years as I grew into an antipodean version of an American football linebacker. After a few months on my diet I realised that all that 'big-boned' stuff was nonsense. An absolute cop-out. At my height I'm no more 'big-boned' than Nureyev.

In fact, I would now qualify as a medium to smallish man. Narrow of shoulder, muscular but thin in the arms and legs, tiny (by my family's standards) in the waist. And no bum.

Such a weight loss does make you feel so much

better – it maybe saved my life. It certainly changed and extended it. In December 1990 on the annual pilgrimage to Hawaii I bought myself a new pair of jeans for Christmas. It was the first time I had bought a pair of Levi's with a 34-inch waist in decades. Felt great. Christmas '91 I went back to the same store and bought another pair of jeans. This time with a 32-inch waist. On that holiday I tucked my casual shirts inside my trousers for the first time in ten or fifteen years. Maybe longer. Males who try to kid themselves and try to hide the spreading beer belly know what I'm talking about. So do women who, as the scales start to creep up, start wearing their blouses outside their skirts and the wardrobe features more and more floppy culottes, baggy sweaters and shapeless dresses bought supposedly on the grounds that dresses without belts are not only comfortable they are a personalised fashion statement. They are usually an 'I'm fat' statement.

Speaking of the Hawaii pilgrimage: a lot of people drop off their diets around Christmas/New Year because they feel it's impossible to diet during the holidays. That's rubbish. That's just an excuse for a blowout. I spent all of December 1991 and some of January 1992 in Hawaii. Some of it alone. Some of it under stressful conditions because I had suddenly, unexpectedly, been sacked by the Seven Network and arrived in Hawaii not knowing if I would be on television anywhere in '92. I stepped off the plane at Honolulu weighing 79 kgs (12st 6lbs). Six weeks later back in Australia I stepped on the bathroom scales and weighed 79kgs. In those six weeks I drank beer every day, drank Australian wine every day, lunched in restaurants every day usually eating Mexican quesadillas, corned beef or pastrami on rye with French fries, or fried chicken – because Americans make the best southern fried chicken in the world. I did not have one swim. My only exercise was a forty minute walk every morning on the golf course (without clubs). I not only didn't put on weight I also saved money because, at home or abroad, restaurant dinners are much more expensive than restaurant lunches.

The dramatic weight loss has had it's lighter, occasionally macabre, moments. I have heard the AIDS, anorexia, cancer rumours. I once weathered a *Truth* newspaper street poster that said 'HINCH CANCER SCARE.' I also weathered a *Truth* street poster that said 'HINCH – THEFT CHARGE' when a man who had robbed my house was in court. That was the one time I got so angry I sued and won. *Truth* paid me substantial damages in 1991.

The best/worst rumour I encountered was during the Gulf War in 1991. Instead of the usual creature comforts of the Sebel Town House in Sydney I was staying in a hotel close to Channel Seven in Epping. After a long day, including six hours on air non-stop after war had been declared I shuffled back to my hotel room. You had to pass the bar to get to your room. An earnest drinker flagged me down with that approach that scares any and every so-called personality, 'Can I ask you a personal question?' My intense, alcohol-fuelled, bar 'mate' then said:

'I have it on good authority that you have cancer and have only 12 months to live. Is it true?'

I picked up my light beer, looked him right in the eye and said, 'No, it is not true, but I admire the sympathetic way you asked the question.'

Once the diet book started to sell, and after I had done the TV and radio talk show circuit, I had some amazingly frank conversations with other dieters. Especially around airports and on planes. On one Sydney-Melbourne flight a gay flight attendant swept by me as I was having my breakfast of fruit and tea. 'I had my Draino this morning,' he shouted, to the consternation of some of the other First Class passengers. (It was a reference to my confessed use of Diet Coke for breakfast instead of orange juice. Lower calorie count – not that it matters – but my diet book mentions the hangover-curing qualities of cola and the cleansing 'Draino' effect that eye-watering Diet Coke can have in the mornings).

Another extraordinary thing started happening on planes. It happened so often that my diet guinea pig and oft times travelling companion, Dermot O'Brien, started asking, 'How long has this been going on?' Weight-conscious, figure-conscious female flight attendants started leaning over my seat, or crouching in the aisle, to discuss failed diets and body shapes. They would, literally, turn their backside my way, or pinch a midriff, or point to a breast and say things like, 'I have to lose a bit from here' or 'I'd be happy if I could just get rid of this' or 'I'm too big here . . . what do you think?' Some even asked me to do the pinch test and it wasn't a come-on. Pretty women living a crazy, frenetic lifestyle of airports and schedules and snatched meals in a career where it wasn't that long ago that overweight women didn't get the job and 'hosties' who put on weight were suspended or even fired. One flight attendant told me she had put on nearly 13 kilos (two stone) since she started flying.

Pretty women but so many of them sounded so unhappy. I wondered if the men in their lives resented their lifestyle and disliked the fact that they were away so much, met so many people, and spent so much time staying in hotels interstate. And I say that as a man who once married an American flight attendant with laughing eyes.

It is now nearly three years since I have had a dinner that consisted of more than bread, soup and white wine. That's around 1000 bowls of soup. Think of it another way: if I were still living in New Zealand and not on the diet, that would mean about 1000 lamb chops and because you always have two it actually would mean 2000 lamb chops. Imagine all that meat. All that fat.

Maybe that's why I do not feel, and have not felt, at all deprived. There have been nights when I have gone out for dinner. I've had some great bread, the soup of the day, some wine and good conversation. It proves, at least to me, that the food is not the reason you go out to restaurants. It is the occasion, the ambience, the company, the event. But, in truth, my dinner visits to restaurants have shrunk from about three or four nights a week to once every two or three months.

You also notice some other changes. Losing more than twenty kilos and taking your weight from more than 100 kilos to less than 80 sounds a lot. When you describe it as losing twenty per cent of your total body weight it sounds humungous. It taught me a few (brutal) facts about my life and my body. When you are twenty per cent smaller you cannot drink as much alcohol. You cannot 'hold your liquor' like you used to. Maybe that's a combination of shrinkage and age. My theory is that you no longer have all that extra weight to 'park' the alcohol. Not a scientific explanation but it will do me. On the down side I also found for the first time in memory that I really felt the cold. I had never felt the cold. Not even when living in Montreal where the snow was so deep and falling so thickly that they used to brush you down with a straw broom before you went into the movies. I didn't feel it in New York City or in the countryside when we went ice-skating on frozen ponds. Didn't even feel it at my farm near Hanging Rock. When everybody else was swathed in thick jerseys and scarfs I would still be in shirtsleeves. The fat obviously was insulation. My blubber, whalelike, kept me warm. Now the fatless sinews and muscles really feel it. For the first time in memory I get cold hands. And at the risk of sounding like a pain in the arse, losing a lot of weight is a pain in the arse. Literally. After having a plump rump for years I feel like a bag of bones sitting on hard chairs or stools for even short periods. Not a complaint, just a weight-loss observation. After all fat people may not get a sore butt from sitting on a hard chair but they do get painfully chafed inner thighs from fat legs rubbing together. And they can't stop those crazy, baggy shorts from riding up into their crotch, as if some frantic, fabric-muncher was after them. See how judgemental former fatties can get? And that's the truth.

Since the diet I have become super critical of overweight people. When I was carrying excess weight, as my belt buckle kept inching out another notch, I paid scant attention, if any, to other people's bulk unless they were grotesquely overweight. But as the diet progressed I did become increasingly aware of other people's shapes and sizes and increasingly intolerant. I saw a mountain of a man in a Canberra hotel restaurant at breakfast one morning. He was carrying so much weight and was so out of condition that at 8 a.m. the collar of his shirt and a large area of his shirtfront were already soaked with sweat. I couldn't help thinking why didn't he do something about it. Surely the strain on his heart would eventually kill him. Surely he knew that?

One of the problems of course is that so much of life revolves around food. Not only in real life but in magazines, in movies, and on television in programmes and in TV commercials. The hours spent advertising food on TV must swamp the total of commercials for almost all other products. The one that angered me the most over the years was the Mars bar commercial. 'A Mars a day helps you work, rest and play.' Oh yeah? You mean 365 chocolate and caramel bars a year are good for your waistline, your sugar levels and your skin?

Three years into the diet I have decided on a couple of minor changes to the daily routine. One of them makes the diet cheaper. Instead of expensive and often hard-to-buy papaya for breakfast I now just have a large orange. I like fruit cold (my wife hates it) so I keep her fruit in a bowl and mine in the fridge. A glass of Diet Coke (I know, I know, I've been lectured endlessly over even admitting to that habit), an orange and a mug of black tea for breakfast gets me through to lunch-time quite easily. I still drink gallons of soda water, day and night, starting around 11 a.m. and with my nightly soup (which is now sometimes only a cup rather than a huge bowl) I like a variety of onion, or cheese, or herb bread. Maybe a crunchy roll or a bagel.

Early in 1992 I decided to mark some specia

occasions when a dinner (other than soup) would be appropriate, would be permitted. I came up with four nights: my birthday, my wife's birthday, our wedding anniversary and Christmas Day. It didn't quite work out the way I planned. On my birthday Jacki threw a surprise lunch for me with about 25 guests at Champagne Charley's in Melbourne. The food and company (and wine) were all so good that by the time dinner came around I not only didn't break the diet I didn't even have the supposedly mandatory soup!

On our wedding anniversary we went out but after three years of not having a regular dinner I had got so out of the habit I spent most of the night pushing an entree around the plate and eating some great crusty mini-loaves of bread. On my wife's birthday the traditional dinner abruptly turned into a lunch at Lynch's because I had been invited to be a guest on Steve Vizard's 500th edition of *Tonight Live* (my first time back inside the Channel Seven building since they sacked me) and I ate nothing. Christmas Day will also be a bit of a non-event in the diet-breaking stakes because, from experience, we have such a huge late Christmas dinner in the afternoon that a night-time meal on December 25 is usually out of the question for most revellers. It's a time to attempt to sleep off the turkey, the ham, the Christmas pudding, the eggnog, the champagne and the sweet things found under the Christmas tree or in the Christmas stocking.

Late in '91, back at the Sebel Town House in Sydney and dining at the same table where it all started, I skipped the soup and instead had half a dozen oysters and a small caesar salad. Only a couple of times though. Just testing to see if the weight would stay off, which is most dieters' main complaint. One man wrote to me, praising the diet, but asking for advice on how to now STOP losing weight. My best advice is try some of the above. Have something small, apart from soup, at night occasionally. If the scales start to show an increase then go straight back to the bread, soup and wine for a month straight. Remember, you only ever want to lose half a pound a week.

Another bit of fine tuning I have done involves vitamins and mineral supplements. I know I have joked on radio (and in my diet book) about having the most expensive urine in Australia and that may well still be true. As a drinker I still take a lot of vitamin B and I take daily doses of vitamin C plus a vitamin E time-bomb containing, among other things, d-alpha tocopherol. In case I missed anything I also have a daily cocktail of vitamins and minerals that has everything: magnesium, iron, folic acid, riboflavin, manganese, thiamine. Since the diet I have also added a daily calcium pill. I started taking extra calcium because in the past few years, in my changed life, I have drastically reduced my daily intake of calcium. I don't drink milk. Wouldn't have it in the house if it weren't for my wife (low-fat milk) or for guests. I don't have cheese in the fridge any more. Don't use butter at all. And certainly have no use for cream. The drastic and dramatic cutback on dairy products has been a major shift in my eating habits. It has also meant a huge reduction in my calcium intake. So, like so many middle-aged women who must take calcium supplements because of the brittle-bone disease called osteoporosis, I now take calcium tablets daily. Maybe I'm about to rattle when I walk but I think it is worth it.

A Low Blow

A couple of flesh-thumpers, face-mashers, brain-scramblers turned a quiet Melbourne Sunday into a day of carnage in March 1992. I didn't actually go there and sit in the rain and watch world champion Azumar Nelson turn our own Jeff Fenech into cannon fodder. And for a few minutes turn his brain into mud. I didn't go, not through some deeply-held pacifist protest, I just didn't bother to get tickets and didn't like the outdoor venue. And anyway, Fenech's clutch of title belts has always been a little suss. The IBF means fuck all to anybody in the real boxing world. And add to that the scepticism that no antipodean joust in one of the new 'designer divisions' can hope to compete in the real world of boxing's big bruisers.

Not that I am anti-boxing . . . although I would love to be. I wish I hated boxing. It is barbaric that grown men get paid money, staggering amounts of money, to try to turn each other's brains into silly putty. It is a violent, despicable and often corrupt sport. And yet, over decades, I have supported it. I have been to some of the most brutal, most passionate fights in recent history. Like seeing Muhammad Ali, the former Cassius Clay, fight people like George Foreman and 'Smokin' Joe' Frazier and Lester Ellis and Jerry Quarry and George Chuvallo and Joe Bugner and Buster (the whale) Matthis. I covered the Lionel Rose fights at Jack Kent Cooke's Forum on the outskirts of Los Angeles.

There is nothing like the emotion and the build-up and the expectations for a heavyweight title fight at Madison Square Garden in New York. It is sheer theatre. The movie stars, the sports heroes, the former boxing champions, the politicians, the tycoons, the black pimps in their big hats and raccoon coats and women showing almost as much flesh as the contestants. It is glitz and glamour. In the lead-up it is almost possible to forget that the reason everybody has got so tizzied up and spent so much money on clothes and fight-night tickets is to sit for a few minutes – or maybe an hour – watching two men trying to turn each other's brains and other organs into soup. At the champagne parties before and after the fight, and in neighbourhood bars with the TV blaring, it is easy to forget, or ignore, that even winners sometimes end up in hospital and dozens of winners and losers pee blood for days. The whole spectacle is an awesome thing to watch. Especially the way that boxing changes people – and I don't mean the re-arrangement of the features of the faces of the men in the ring. Some boxing fans are primal. As a kid one of my favourite, girl-next-door actresses with a funny voice was June Allyson. Several decades later I sat in front of June at a fight. I told her, in a later radio interview, I'd stumbled on her secret as to how she'd got that voice. From bellowing like a fog horn round after round at ringside. The woman was transformed from the 'butter wouldn't melt' screen star into a fishwife. And then there are the boxers' wives and girlfriends who must steel themselves to go to the fights to watch a loved one being battered into brain-numbing oblivion. Sometimes they would hide their heads in their hands. Other times you could see them flinching and twitching, real-life voodoo dolls, as if every punch being absorbed by a lover was also ramming a sharp pin into them too. Of course, they got to share the spoils even if their man was physically spoiled along the way.

I have two lasting impressions of the downside of boxing. One involved the great Joe Louis, one of the greatest champions in the history of, what is so wrongly called, 'the game'. I never saw him fight. Never saw him fall in the ring. But I saw him fall once he was out of it. It was in Las Vegas. I was there to cover the crash of yet another of the controversial, super-expensive, cost-overriding fighter planes called the F-111. We dubbed them the 'swingwing lemons'. The crash I was covering left the remains of one Australian F-111, out of Nellis Air Force base, strewn all over the Nevada desert. Luckily the two pilots managed to eject and parachute to safety.

Covering a story in Nevada meant a great chance to visit the Vegas casino strip on your newspaper boss's money (thank you Warwick Fairfax, who now knows something about the perils of gambling on a larger scale). I made a beeline for the newest and most opulent casino-resort complex called Caesar's Palace. It had more fountains than Rome and, for some reason, there was a huge replica of the statue Winged Victory in the driveway. There was more braid and spangles on the foyer staff than on an American college brass band. At the reception desk the hotel's public relations man miraculously materialised the minute 'journalist' was entered on my check-in card. He took my elbow and steered me across a football field-sized foyer.

'I want you to meet someone real special,' he said. 'You'll love it.'

That's when I came face to face with a legend – a large, obviously disoriented, old black man. 'Hi,' he said slowly, in a voice that sounded like he was talking through treacle. 'I'm Joe Louis.' The champ had been reduced to being a shuffling 'meeter and greeter' at a Vegas gambling joint.

A spookily similar thing hapened years later with one of the greatest, most gutsy, athletes, the world has ever seen. The comeback king: Muhammad Ali. I interviewed Ali around the time of his first real comeback fight against the Great White Hope, Jerry Quarry, in the Houston Astrodome. Ali had endured a forced three-year lay off, stripped of all the titles he had won in the ring, because of his newly-found religious opposition, as a conscientious objector to the Vietnam war, and his refusal to be drafted into the Army. His ageing, white, southern draft board was apoplectic. America's earlier favourite son, Elvis Presley, had had his duck-tail haircut shaved off and joined the Army but he only went to Germany. In peacetime. Ali, who is possibly, probably, the greatest heavyweight boxer who ever lived, actually summed up what should have been the United States' official policy on Vietnam years before the politicians (safe in Washington) decided that more than 55,000 body bags was too high a price to pay and finally just pulled out of Saigon, leaving Vietnamese friend and foe to their own devices. Ali, in his sometimes mangled, but often eloquent, turn of phrase, said, 'I ain't got no fight with no Viet Cong.' For that he was ostracised and stripped of all the belts he had been belted for in the ring.

When he was finally forgiven and made his comeback in Houston I interviewed him. He was still a black Adonis. He could still do the 'Ali Shuffle' and the taunting 'rope a dope' trick and still 'float like a butterfly, sting like a bee' as his hyperactive and agitated Second, Drew 'Bundini' Brown, would shout from his corner. The face in those days was unscarred, virtually untouched. A far cry from the gristle that thickened it after taking some merciless punishment in later years when, in comeback after comeback, Ali couldn't comprehend the lead in his legs or the blows his older body could not absorb. Whatever the cause of his illness it was sad – and an indictment of the very 'sport' itself – to see a caricature of the old Ali painfully climb through the ropes and struggle to raise his arms, just like in the old winning days, to acknowledge the cheers of the crowd before somebody else's attempt at boxing glory. Any wonder so many people hate boxing and want to have it banned.

When I was a teenager I joined the Zambucks, the St. John's Ambulance Brigade. A couple of times a week we'd have classes on first aid and on Saturdays in our black tunics, short pants, long socks and a beret we would get to sit on the sidelines at the football and carry the heavy first aid kits for older officers when the referee signalled us on to the field to give assistance to an injured player. It was a world of liniment and bandages and blood and mud every Saturday afternoon in winter. One night after training I arrived home with a special present I had been given, or lent, by a senior Zambuck. It was a pair of huge, red leather boxing gloves. I slid them on and laced them and shadow-boxed in our back shed. To this day I can still remember the surprise when I realised that boxers don't actually fight with fists. Their hands are sort of cupped inside the gloves and it makes you understand why their knuckles take such a pounding. Why somebody could write recently that every time Jeff Fenech fights his battered knuckles run the risk of 'crazing like porcelain'.

I didn't get to throw a punch in my new gloves. My mother saw them, threw a fit, and ordered me to take them back after school next day. I wasn't even allowed to keep them for a week until the next St. John's bandage class. She reacted with such shock and vehemence you would have thought she had caught me wanking. Flash forward only ten years or so and the 12-year-old posturing and poking the back shed air with the red leather in New Zealand, is at ringside with Hollywood stars in Los Angeles for world champion Lionel Rose's title defences against such determined and tough Mexican fighters as Reuben Olivares and Chucho Castillo. On the night before the Castillo fight I predicted in a piece for the *Sun-Herald* that if the decision went against the Mexican there would be a riot in the stadium. How a 23-year-old foreigner, who had been in LA for all of a week could make such a prediction is, a long way down the track, quite beyond me. Maybe it was a slow news day and the eggbeater had to be applied to the story. As it turned out, and you would know if you saw that TV series on Lionel called *Rose Against the Odds*, the points decision DID go against Castillo and there was a riot. When the fight ended and the decision was announced I looked at my ringside colleague, the Melbourne *Herald*'s Peter Costigan, who (like me) thought Rose had lost and shouted, 'This is going to get ugly.' We soon had a ringside taste of it. Costigan was shouting his copy down a phone to Australia when he suddenly sensed a group of disgruntled Mexican-American fans looming over him. They obviously didn't like the way he was reporting the fight and I remember seeing a large brown hand come down like an axe, chop his call off in karate fashion and then rip the phone out of its socket. That was the least violent action of the night. Suddenly all hell broke loose. An angry boxing crowd, fuelled by tequila that had been smuggled into the stadium in those miniature bottles they serve you on airlines, went absolutely berserk. They set the bleachers on fire. They hurled hundreds of empty tequila miniatures down on the hundred dollar seats and the Press at ringside. They pried seats loose and started lobbing them down on us. When the metal chairs started flying I decided (as one of only a handful of Australians there) to make a run for it. The security guards had totally lost the plot. The stadium was full of noise and smoke and the sounds of breaking bottles. Just ahead of me I spotted the unmistakable burly frame of Lionel Rose's dedicated trainer Jack Rennie who obviously had the same idea that I had. Suddenly he went down, skidding on the slick and deadly mixture of spilled alcohol, urine and broken glass. Within seconds my feet had suffered the same fate as we skidded through the muck and the glass. As the crowd closed in and the noise was ghastly I shouted in Rennie's ear and pointed to an exit door about thirty feet away. We got to our feet and, like a couple of old drunks in a three-legged race, wrapped our arms around each other and buffeted our way through the angry crowd to the safety of the corridor and the dressing rooms. Both of us were bleeding from cuts. I thought Jack was going to have a heart attack until somebody told him that Lionel had also got out safely.

At the best of times the Inglewood Forum, on the outskirts of LA, can be dangerous. We were told at a cocktail party before the fight that armed security guards would escort 'celebrity' guests to their cars. That a lot of people got mugged, got hit harder than some fighters in the ring, in the car park after the fights. I had also been warned by a Hollywood gossip columnist who was my date that night to 'dress down' for the event. No gold chains, no jewellery. I knew she was serious when she showed me the small and ugly pistol she had in her handbag.

When we left the Forum, after a few nerve-settling drinks, I could not believe the damage. Inside, the stadium had been trashed. Outside there was a pea-souper of a fog but you could still see the damage. At least six cars overturned. Most of them expensive Cadillacs. Several of them torched including the wheels of the free-wheeling entrepreneur who owned the place, Jack Kent Cooke. Another Jack, a shaken Jack Rennie, vowed to me he would never have a fighter there again. I doubt he ever did.

Having been to so many title fights it must seem strange to a reader for me to say I abhor violence. But it is true. In the past 35 years I have only ever thrown punches a couple of times. Maybe three or four times. I'll admit I have had to talk my way out of a few barroom brawls in several countries over the years and some of them were my fault. Despite the reputation, I am not a violent person. Thankfully, I am a happy drunk. I would far rather make love than war. Twice I have hit people to (stupidly) protect property and once to protect a lover's honour. One of the ironies of having lived in that violence-ridden place called New York City is that I have been mugged twice – once in Washington, DC and once in Newport, Rhode Island. Never in New York. Not even when heading home, full of giggle-juice, and walking on the wild side (Eighth Avenue at 44th Street) at four o'clock in the morning. The Gods must be crazy.

A punch I threw in Washington was a real doozy. I was lucky not to be shot. Ironically, I had flown there from New York to do a story on 'violence in the nation's capital.' A Kennedy staff member, a researcher, had been raped as she left Capitol Hill after work one night. Assaulted in the shadow of the White Houe as the tabloid newspapers put it. For once, no Kennedy was suspected but it was back in the days when the Kennedy clan's sexual appetites went unreported.

At the National Press Club on F Street I met up with an old journalistic mate, Peter Barnett, from the ABC. He invited me to dinner at a restaurant on the ground floor of the snazzy apartment building where he led the bachelor life of an airline hostess-chasing foreign correspondent. We talked about my reason for being in Washington. Not a conflict of interest because he covered Congress and Lyndon Johnson's White House. At the end of dinner he insisted on calling me a taxi. 'Don't want to add to your beat-up old boy but the violence around here is serious.'

I did take a cab back to the Fairfax apartment near the *Washington Post* – not the most salubrious area in town. It was only a couple of blocks so I decided to venture out again and walk to a drug store to get some toothpaste and the first edition of the *Post*. On the way back, less than 100 yards from the apartment, a young mugger came at me from behind a hedge. It was actually in front of a church. The street thug, sixteen or eighteen, demanded my money in explicit four-letter fashion. A month earlier I had absent-mindedly left my wallet on the seat of the car after paying for a book of toll tickets for the Lincoln Tunnel linking Manhattan and New Jersey. The car jockey who parked my car nicked the wallet and the money. With that still in my mind, and not being paid much by Fairfax in New York, I resented another attack on my fragile finances. Recklessly, foolishly, I resisted and threw a punch at him. Not a good one. What they call a 'glancing blow'. It was hardly a king hit. He responded with a fist that made my eyes smart and my cheek swell. Suddenly out of the dark, near the church, a second mugger appeared. And, just as suddenly, I had a short, black pistol rammed hard into my stomach.

When people ask me what do you say when a gun is rammed in your guts, I have to be honest and say, not much. All I could come up with were some strangled, mangled, non-words. A sort of a bleat like a terrified goat. And a feeling of gorge rising in the throat. I had read about gorge. Let me tell you, when you are shit-scared, it does rise in your throat. And I don't even know what it is.

I had not been so scared since having a rifle muzzle to my neck during the Detroit race riots in 1967.

After bandit No. 2 pulled a gun on me in Washington and rammed it into my Aussie beergut I was ready to do anything for them – 'What size shoes do you take? Can I call a cab to get you home?' I handed the older, gun-toting mugger my wallet. Then they fled. I was only a few blocks from my office apartment but I was shaking and flagged a cab. I didn't call the Police, figuring there wasn't much point. I had a bourbon and went to bed. Next morning, with a decent shiner, I went to the club of the *Age/Sydney Morning Herald* White House correspondent Roy Macartney to have lunch and to borrow enough money to get home to New York.

It was the first time I had thrown a punch since I was at school. The last time had been when I thumped Jimmy Forrest. We were at primary school together. He was eleven. I was twelve. He was a new boy on the block. We were mates. (He ultimately became a policeman, a crooked one, and went to jail but that was light years away.) At the West End Primary School we got into fisticuffs because we were both vying for the (unrequited) attention of a young girl, also a newcomer to the school. We would both hover at the end of the school track to meet her and walk her back to school after she had been home for lunch. Most of us lunched on Vegemite, or pungent banana, or jam sandwiches at school. Going home for lunch was really ritzy. One day, out of the blue, the inexplicable sexual tension got the better of us both. What started out as horse-play in the schoolyard turned into a real, physical shitfight. The problem was that I was a school prefect, a House Captain. The unseemly brawl cost me my badge. I was called to the principal's office, given six of the best and ordered to hand over the badge as head of Grey House.

Looking back they really were primitive days when it came to social skills. As prefects we got to hand out demerits and punishments to other pupils. At 11 and 12 we were making seven and eight-year-olds quake in their shoes. We would have prefects' meetings every Friday and everybody on report would be hauled up before us. (I was up a number of times before I made it to the final year of primary school and got elected head of Grey House.) Twelve-year-olds would sit around a refectory table while younger students literally shivered and shook in front of us, often in tears. We would listen to the evidence and then send them outside while we decided whether or not they should write umpteen hundred lines or spend several hours a day after school for a week picking up garbage. It was terrible. Some kids, and they were kids, would pee themselves when called up before the prefects. I remember, as a transgressor, waiting my turn for the New Plymouth version of the Spanish Inquisition. I spent ages in the school corridor staring at a pathetic display case of the school's treasures: a couple of bits of nondescript colourless coral and a mangy, bug-eyed, stiff as a post, platypus.

My second punch-up in around twenty years was in Newport, Rhode Island, covering my second or third America's Cup. Actually the Cup was well over. Australia had lost yet again. But the Fairfax apartment I had hired for the yachting correspondents was still there, still furnished, and still being paid for. I went there alone to shut it down, finalise the lease, and to start writing my first novel. I spent several weeks in a deserted post-Cup and economically-dying town. I lived on toasted tomato and black pepper sandwiches. And wrote my fingers off. One night after about ten hours hunched over the typewriter with a head reeling from so much fictional dialogue I decided that I was all 'tomato-sandwiched out' and decided to treat myself to a pizza.

I went and had a few beers first at a couple of old haunts like The Black Pearl and the Candy Store on the waterfront, on Thames (pronounced Thaymes) Street. I ended up, deliberately, at a favourite pizza joint, the all-night II Capri. Leaving the men's room I suddenly had an alarm bell go off as a young American in jeans and T-shirt bumped me. At the door I checked my wallet which had been stuffed in the front pocket of my jeans. It was still there. For some reason though I took it out to check the billfold for my money. The wallet was there. The money was not. I spun back into the men's room and confronted the only other occupant. As I put it in the fictional version, in the novel *Death at Newport*.

'At an earlier hour and with less alcohol in him, and probably if he were in a better mood, Hunter would have hesitated before accusing a stranger of picking his pocket. In different circumstances he might have gone back to the table and asked his colleagues if they had seen it; or maybe even tried to retrace his steps before risking a confrontation in a seedy men's rest-room at an all-night pizza parlour.'

That incident DID happen. I did confront a mugger

in a men's room in Newport and, recklessly, slammed him against the urinal. All the time using language of the New York streets to show him I was not a foreign tourist. Not an easy mark, which of course I was. I called him a cock-sucker and a mother-fucker. A scumbag. And threatened to ram his head through that shit-house wall. And I got my money back.

My only other personal involvement with violence was at the start of the Singles Bars on New York's Upper East side. There were places like Maxwell's Plum, Flanagan's, My House, TGIF (Thank God It's Friday). A lot of British and Australian foreign correspondents made midtown Costello's their sleazy, after-work, watering hole and then, for late night drinks, headed further uptown to Flanagan's, formerly Sullivan's Tavern. It was on First Avenue just above 66th Street.

For me it was the time of 'Obbs. Carol Hobbs. She was 'Obbs. I was 'Inch. She was nearly six feet tall, a stunning photographic model turned fashion photographer to whom I was introduced by her flat-mate: a blonde and buxom Joan Kennedy lookalike photo-journalist and sometime date who was fascinated by foreign journalists. Her name was Sara Webb-Barrell. She salvaged her hair curlers when on one of the last planes out of Indo-China during the Vietnam war and finally took a pistol and blew her brains out when her latest boyfriend, a mercenary, was killed in Zimbabwe. I think she was 29.

'Obbs was not only beautiful and witty. She was black. One New York summer passed in a blur of booze and bed. In retrospect I loved her more than I let on to either of us until it was too late.

The only really racist reactions we got, except for

the surly old bigoted Irish bartender at Costello's when we might kiss each other at the bar, was from the pimps and other black dudes mid-city. Especially around Times Square when this flashily-dressed foxy black lady would come to my office in the New York Times building to pick me up.

The last punch I ever threw – the last punch I hope I ever throw – was because of 'Obbs. It happened uptown at Flanagan's. A bunch of us, the ragtag Brit/Aussie army of foreign correspondents had been drinking at Costello's, moved through a Szechuan Chinese meal in mid-town and then headed uptown to our regular late night spot. Often the troops picked up a few ring-ins – visiting reporters or editors from Down Under or across the Atlantic. This night there was a ring-in . . . a Fleet Street 'heavy' in more ways than one, a John Bull lookalike wearing a Saville Row suit. He was quick to deride anything 'Orstralian' or antipodean. Especially anything to do with the Press Down Under. Lord knows why.

As the night got longer, John Bull got increasingly unsubtle. From the minute he had set eyes on 'Obbs he had zeroed in. Had become increasingly loud and pompous as he monopolised the conversation. And increasingly drunk. 'Obbs and I deliberately left the table and retreated to the bar in another room for a traditional Irish Coffee nightcap with a difference. I would always order it without the sugar and without the cream. It wasn't for health reasons in those days. I was just sick of sipping through an inch-thick layer of cold (real or synthetic) cream and then getting to a tongue-blistering glass of scalding hot coffee.

This night John Bull tracked us down at the bar and came on to 'Obbs like a seagull on a piece of hot fat. Warnings to back off were ignored. As I called for the check and prepared to leave he bluntly told 'Obbs that she could do much better than being with a descendant of a convict.

It was like doing tai chi underwater. I could sense and see what, inevitably, would happen next. The fight, like the recession, you had to have. And late at night when you haven't thrown a punch in more than twenty years, except when trying to fend off two muggers, it is a ghastly feeling.

I remember asking him one more time to leave. Although that is probably cleaning up history. I probably told him to 'fuck off'. He then turned to 'Obbs and said 'I'd love to. If you would come with me. I've always wanted a bit of black velvet.'

In my mental video of what happened next 'Inch came to 'Obbs rescue and defended her honour by unloading a Neanderthal punch that started about two inches off the ground and tore the obnoxious Saville Row man's head off. I have since been told, and I must accept it, there was not one but two punches and neither travelled more than about six inches. Two jabs that luckily caught him right on the nose. If you had had a video you would have missed them. He must have had high blood pressure because his nose exploded and he bled like the proverbial stuck pig. Gushes of tomato sauce, or ketchup as Damon Runyon would have said, poured all over the pinstripes. His own blood drenching his expensive lapels.

Before he could respond, and while still looking at his blood-stained London suit in horror, there was a blur of further action as the bartender leapt over the old wooden bar. He had to weigh nearly 300 pounds but, like a lot of fat men, he was very light on his toes. This guy, who made Jackie Gleason look like a featherweight, came over the bar in one sweep and threw the other guy out into the snow. I guess he figured I was the local. How many times would the blow-in be around to tip him?

A postscript to all this, if we are trying to be really honest here. After the punch-up, which was really a two-punch king hit with the victim getting tossed out into the white stuff, I can remember being guilty of a sort of Cagney-style shrug and a squaring of the shoulders. Then a shooting of the shirt cuffs. As I reached for the Irish coffee I saw flecks of blood on both cuffs of the white shirt and made sure 'Obbs saw them too. Didn't need to. As she admitted later she was already moist over a lover physically defending her honour. We went home and had a great sexual romp. Admittedly we left by the back door. After all, when you've won it, why risk a bruising re-write of the ending?

On the Rocks

I watched a marriage go through its death throes one night. Not mine – although I have been through it. I watched a couple absolutely carve each other to shreds.

I was sitting at a table in an expensive, international, holiday resort – it was like being an innocent bystander at a Mike Tyson date. She was fiftyish in yellow pants and a red and gold top, blonde, good body. Probably cosmetically remodelled. Not really attractive but had the look and the feel that she had been around money for a long time. A hint of actress Clorice Leachman. She sipped at a pink cocktail with a bamboo umbrella on the rim of the glass. He was drinking light beers from the bottle with beads of sweat around the neck – his and the bottle's. He wore a tropical, fake-faded, shirt and he was angry. Old, tanned, rich and angry.

The woman unleashed a myriad of complaints about their life. The litany was peppered with, 'We begged you . . . I begged you . . . the kids begged you.' They sat there and snarled at each other as a relationship died. Or, to be pedantic, as they probed the carcass of a marriage that was obviously long dead. I suppose this was the classic tale of the rich man's wife left to bring up the family while he worked to keep them rich. When the children grow up and leave they are left with each other. Something they obviously weren't enjoying.

Sitting a table away in 'paradise' you wondered why she didn't just leave. Piss off. Flee. Thanks, but no thanks. As one ice-hockey stick said to the other ice-hockey stick – 'Let's get the puck out of here!'

As they sat in the bar their argument got nastier, more sordid.

She said, 'I've spent twenty years, twenty years of my fucking life, to keep this fiction going.' His response, 'You talk like a child.'

I wondered, did they, would they, sleep in the same bed that night? The private hell, the public vitriol, was still going on when I paid my bill and left.

The last words I heard her say were 'For crissake, I didn't marry you for your class or your charisma.'

Watching them fight so publicly, so rancorously, actually took me back (I think incongruously, you may not) to a private time when, before we were married, my second wife Eve and I had a rare, but verbally bruising, joust. Shackled by a hangover I was packing a suitcase, for an unexpected and fast journalistic trip from New York to South America. I don't remember what the argument was about but I do remember her, understandable anger when she said, 'You're winning this argument and you aren't even concentrating.'

It was true. I was thinking: socks, underpants, how

many suits, need a good jacket, don't forget the hairbrush. And still 'winning' a lovers' quarrel.

In *They're Playing Our Song* Jacki Weaver's character (read that as Carole Bayer Sager) gets embarrassed when she invites Vernon Gersh (read that as Marvin Hamlisch) to her apartment and has to apologise for the mess. His response, in words akin to these, 'That's okay, you could eat off my mother's floor. She and my father didn't speak for 35 years.'

Says much for a lot of relationships. Especially with my parents' generation who, for religious, community and social reasons, even through misplaced pride, knew that (even if it didn't work out, even if the rose garden had more thorns than flowers) their 'lot' was 'til death us do part.'

Much is made of the fact that in recent decades the divorce rate in Australia has gone from one-in-four marriages to one-in-three. By the turn of the century it will probably be one-in-two. Several reasons and not, I believe, because relationships are all that different these days. There were stacks of people of my parents' age who would have called it quits if they could have. The stigma of divorce was the glue for many a failed relationship to stick together, often to the woman's detriment and mental and physical suffering. Plus 'for the sake of the children' or the harsh economic reality for a lot of women who lost a career when they married and, once the first child came along, lost, totally, any semblance of financial independence.

It is easy for a wage-receiving male to ask why abused women don't just pack up and leave. Why bashed women, who are the prisoners of drunken, violent husbands, don't take the kids and run. The simple answer is often that they can't afford to. They don't even have access to enough money for bus fares, let alone plane fares, to safety. And this applies, increasingly, in mortgage-ridden recession days when financial pressures put even more intolerable weights on families and relationships.

I remember women my mother's age (including my own mother on occasion) joking about 'escape money' – a secret nest egg for the day when the kids had left and the woman could contemplate a taste of rare independence. The truth was, and this applied to all my working-class family friends, there was never enough left at the end of a week for any sort of nest egg. Not even a few shillings for a wife's holiday fund. In all her adult life from the time she got married, my mother never, ever, had her own bank account. That's not to say my father was mean and controlled the purse strings. Far from it. Survival actually controlled the purse strings. Every week, for the whole of his married, working life my dad brought home his weekly pay envelope, in the days when workers were always paid in cash, and gave it, unopened, to my mother. She then gave him a few shillings 'pocket money' to buy beer and cigarettes but the rest was stuffed into envelopes in the weekly pay night budget ritual. Mum would put so much aside for the 'State Advances' – the autocratic New Zealand government body that provided state housing loans. (There was a time when my parents got hooked into a fledgling building society lottery in which, supposedly, some lucky investors every month won the right to a cheaper housing loan. I know they were in it for years, carped about it constantly, didn't really understand it and didn't win anything over about ten years. When they finally decided to get out it cost THEM money.)

Some pay nights my mother cried. I can still see her – making roll-your-own skinny cigarettes in one hand, a 'racehorse' she used to call it – trying to stretch a pay packet not only through seven days but further ahead for projected expenses like the newfangled 'partyline' shared telephone, the light bill, petrol for the Morris Minor, car insurance and house insurance. Then she would stuff all the brown envelopes back into a cardboard concertina file on the floor of the hall cupboard. The food money for the week fluctuated. It all depended on how much she was forced to cram into the envelopes for other things. And that wasn't unusual at all for that generation. It went on every week in thousands upon thousands of houses on both sides of the Tasman.

So what chance was there for an unhappy, harshly-treated, woman to leave a wife-basher or a drunk? Even if they had grown so far apart from the unfeeling, uncaring husband, that it was like living with a stranger.

As a professional people-watcher I have observed non-communicating couples in restaurants. Not the embarrassed youngsters on a first public dinner date; not the tongue-tied couples with their tongues tripped up by awkwardness. I am more intrigued, and saddened, by the middle-aged couples – often spending a small fortune – who sit there through a whole dinner, hardly exchanging a word. I wonder – do they talk at home? Do they ever get animated about anything? Any issue? Any subject? I watch a couple at a stonily silent meal and wonder, why do they do it? Why pay for such an expensive, surely ultimately unsatisfying, ritual? Especially when the husband seems more animated with the waitress than with his wife.

In one of my novels, writing about the break-up of a relationship, the death of a marriage, I advanced the Hinch theory (only a theory) that most adulterous relationships end at Christmas and during school holidays. No matter what a married lover may have promised his mistress, the crunch always comes at Christmas and when school holidays loom. At Christmas if the mistress is single she, inevitably, sits alone on Christmas Day, with her champagne or her vodka and tonic, while he 'only because I have to . . . only because it's for the sake of the kids' spends it with his family. The promised divorce, the fervently pledged disentanglement from my 'wife who doesn't understand me', somehow hasn't happened. At school holiday time he just has to, can't avoid it, go away camping with the family for the sake of the children.

Holidays nurture another theory about a crucial, testing time for relationships, especially when people have been married for a long time. Watch how some married couples fight and snarl and spit at each other on holidays. And I'm not talking here about lost passports or misplaced tickets or a stolen handbag. You eavesdrop on some of the savage, high-tension, accusations and you wonder if the couple can get through the holiday without one of them pulling a gun.

Maybe in the high-pressure, demanding, daily work routine people don't have time for all the snipes and the swipes. But on holidays – when people are supposedly being rewarded for all that work – when people are supposed to be laid back and relaxing, it all hangs out. Vitriol village.

In one Hawaiian resort I watched a middle-aged, florid, American couple going fifteen rounds across the table totally oblivious to the fact that the band – for which they had paid a cover charge to listen to – was playing an old Eagles classic, 'Take it Easy'. They sure as hell weren't. He was pot-bellied and bug-eyed. She was blonde, overweight, with a verbal quiver full of arrows and Christmas colours in her hair.

The husband attacked the ice in his dark rum and pineapple mai tai with a straw. 'What's wrong? Was it the restaurant?' No answer. 'The wine? Is that the argument? The lady?' (whoever she was.) 'Is that the argument? Come on. Gimme a break.' He sucked on his drink, gave a giant, exasperated sigh, and sounded like a dying vacuum cleaner. She gave him a classic 'get fucked' look. He paid the bill and they left.

'You know,' the waitress said, as she removed their glasses and the half-eaten bowl of nuts from their table, 'they just got married. Here in the hotel, yesterday.'

What chance would that union have? Personally, I have never been a believer in the theory that it is great to have fights because making up is so much fun. The self-serving male theory that a lot of women like to fight because making up can be such a frenzy of passion doesn't make sense unless one of the pair is a masochist. Or maybe both are.

Within minutes of those 'happy' newlyweds heading off to their bedroom in a tropical paradise another, younger, couple and entourage turned up for post-wedding drinks. She was still in her wedding dress and about twenty people, including the marriage celebrant pushed about four tables together. The bride was buxom, broad-beamed and flushed in the face. The groom was also red-faced but it was hard to tell if that was because he was excited, emotional, or just physically beat from walking through a tropical garden in a tuxedo while almost disappearing under a pile of tripods, lenses, cameras and video gear. Forget enjoying the moment – preserve it at all costs. He had more gear than a camera store and spent the whole time (apart from one brief toast when somebody else filmed it all) staring down the viewfinder of a video gadget. A bit like those hordes of camera-laden Japanese visitors who don't know what they have seen on their holidays until they get home.

I wondered if any of those three couples would make it. Couple One at the Princeville Resort Hotel probably would – although a Pyrrhic victory because the wife had led the self-sacrificing life for so long that she would probably keep putting up with the philandering and the personal put-downs from a wealthy husband. Seize the Pay rather than Seize the Day. Couple Two, if they were snarling and snaking at each other with such vehemence over what did or did not happen, what should or should not have happened, at a restaurant in the first days of their nuptials, are probably apart by now. Couple Three could make it. And if they don't, well at least they have it all in meticulous detail on video.

TV or not TV

Somebody recently came up with a crude but telling definition about people who work in television. Two categories: people who have been sacked, and people waiting to be sacked.

Not far wrong and I have tasted the bitterness myself. It is an ego-driven, money-mad, power-hungry industry that has more byzantine politics than you will ever find on the shores of Lake Burley Griffin in Canberra. Television is not a dog-eat-dog world – it's a rat-eat-dog world.

It plays an amazing, frightening, role in most of our lives. And I am talking about the people on the outside looking in – from their kitchens and living rooms – not about the people inside trying to stay afloat.

Television is a tool, a weapon, a distraction, a baby-sitter, a time-waster, an escape, a diversion, that captures people from the time their eyes can focus as babies.

It still feels strange to me, even though I am in it and have thrust more than 600 hours of live prime time television into Australians' living rooms. It feels strange I guess because I did not see any television until I was 17 years old. I did not grow up on *Romper Room* or *Play School*. I did not pop my teenage pimples while watching Jacki Weaver, (whom I later married) or Johnny O'Keefe, Bryan Davies or Brian Henderson on *Bandstand*. I didn't huddle around the local music and gramophone shop to gaze at the whiz bang new invention called television that gave Australia a grainy, black and white, version of the Melbourne Olympics in 1956. (In 1956, in New Zealand, we were lucky to get a Bill Haley or an Elvis Presley record played once a week on our government-controlled version of Siberian radio let alone seeing pictures on a screen in your living room.)

In 1962, aged 18, I impatiently moved to my third paper in less than three years of journalism. I went from New Zealand's oldest daily newspaper, the *Taranaki Herald*, to the big time, the *Christchurch Star* in the South Island. After eight months as the assistant sports editor, I fished for, and got, a huge jump in grading to join the *Waikato Times* in Hamilton as a general reporter and writer of a 'man about town' fashion and style column called 'In Vogue'. I remember, as the owner of one suit and two sports jackets, lecturing readers about the sins of hanging coats on wire hangers.

In Hamilton I boarded with a dictatorial old lady. In fact my bedroom was a concrete slab converted garage. The nightly dinner of roast lamb, potatoes, pumpkin and cabbage was served at 5.45 p.m. on the dot. It made it hard when the pubs didn't shut until 6 p.m. and you didn't get to drain your last glass of flat, warm, Kiwi beer until 6.10 with a ten minute walk home across the bridge. I ate a lot of cold lamb and claggy vegetables. In stony, septuagenarian silence.

After dinner Mrs McGerkinshaw turned on the telly. There was no argument over what we would watch each night. We only got one channel: Auckland. We would sit there: the white-haired landlady, another boarder and me and watch the television. English comedies, clumsy, fault-ridden, often out-of-date news, a cooking programme hosted by a gushing geek called Graham Kerr. The TV viewing was done without booze or cigarettes and virtually no conversation. Around 10.15 p.m. some unctuous prelate with his collar back-to-front would pop up in front of a stained glass window and close the station down for the night. Actually he was followed by a fluttering Union Jack, or New Zealand flag, and strains of 'God Save the Queen'. And I would head out to the cement brick garage to have a wank and get some sleep.

That was my belated introduction to the communication, information and entertainment medium that now rules my life.

My prime-time current affairs TV career was only a couple of weeks old when one of my would-be studio guests was stabbed in the foyer of Channel Seven in Melbourne. A revenge stabbing by the son of a man bludgeoned to death in a drunken binge argument many years before. My studio guest, the killer, had just been released from jail after a long sentence and was trying to avoid being deported. The stabbing attack stunned and traumatised several of my staff members who saw the knife being thrust repeatedly into the victim's body. (There was one lighter moment when somebody said we should contact the *Guinness Book of Records* on the grounds that it was the first time in television history that anybody had ever been stabbed in the front.)

It also gave me a personal AIDS scare. I had run downstairs and become smeared with blood as I cradled and comforted the victim. He was losing blood from about four or five stab wounds to his upper torso. AIDS didn't enter my mind, as a former teenage member of the St John's Ambulance Brigade, until the emergency medical team arrived. Before the ambulance officers came anywhere near us, even though a man was oozing blood (and life) all over the foyer at Channel Seven, they opened their medical kits and pulled on plastic gloves. Four years later, figuratively speaking, I felt the knife when the Seven Network killed off my programme.

I copped it right between the shoulder blades and didn't even see it coming. In fact I was one of the last two people to know. I should have known. Weeks before I had heard a crazy rumour from another on-air Seven Network star that some young, former ABC and virtually unknown, guy called Stan Grant was swaggering around the Sydney newsroom boasting that he was about to host a new nightly current affairs programme in 1992 'in your time slot'.

For months and months newspaper columnists and radio gossips had been sowing the seeds. They were a constant water torture of rumours that were not killed off by the Seven Network's management. The warning bells should have been louder. Phone calls to top executives that had always been returned promptly just weren't returned at all. A casual end-of-year-dinner-date request featuring network star and network chief executive is suddenly not possible because the executive is 'just so busy this week'. Secretaries never get paid enough for the lies they have to tell.

At the Perth Telethon in aid of the Royal Children's Hospital, a man I considered a friend, Seven's chief executive Bob Campbell, could not look me in the eye and desperately found excuses 'to circulate'. Approval to hire a new Associate Producer from a rival network suddenly dissipated. It wasn't withdrawn but a tortured network senior executive, Alan Tyson, had to tell my producer that it was 'on hold' that 'the decision is that no decision has been made'. Why? 'Look it just is. The decision is NO decision. I can say no more.' Blindly and blithely I kept fronting up at seven o'clock each night. Did I not know? Or did I not want to know? In truth, I really did not know. In retrospect I believe I would have been given the old 'go on holiday and don't come back' routine if I had not flown to Sydney to do one more week of programmes from that city and one more from Melbourne before shutting down for 1991.

There were other clues, abundant clues, that I didn't know about then but found out about later. Behind my back, the wardrobe mistress was given some cockamammy story about budgets not being finalised, breakdowns not broken down, and told straight-faced not to go ahead and order the new suits for Hinch for 1992. Use one of the old ones for the coffin.

Memos about possible time-slot changes (to have a national crack at a vulnerable Jana) go unanswered. Invitations to senior executives to attend a party they were paying for at Melbourne's Cafe Neon to celebrate the milestone of 1000 programmes go unanswered and not one turns up. A 'herogram' from Bob Campbell to acknowledge that 1000 milestone is, in retrospect, so cleverly, so cunningly, so deliberately, ambiguously, worded. And why not? He sacked me after programme 1001. (I can't say much more about it because, as I write this, I am facing a court battle with the Seven network over my claim of a breach of contract.)

It is a ghastly feeling being sacked. It puts a great gnawing hole in your stomach no matter if you are jettisoned from an assembly line, a checkout counter or as host of a national TV programme with your name on it. Suddenly, you are told you are no longer wanted or needed. They can dress up the decision in as much tinsel and as much rhetoric as they like. They can tell you that you are wonderful but the number crunchers have come in. They can tell you it is nothing personal – just a 'rationalisation', or a 'productivity reoganisation'. In my case I was never really told why I was sacked. Still don't know. I actually flew out of the country the day after the last programme with Seven and, on the plane, went through the figures for Survey Ten – the last ratings survey for 1991. The 'HINCH' programme won Sydney, Brisbane, Adelaide, Perth (by a streak head-to-head with Jana Wendt on 'A Current Affair') and lost Melbourne by less than half a percentage point.

You're only as good as your last programme? Bullshit. You are only as good as your next programme, or somebody's perception of your next programme. Bob Campbell sent me an effusive note on a Friday in November 1991 to congratulate me and my staff on reaching the milestone of 1000 programmes on prime-time Australian television. He personally sacked me after programme number 1001. Emotional, political, stuff. The morning the axe fell there were two of us in the room and only one person cried. It wasn't me. At least I wasn't given the heave-ho while on holiday which is what happens to most people in television. It is what happened to friend and colleague Richard Zachariah who had been sharing a two-hander on Seven's Sydney news with the beautiful and talented Ann Sanders. He got the chop while holidaying at my house in Hawaii. And he only got the word because his principled former partner wouldn't go along with a sneaky deal. Sanders turned up at the Seven studios in Epping to shoot some fresh promos for the new year and found not Zachariah but the former newsreader, and AMP insurance spruiker, Roger Climpson. Sanders had the decency and the gumption to threaten that if an executive didn't call Zachariah that day she would.

In 1981 Mike Willesee went off to London to cover the wedding of Prince Charles and Lady Diana Spencer. His relationship at the time with the Seven Network was about as friendly as Charles and Di are now. Willesee's Transmedia company had a multi-million dollar packaging deal with the network that could easily have choked one of the thoroughbred horses he went on to buy, ratings were slipping for 'Willesee '81' and rancour was rife. Willesee's producer, Phil Davis, was spending as much time fighting the corporate battles at Epping as he was fighting to get stories to air. Out of the blue I was asked to 'fill in for Mike' for three or four nights. A big ask for a newspaper man turned radio commentator with no real television experience.

I think I had been on television twice in my life. Once

in a tabloid newspaper circulation shitfight as a guest on the ABC, with the other bearded bookend Mark Day, when he was editing the Sydney *Daily Mirror* and I was editing the Sydney *Sun*. And again when I appeared on New York television in the 'Would The Real Joe Blow Please Stand Up' quiz show in which I successfully conned a CBS studio audience into believing that I had crossed the Atlantic in a 13-foot boat to prove that Saint Brendan had made it from Ireland to New York. The scrawny, but undoubtedly brave adventurer, who had actually fought the elements in a cockleshell and made it across the Atlantic, was so pissed off when he didn't win that he walked out in a huff without even saying goodbye. I didn't mind. It was 1967 and I had just won $300. Nearly two weeks wages.

My stint on 'Willesee '81' triggered a couple of my worst experiences in TV. The first was when the Seven Network told Willesee that he was being 'rested' as host. That my four days, which by then had become three weeks, would extend to some months. I didn't mind, despite the daily inter-city rat race. In 1981, either Willesee or the Seven Network (I never found out which) was paying my private company $5000 a week and I still had my top-rating radio job on 3AW in Melbourne. One frenetic day in Sydney, after three-and-a-half hours of live radio in Melbourne, I had a heady meeting with Channel Seven honcho Ted Thomas and suddenly I was, supposedly, the new Willesee. (Maybe that's why Mike hates me ten years down the track). With the arrogance of ignorance I told Thomas I would do it for another three months only. That night I was due to have dinner at the Hilton with a good friend, and good actress, Rowena Wallace. After a series of oblique, almost coded phone calls, Phil Davis insisted he had to see me even if it meant crashing a dinner 'pour-deux'. I remember a strange threesome crammed into a leather banquette at the San Francisco Grill. Davis, and I say this with no disrespect because he was, and is, a great TV producer, was faced with making a silk purse out of a sow's ear. He had to put to air in Sydney every night a current affairs host who worked in Melbourne on radio every morning. Somehow, somebody let it slip about the $5000 a week for my services. I know Davis thought it was highway robbery to pay that much to a TV novice. And it was. Judging by the reaction I suspect that Ted Thomas had readily agreed to the high weekly fee because it was coming out of Willesee's budget (as in pocket). Rowena Wallace, who was experiencing a trough in her acting career, let it be known that she had earned a total of $200 that year. It didn't help the digestion. Suddenly Mike Willesee turned up. It wasn't the most comfortable of dinners for any of us. Finally I said and, in restrospect, it must have sounded like an unctuous comment from an upstart, 'This isn't easy for me Michael.' His reply, in that copyrighted Willesee undersell, 'It isn't easy for me either, Derryn.' It was a 'words hanging in the air' heavy night for everybody.

The second nightmare stemmed from the first. One night on the Melbourne-Sydney-Melbourne radio/TV merry-go-round I was in my dressing room at Channel Seven in Sydney. It was a tiny changing room with a hand basin and a shower but it had one advantage over all the others – it was only feet away from the make-up room, and the Willesee studio.

My daily routine had become a treadmill. I'd get to 3AW's studio in Melbourne just before 6 a.m., read the newspapers and write eleven foolscap pages of news and editorials by the time Frank Sinatra started singing 'That's Life' at half past eight. I would then sprint down a series of steep stairs from an office the station management called 'the penthouse' and we called 'the attic', along several corridors and down more steps until I got to the studio laden with papers, scripts, books, earphones and a cup of Chinese tea.

I would get off air at noon, do radio and personal business for thirty minutes and then dash to an American-style restaurant I owned called Sardi's. I'd talk to the manager (who would deceive me), the maitre d' (who lied to me with breathtaking pork pies), the barman (who stole from me), and the chef (who was often drunk, at my expense, by six o'clock.)

I would inhale a lunch-time meal at Sardi's before leaving at 1.17 p.m. to catch a two o'clock flight to Sydney.

Sometimes lunch, short as it was, would be more exciting in 47 minutes, than the three-and-a-half hours I had just spent on live talk-back radio. Like the time the maitre d' told me that there was a problem. The chef couldn't handle it, the kitchen staff had fled and he, the maitre d', didn't blame them. His lengthy protestations sort of boiled down to: your restaurant, your problem. So one October afternoon, with my eye on the clock for my flight to Sydney, I was edging into the restaurant kitchen where the second chef had gone troppo. He was talking in tongues (as far as I could make out) and was waving a meat cleaver around with expertise and flair.

Eventually, I talked him into a corner near the greasetrap and got the meat cleaver away from him. I even made my flight to Sydney. It just added to the madness.

In Sydney they would have a helicopter parked on the tarmac and I would reach it by being diverted down the stairs of the air bridge as I got off the plane.

This night, as I was getting changed before heading for the car, the airport, and the flight home, I heard a conversation about me. I wasn't meant to hear it but it hurt. The conversation was between a male and a female, obviously professionals. 'Experts' in the world of television.

He said, 'I mean, not wearing a tie. That's just not on in prime time television. He should be doing a late night show.'

They started to walk away but not fast enough for me not to hear her response, 'Let's face it, he's not television material at all.' I had never had a camera test and had never been told how to use an auto-cue. I didn't even know how the mirrors got the words in front of the camera lens or how the viewers at home didn't see them. I had received not a skerrick of advice about camera heights or camera angles. I know now, in TV terms, my hair was too long, my beard too bushy, my moustache too droopy, my clothes unfashionable and not flattering on television. But nobody from wardrobe offered any advice, let alone a jacket or a decent shirt. And this was prime time television on a major network.

I didn't know whether to run out and confront my detractors or do nothing. I did nothing. I slowly, very slowly, got changed and thought about it all the way to the airport in the hire car. Thought about it while eating crackers and cheese in the first class lounge. And on the flight back to Melbourne on a night when, for once, I couldn't sleep. It hurt.

In late 1981, while I was filling in for Willesee – his name still appeared as executive producer on a programme I was writing and fronting – the Seven Network approached Fairfax to have my Fairfax-owned radio contract waived and have me seconded to Channel Seven. All part of the family etcetera. Brian White, fighting a tough, but ultimately successful, radio war in Melbourne was singularly unimpressed. He wasn't even happy that I was playing shuttlecock between two cities and two arms of the media every day and every night. One, or both, had to suffer. And he was right.

However, Seven was so impressed with my Willesee fill-in months that they offered me a regular spot in 1982. Not exactly a Seven version of 'Sixty Minutes' or a new-look current affairs programme but a job as host of yet another revamped version of the oldest of daytime television shows 'Beauty and the Beast'. Obviously I was the Beast. The beauties included Jane Priest, the statuesque model who kissed Prince Charles (in one of the most audacious publicity stunts ever plotted by the Palace), that wonderful comic actress and great lady Noelene Brown, singer/actor Geraldine Turner, the delightfully warm but naive Bernadette Hughson and the battle-axe from previous 'B and B' programmes Freda Leslie. It turned out as I privately predicted. In 1982 I was more of a feminist, more of a 'women's libber', than most of my panel on most issues. And unlike one of the original 'beasts', Eric Baume, several decades before, I wasn't prepared to take a position or suppress an opinion for the sake of TV 'entertainment'. Baume, a real chauvinist beast, would happily change an opinion overnight if he thought it would make his show more entertaining. He was shameless.

At the end of our first year of 'Beauty and the Beast', we finished our last pre-recorded show, drank some champagne, wished everybody Happy Christmas and went into recess. We never heard from the Network again. I was never fired. Never re-signed. Did not resign. Just nothing. Ten years down the track I have never had a conversation with the producer of 'Beauty and the Beast' since our 'Happy Christmas – see you next year' break-up in November 1982. The lack of a start-up date in 1982 probably should have warned me. But then in late 1991 I was given the re-start date for the 'HINCH' programme on the Seven Network of January 13, 1992. As it turned out it was rubbish. Re-start in January 1992. Sacked in November 1991. The day before the sacking, while broadcasting from Sydney, Dermot O'Brien had heard strong rumours about our demise and he made a ritualistic wander through the corridors and various departments.

He had a pleasant chat with Chris O'Mara, the second most senior programmer. They talked about their two families going away together at Christmas to O'Brien's favourite fishing spot in Merimbula. The rumours came up. O'Mara, obviously adept at the make-believe world of television, told O'Brien he had not only heard the rumours he had gone out of his way to check that they were not true. 'Absolutely not true. You've got the summer series, and then 'HINCH' comes back on Monday, January 13.'

After some more chat about possible holiday venues and it being time for a long overdue break, O'Mara said, 'Mate, believe me there is no hidden agenda. If there was, obviously I would know about it.'

Less than 24 hours later Hinch, O'Brien and most of our staff had been sacked. Heaps of the replacement programme's staff were, we discovered later, already working at O'Mara's station. Chris 'no hidden agenda' O'Mara oddly enough wasn't seen around Merimbula that Christmas.

But then no knifing, no skulduggery, no betrayal, no back-stabbing or undermining should ever surprise anybody in television. It's not a mug's game. It is a highly-paid thug's game. My programme had been national (well, Melbourne, Adelaide and Sydney) for only a few weeks when I had a showdown with the network's most powerful programmer and skilled TV politician, Glen Kinging. I was running interference for a talented but vulnerable political novice, Dermot O'Brien. Kinging, whom I had known for several decades – and had in fact driven him, his wife Sue and their young baby around New Jersey and Connecticut, looking for an apartment in the late 1960s – was incensed that his network's new owner, Christopher Skase, had hired, and slotted into the programming schedule, a new prime time current affairs programme and host, without Kinging's permission. He had been told, not asked. It burned. It riled. People seemed to forget or overlook the fact that the Seven Network had never been Number One and didn't even seem to try harder. I actually heard Seven people say openly that it was better to be Number Two than a trail-blazing Number One.

Kinging, a man I later dubbed a 'prince of darkness', faced me one morning in a florid showdown at the Epping headquarters in Sydney. I admit I had pushed for the confrontation. He said that with thirty years of television experience, 'I know of 83 ways to kill you in television without you, or Skase, ever knowing. You will never know.' And we were supposedly on the same side.

I tried to tell him that his fight was with Skase not with me. On my last day at Channel Seven I was tempted to send him a fax that said, 'Okay, you win. But it took you four years and all 83 ways to do it.'

One of the most bizarre anomalies, and the 'wrongest' rumour, was that I was a 'Skase mate'. And this is not a rewriting of history cop out now that Skase has fallen into such a humiliating financial hole. I had never met Christopher Skase until he approached me at Melbourne's 3AW and told me that, with him, I could be, would be, 'Australia's Walter Cronkite'. In our first phone conversation, setting up an appointment, I offered to meet him at his Melbourne office. Indicatively, characteristically, he adopted a Mohammad and the Mountain routine. He would come to me.

He swept in, full of boyish charm, confidence and enthusiasm, took off his suit jacket and in shirtsleeves (and execrable tie) perched on the edge of my office couch and started drawing diagrams, arrows and boxes to show me where and how he was going to take the Seven Network (and the Australian TV industry) by the scruff of the neck and shake it into a wonderworld. Remember this was after the heavy-handed Fairfax goon squad had been in there dumping Australian Rules football and trying to turn Melbourne into a Sydney relay station. Seven's news was rating an asterisk – that means less than one per cent of the market.

I believed Skase. When it comes to vision in media, and resorts, I still do. I can't explain, and would not apologise for, the way his empire crashed. A lot of people got financially burned. Personally it cost me more than half a million dollars. My own producer, Dermot O'Brien, has the unenviable record of being the last person in Australia to buy Qintex shares. I advised him to do it. Less than fifteen minutes later the shares were suspended from trading. But Skase had charisma that would have you crawling over broken glass. At the Seven Network – and leaving me out of this – he did breathe some magic into the place. He took a punt on the radical late-night lunacy of Steve Vizard's 'Tonight' show. He embraced 'Fast Forward'. He got Australian Rules football back and played a high-price poker game to win the Barcelona Olympics for Seven. He went broke, went belly-up, after mixing it with the big guys in Hollywood but he gave it all one helluva shake.

In my time at the Seven Network it is true I rubbed some people the wrong way. Obviously not Skase. In fact, the best Skase quote that I will take to my grave was made at an opulent, black tie, Christmas party, at the home of former Melbourne Lord Mayor, Ron Walker, just before the Skase freefall. Christopher Skase, who would never drink before 8 p.m., would never even have one glass of wine at lunch-time, sucked on a late-night cigar and sipped on a glass of his favourite drink, bourbon. I was having trouble, was being seriously sabotaged, by resentful executives inside the Seven Network. Skase drew on his cigar, looked out over the fairytale Christmas party tableau and said softly, 'Keep one thing in mind. We'll both be here long after they have all gone.' He was wrong. We weren't. Just like bureaucrats outlast prime ministers and governments, television's second echelon hangs on like a limpet. The anonymous losers end up winners.

One of my, ultimately insurmountable, problems in four years at the Seven Network was that I had not paid my dues. I had faced the same thing in radio. (There was a touch of it too when, unexpectedly, I came back from New York to be editor of the Sydney *Sun*.) When I popped up on 3AW in Melbourne, challenging Bert Newton's alleged invincibility, a newspaper man was criticised for trying to muscle his way in on big-time city radio when he hadn't done Orange or Katoomba or Geelong. Hadn't 'paid his dues'. In television I hadn't chased fire engines, hadn't done stand-ups, hadn't even done a 'live cross from a court' for crissake. And to add to the lead in the saddlebags I hadn't been auditioned, let alone anointed, by the network heavies, the programmers. Those faceless, manipulative and often poisonous, men who never risk their own faces and reputations on camera or really put their careers or reputations on the line. Some of them have spent expensive, decadent decades with snouts in the network trough, their homes bedecked with network contra, without even being able to say they had programmed a winning station. A Numero Uno Network.

Adding to my network baggage (and to the seething undercurrent of executive discontent) was the fact that I answered to Skase. Nobody else. And, I'll admit, I used it. When months went by before I could get vital TV monitors installed in my reporters' room, so they could see the comings and goings around the world, I sent a five-word memo to a senior executive: 'Where are my fucking monitors?' In retrospect I'm not proud of it . . . but it worked.

After Skase left I answered to the new managing director, Bob Campbell, and felt no shame that I was still operating at the top of the tree. When you've been a top level executive, when for years you have answered only to 'mahogany row', when, in radio and television, you have fought for and won the precious freedom and independence of 'editorial control' why fight, and risk strangling yourself, in the often-mediocre middle management seaweed? It is true, and I made no bones about it, that I did not answer to individual station bosses. Did not answer to station programme managers who, in a network sense, were not programmers at all. They were mere schedulers of commercials despite the grand titles. In the Seven Network in the late 1980s and the early 1990s, station managing directors were not 'managing directors' at all, despite what the Broadcasting Tribunal might think (or be told). They were at best 'general managers'. In reality they were network 'rubber-stampers'.

I remember, in the middle of an early political shitfight, telling Kinging, 'Your argument is not with me. It is with Christopher Skase. If the network owner says to me, "Derryn, you answer to me, and only me" then I am happy to answer to him.'

The day Skase was gone from Seven my own days were numbered, despite the good ratings. The clock was probably ticking for a year before they sacked me. I've admitted I was, virtually, the last to know which is a chastening admission from a person whose career for more than thirty years has involved finding out things that people don't want others to know.

I should have known something was up because, among other things, for some months I had been under a ban – ordered not to broadcast my programme from Sydney. 'Too expensive, don't need to, who cares etc.' It reached such a bureaucratic stage that I had to get personal permission from the network's managing director before I could even visit my own Sydney office. It got so subterranean and so ludicrous that in December 1990 I personally paid the airfares and the accommodation so that my producer and I could visit Sydney to have an end-of-year lunch and drink and chat with my Sydney staff. I guess I should have known then the Welcome mat had been withdrawn. At one stage in 1991 I personally spent more than ten thousand dollars to send Channel Seven reporter David Richardson to Bangladesh for an interview with Malcolm Fraser's daughter, charity worker Phoebe Fraser, and for a heart-breaking series of stories about the suffering in that stricken country. Months later the caring, sharing family network – which had put all those Bangladesh stories to air on the 'HINCH' programme – finally reimbursed me for less than half of it.

In January, 1991, I returned from holiday early because it was obvious the Gulf War was about to explode. I tried to go straight from Hawaii to the Middle East but was turned down. Then, back in Melbourne, I started making plans to be in Sydney despite the ban, so that, at least, I would be close to network headquarters if the balloon went up. I was ordered by the Sydney managing director, Alan Tyson, to stay in Melbourne.

In the end, after a lot of huffing and puffing and posturing on all sides, I got to Sydney, set myself up in a hotel near the station in Epping and when war did break out I was on air in minutes and spent the next six hours straight anchoring the network's coverage without even a toilet break. But I should have known then my appearance was under sufferance. Out of left field they suddenly brought in George Negus to supplement our Gulf coverage. He had the decency to be embarrassed. Predictably it started a new wave of speculation about the future of the 'HINCH' programme. In hindsight it was pretty big writing on a very public wall.

Campbell came to my Sydney office on a Tuesday morning. A jolly, matey, handshake as he walked into the reporters' room and I ushered him towards my office. It must have been a long walk for him. I have since learned Campbell doesn't like the face-to-face shootout. He sat down, on the other side of my desk, and said, 'I've got some bad news.' I guessed it and from memory said something inane like, 'Well, I know the dog hasn't died because I don't own a dog.'

Campbell said the Network was not bringing the 'HINCH' programme back in 1992. It was over. In a way I let him off the hook. Didn't have a tantrum. Wasn't histrionic. I did not and would not beg. Did not and will not crawl.

I do recall he called me Hinchie. I do recall saying, 'Well, we gave it our best shot.' To which he replied: 'You did better than that. You did incredibly well. The ratings around the country . . .' and he tailed off. As well he might have. We were winning in four out of the five major markets. He also said it was not a unanimous network decision. And he wasn't really sure himself if he was making the right decision.

When I asked, 'Why then?' he trotted out a parade of TV-speak theories. 'The network believes, although I am not wholly convinced, that Gerald Stone can take us, long term, more confidently, more successfully, in the direction we want to go, into the 1990s.' 'HINCH', he said, had peaked, or was about to peak, in '92 or '93. Opinionated hosts, tell-it-like-it-is hosts like me, had a faster burn-out factor in television than 'safer people like Andrew Olle or Peter Couchman.' That comment seared into me: Olle! Couchman! Two TV 'hot-shots' riding on the ABC's magic carpet, fuelled by the taxpayer, and never having to worry about that cruel, demanding, commercial villain called 'ratings'. That really hurt. I had watched, over the years, as a gaggle of ABC 'stars' heaped buckets of muck on people in commercial television. They changed their tune when a fat cheque was waved in front of them, ran away from under Auntie's skirts, tried to dance in the real world, fell flat on their faces, and then sprinted back to the ratings-free safety zone of government television. Geraldine Doogue, Chris Masters, Ian Carroll. The roll-call is staggering. And Auntie ABC always welcomed them back with open arms as, fingers commercially burned, they insisted that commercial networks could not really do justice to their sort of committed, respectable, journalism. Masters – who did not cause the Fitzgerald Royal Commission into police corruption in Queensland but coat-tailed a brave print journalist called Phil Dickie – actually made some preposterously, pompous claim that he needed to get back to the ABC because commercial television wouldn't cover stories about aborigines.

Jacki Weaver, having worked in theatre, on radio, and in television – ABC and commercial – for 30 years summed up my own sacking in three, admittedly biased, words: Malice beats commonsense.

One of the saddest, most bewildering, moments after the axe fell involved my producer Dermot O'Brien. He was the Channel Seven Chief of Staff, holding down the stressful 'suicide slot' in the Melbourne newsroom, when seconded to 'HINCH' late in 1987. Supposedly he was going to produce four international documentaries, hosted by me, every year for three or four years. He was shanghaied to help us get the five nights a week current affairs programme off the ground. We did not make one doco. (The projected budget was so laughably low we couldn't have made a doco even if we had somehow found the time.) O'Brien became the producer of the 'HINCH' programme in early 1988 and became co-executive producer, with me, when we resurrected the abandoned package and took it to the Ten Network in 1992. O'Brien had spent fourteen years working for the Seven Network. A former *Herald and Weekly Times* reporter and the Seven reporter he survived the ownership turmoil of the 1980s. Copped the abuse, the insults, and the threats, especially when a swaggering team of Fairfax executives hit Melbourne and started sacking waves of people. They got rid of Aussie Rules and almost turned the once high-flying and proud Channel Seven Melbourne into a relay station out of Sydney. It was Noddyland. Egos out of control. Inter-city rivalries and revenge in full flight. Within weeks Channel Seven's, once proud, once top-rating, news rated an asterisk. Meaning no viewers.

When I was suddenly sacked so was O'Brien. Guilt by association. Network boss Campbell actually told me that morning that virtually all fifty of my staff would be chopped. My on-air reporters? Out. Talented, dedicated, crawl-over-broken-glass, journalists? Out. He did say, 'Well, Gerald might look at one or two . . . but to be honest I doubt it. He wants his own team.'

Malice before commonsense. How could talented, really skilled, TV reporters, who had held down sought-after slots on a successful national prime time current affairs programme for four years, no longer be good enough to even front up in any Channel Seven newsroom anywhere in the country? David Richardson, Jackie Quist, Chris Smith, Pamela Graham? Their crime: Guilt by association. The same with O'Brien. Fourteen loyal years with a network and a year after his sacking, in breach of his contract, he still does not have a letter confirming it or explaining why. In fact, although a sub-contractor, I actually sacked O'Brien and he did not, technically, work for me. I was not a Seven Network executive.

When you are ambushed, you go into defence mode. At the execution I asked Bob Campbell how many people knew of my fate. He said eight. I said that if that were true, then the whole world knew – having worked on the theory for years that if more than two people know something it is no longer a secret. It was time to make it official.

He offered me an out, a face-saver. I could announce that in the wake of my successful diet book for Penguin I could say I was going off to write books full-time. I told him that wasn't on. It wasn't true and wasn't fair to my viewers or to my staff. I told him I wanted it to be announced that I had been sacked and I wanted to announce it myself. Campbell wasn't surprised. 'I thought you'd be Hinch right through till the end.'

After he left O'Brien was quickly at my door. I said something rattled and inane like, 'Let me grab a cup of tea and then I've got a couple of things to talk to you about.' I went and had a pee, made myself a cup of Earl Grey tea-bag tea, walked back into my office, closed the door behind O'Brien and said, 'We're down the road. We've been sacked. The programme isn't coming back next year. We're kaput! It's over. We finish Friday week.' It came in a gusher of words. For a variety of reasons, and because I had to get a professional programme to air that night I decided not to tell my staff until about an hour before we went to air – more than seven hours away. One of the hardest things happened a minute after my conversation with O'Brien when I walked out into the general reporters' and researchers' room. An astute and canny Chris Smith (that's one of the reasons I hired him) cornered me. He wanted to know if the rumours were true. And was it true that I was negotiating with the network for a new one-hour-a-week Parkinson-style interview show that would not involve the 'HINCH' reporters? 'The newsroom is full of it,' the former Sydney news reporter said. 'There are rumours everywhere. Stan Grant is even telling people he is going to front the new programme.' Less than five minutes after being sacked I lied to Smith. In a performance my actess wife might have been proud of I told him it was rubbish. I told him we had a re-start date for 1992 (Monday, January

13) and, until a few minutes earlier I believed that to be the truth. I also told Smith that it was true a new production company, involving both Hinch and O'Brien, had made a pitch, a submission, to the network for a new, once-a-week, one-hour interview/variety programme but if it, in any way, interfered with or harmed the five-nightly current affairs programme I would walk away from it. Promise.

Every second of that bullshit is etched in my mind. I remember where I was standing, where my loyal and keen, but troubled, reporter was sitting. It was a replay, after the massacre, of what I had told my Sydney producers (in good faith) the previous day. They too had heard rumours. Seen new staff being brought on board. On that Monday, pre-sacking, O'Brien and I took Andy Nieuwenhof and Terry Hill to lunch at a small Thai restaurant in Epping. They were closer to the Sydney gossip and both were understandably, desperate for reassurances about the programme's future. Like a broken record I told them the 'HINCH' Summer Series was about to go to air hosted, as usual, by Peter Luck and produced, as usual, by my deputy producer, Warren Wilton. And we had a start date for 1992: January 13th. Terry Hill, a mountain of a man and a veteran TV cameraman, said, 'I'm about to sign a mortgage for more than $100,000. These rumours scare me. Do I have a job with you next year?' Twenty hours before I was sacked I assured him he did. I repeated the '92 start-up date. And I believed it.

After Campbell sacked me, after I talked to O'Brien and before I was bailed up by Chris Smith, I called Jacki who was in Sydney doing a great, but tragic, play called *Shadowlands*, at the Sydney Opera House for Wayne

Harrison and the Sydney Theatre Company. One of her best performances ever.

After my boss's strange, evasive behaviour at the Perth Telethon Jacki and I had discussed the possibility of a Campbell-Kinging-Stone triumvirate tearing up my contract even though we were well into Year Five at Channel Seven. I told her I had been sacked, that Dermot O'Brien had been sacked and that virtually none of my staff, it seemed, would hold their jobs through Christmas. Typically, she offered to come straight to my side, straight to the station, but she had never done that before (apart, ironically, from a stint as a Willesee reporter) and I didn't want anybody to suspect it wasn't business as usual. Instead I arranged to meet her and my stepson Dylan, at a suburban restaurant in Sydney's nearby Marsfield. Jacki, Dylan, Dermot and I had an emotional and tearful lunch. It was even harder for him, after all those years devoted to Channel Seven to have his wife looking around their house in Melbourne and, at home alone, wondering in tough times if they would be able to keep it. The lunch wasn't helped by a non-observant waitress who stuck to our table like glue and bubbled, incessantly, about nothing while we contemplated a cold and bleak future. I couldn't divert her because I did not want to alert anybody to the news until I had told my own staff just before going on air that night and told my national television audience the truth at 7 o'clock.

This is how I dropped what to me, and a lot of viewers according to talkback radio the next day, was a TV bombshell. At no stage did any Seven Network executive ask me what I was going to say. I went on air showing more 'couth' than I would probably show now and simply said:

'Good evening Australia.
There are a lot of rumours around at this time of year, especially about the television industry, especially about this programme. Rumours that the "HINCH" programme will not be back next year. Well, tonight I can put an end to those rumours. They are true. A short time ago I was sacked. The "HINCH" programme, after four years and more than 1000 programmes, will disappear at the end of the Summer Series.

Now I could try to con you and say that I'm leaving of my own volition, to write books or whatever and save face, but it is not my style – never has been, never will be.'

I ended the programme like this:

'And on an eventful and sad night for me and for a great "HINCH" team, a loyal team, on Tuesday, November 19th, 1991, that's life. Goodnight.'

Just over a week later I went to air for the last time on the Seven Network. I said:

'For the last time, good evening Australia. Funny feeling, but we will go out with as much of a professional manner as we can but it doesn't mean it doesn't hurt. On a lighter note I have burst a blood vessel in one eye which, on any other night, would keep me off air. One consolation, it is so inflamed you won't know if I cry or not. Not that it matters.

And in the same tone, I went to the dentist today and told him that I am contacting the *Guinness Book of Records* because it is the first time in my life when a visit to the dentist has been the highlight of my day.

Still we will not wallow. On the programme tonight we will look back at some of the highlights and the lowlights of our years of "HINCH".

At a time like this, in a situation like this, there is a lot of black humour with jobs on the line. As I said the night I was sacked, the Network does have the right to do what it did. I just think it was wrong. Stupid, actually. I guess I was caught between a Stone and a hard place.

I just want to thank you, the viewers, for your support over the years and also for the ratings right to the last. To my loyal staff, a huge salute. Thanks team. To the Network, as they say in vaudeville, "Thanks for the loan of the hall." '

Then I showed a compilation of more than a thousand programmes. Something I had deliberately not looked at until that moment. It made the eyes water and the voice more husky than usual as I said:

'So that's it. On Friday November 29th, 1991, that's life. Goodbye.'

Within days of being sacked and having faced the ignominious newspaper headlines I did what I do well – I fled to my holiday house in Hawaii. It is a place that I'm often quoted as saying I cherish because there I am anonymous and regarded as some mildly eccentric, bearded, Australian writer who sits scribbling, furiously, in bars for six hours at a stretch with a wine bottle at his elbow. I realised that, suddenly, that is what I was. I had no job and my only visible means of support (as they used to say when I covered courts as a young reporter) was a moderately-rewarding contract from Penguin to write this book of essays. I also believed I was still, legally, entitled to money from the TV network that had abruptly dumped me. That is why it seemed bizarre, even to me, when, jobless, ten days after being sacked and after an emotional farewell from my fantastic staff I was on a plane from Kaua'i to Honolulu. Suddenly a guy in an Aloha shirt, R.M. Williams boots and faded jeans is in a limo the size of the MCG – heading for a royal suite at the famous 'pink wedding cake' hotel on Waikiki, the Royal Hawaiian. Inside the suite there is Dom Perignon champagne on ice, masses of flowers, baskets of fruit and macadamia nuts. At 6 o'clock this unemployed Aussie journo is heading for a Honolulu TV studio.

(I'd just spent a weird twenty minutes in the women's beauty parlour at the Royal Hawaiian after convincing them I needed some powder, spackle and eyeliner).

It is a time that I have never really, fully, shared with anybody. Not even my wife. I'd been sacked. Told that my programme wasn't 'the look of the 1990s' for the Seven Network even though we were winning in most markets and thrashing Jana and 'A Current Affair'. Part of me wanted to quit TV. I felt betrayed by people for whom I had worked, and more importantly, my team had worked for with passion, for four years. We had climbed fifty mountains and people (especially TV executives) forget how high some of those mountains were: Everest-sized peaks like 'Neighbours' and Tony Barber's 'Sale of the Century'. They were ratings buzz saws to go up against and to the surprise and chagrin of some people – even inside my own network – they couldn't, or didn't, want to believe it when we broke a few of the buzz saw's teeth. There were times we beat both of them. Sometimes, in some cities, week after week.

In Honolulu I went to a local TV station and, via satellite, did a press conference back to Australia and an interview with the Ten Network's rising star Anne Fulwood. I think I quoted Freddy Krueger 'He's back, he's back,' even though I have never seen one of his horror movies.

It was a bizarre feeling. Like, I guess, Wally Lewis suddenly playing for New South Wales. Or Collingwood's captain Peter Moore pulling on a Melbourne jersey. Your enemy is suddenly your friend. Your friend, through no fault of your own, is suddenly your enemy. For me it really was a bitter-sweet feeling because I loved the Seven Network and where I thought it was, and could be, going.

In the back of a Cadillac I returned to the Royal Hawaiian, a rich person's playground. It brought back memories and, in fact, that night although signed, sealed, and expensively delivered to a new network, with a stretch limo at the door at my beck and call, I went nowhere. Didn't open the Dom or throw a party. Instead I went downstairs for a bottle of Australian white wine, a bread roll and a bowl of French onion soup and wallowed in the past. I thought of my first trip to

Hawaii en route to Canada more than twenty-five years earlier. My tip at the bar at the Royal Hawaiian after dinner in 1991 was the same as the cost of my room for one night at the nearby Reef Hotel in 1965. Worse than that, in 1965 I could see the pink palace from my tiny balcony at the Reef but couldn't even afford to buy a beer there. Didn't even have the gall, confidence, or the social graces to walk through it. I remembered walking on the sand on Waikiki Beach and staring, in awe, at the Royal Hawaiian where the rich people lived. Never dreaming that one day I would spurn a $200 bottle of champagne in one of the Royal Hawaiian's luxury suites. Such a rich person's playground was incomprehensible to a brash, and poor kid from a town of 30,000 people in New Zealand. Alone, on that contract-clinching night with the champagne and the limo and the flowers and the Hawaiian expense account, I remembered how scared I had been on my first visit. In 1965 I wasn't only too scared, too intimidated and too broke to set foot in the environs of the Royal Hawaiian . . . I was too scared and too broke to even venture out to a poolside table at The Reef Hotel to order a hamburger and a beer. After all, I had sussed out a menu and a beer was almost a dollar! I was heading for Canada with a bankroll of $NZ 600 – most of it squirrelled away while working as a seagull labourer on the NZ wharves. The minute I arrived in Canada and spent a dollar I no longer had my fare home. It was not scary but it was not a new sensation. My Dad had insisted that, as a teenager, I had my return fare to New Zealand when I booked on the MV *Wanganella* for the big sea journey to Australia. I didn't lie to him. I DID have the return fare of £22 when I left New Plymouth but the minute I arrived in Sydney and my two female room-mates (just mates) took me straight to the Golden Sheaf Hotel in Double Bay for a couple of the biggest, coldest beers I had ever seen in a sun-drenched thing called a 'beer garden', I was suddenly under-funded for any possible trip home. So being broke and far from home was hardly a new sensation.

In Canada I remember spending my last thirty dollars on a filmy, (to be honest, ghastly) short nightie for the young woman who would eventually become my first wife. When I finally made it to New York I managed to get a $700 bank loan so I could fly back to Australia to marry her in 1967. Back in New York, we were so poor, she shivered and shuddered through her first winter. I have never forgiven myself for never taking seriously the fact that she could not afford to buy an insulating, thick winter coat to ward off the vicious cold. She did buy a bright red cloth coat from a downtown discount store but it was like wearing a bikini in a blizzard.

Jesus, we were poor. And the weekly food bill could not have been more than $14 a week. Tell me I am dreaming. I know we couldn't afford a car (although when things got better I bought, an old green Ford Falcon for $200) and we certainly couldn't afford to use the phone for international calls home. My grandad had been dead for two weeks, and long buried, before a letter from my mother arrived in Montreal to tell me what had happened.

Within days of my final programme on Seven prescient gossip items started appearing in newspapers about where the 'HINCH' programme was going and when. It is true that both Peter Meakin, Kerry Packer's TV guru at the Nine Network, and Gary Rice, the new Ten Network honcho did both call me. I had called nobody, in the belief that any so-called TV, or radio, star who loses his or her job and then phones a rival network touting for work diminishes their financial value by about 70 per cent. Neither Meakin nor Rice offered me a job. They were both, in TV jargon, just 'touching base'. The truth was, if I were going anywhere in daily current affairs TV, there was only one game in town: Ten.

In Hawaii I had a fairly spirited exchange with Peter Meakin who called me to tell me he knew I had already signed with the Ten Network (which wasn't true). I did tell him that if I joined Nine they would 'park' me. Another Nine Network eunuch. Meakin denied it. Even when I pointed out that the Nine Network's expensive 'buy them and bury them' formula had taken care of Terry Willesee, Greg Evans and Jo Pearson. I also pointed out they had a popular, successful, five nights a week, current affairs host in Jana. Even though she had made an audacious, personal and, ultimately-misguided, approach to the Seven Network's Bob Campbell in an attempt to break her contract with Nine, package her show, and, in a lock, stock and barrel move, shift to Seven. It was a big league, serious television power play that would have left me up that creek without a paddle. I suspect, now, that it almost happened. It still might.

In December 1991 as television writers scrabbled through my TV carcass a strange thing happened. Critics who had mauled me unmercifully for years – had hated my style, my stories, my opinions, my voice, my delivery, my looks – started saying things like, 'We hated him but we'll miss him', 'He was a shit but at least he had a go.' (By mid-1992, back up and running on the Ten Network, I suddenly became the respectable bookend in current affairs television).

Shortly after my final programme on Seven a diligent network ferret, Ian Duncan, produced a burst of activity to put 'HINCH' and Seven into perspective. The network's Melbourne 'programme manager' sent a burst of personal letters to TV writers pointing out that stories about Hinch being chopped down in his prime were rubbish. Hinch had not been a ratings winner. The programme had, in fact been a consistent third. No mention of the nights we had beaten 'Neighbours' and 'Sale of the Century' for him. No mention of the fact that in the final survey, that was completed the night I finished on Seven, I had won Sydney, Brisbane, Adelaide, and Perth (by a street, head-to-head with Jana) and lost Melbourne by half a percentage point. Funny how I had never seen Duncan burst into print to write to TV critics at any other time in my four years at the Seven Network. Even when we nudged close to a 30 and blitzed the opposition one night. But why should I have been the least surprised? This was a person who once reportedly told a Seven board meeting, 'This network shouldn't even feed this man' (meaning me). The same executive who told a colleague that, 'Hinch lost me forever when he announced at the start of a six-hour federal election broadcast that he had not voted.'

And yet he turned up, smiling and unctuous, for drinks with me and my staff the night I left. Maybe just to reassure himself it was true. Anyway, he will always remain in my TV memories for one of the most coincidental events in my TV career. One morning, my producer, Dermot O'Brien, received an unusual, even unprecedented call from Duncan in London. He wanted to know if we were happy with the placement, and volume, of our programme promos. Such a call had never come when Duncan was only a couple of floors above us. Some flattering attention to station detail. Obviously it had absolutely no connection with a story that had been aired on radio, and appeared in the *Age* that morning. A totally fallacious report that the Seven Network was about to get a new chief executive and his name was . . . Hinch.

Ah, the machinations of the off-air survivors. Television – that concerned and deeply sincere industry. A cannibalistic world where they eat not only their young . . .

The Derryn Hinch Diet Derryn Hinch

Who's Who lists cooking as Derryn Hinch's favourite hobby. To be more honest it should say 'eating'. Especially at long lunches. Call him a toothman, a trencherman, a legend in his own lunch-time, Hinch knows his way around a menu – and a wine list. So it is all the more remarkable that in recent months he has lost more than 20 kilos on a diet he devised himself.

A non-deprivation diet. Because: he didn't stop eating, he didn't stop drinking alcohol, he didn't stop going to restaurants and he did not stop having fun.

What's more he continued to eat 'banned' diet foods such as fried dim sims, pizza, French fries, bread and fried chicken.

The Derryn Hinch Diet tells, in a clear and lively way, how Derryn got his weight under control, and keeps it that way. It's a diet that is so easy, it will also work for *you*.

Nothing ventured, nothing gained Fabian Dattner

Fabian Dattner is one of Australia's leading female entrepreneurs, a woman with a passionate commitment to the future and the opportunities presented by change.

Born into the vibrant and creative family of retailer Stephen Dattner, Fabian moved into the family business, developing it in a number of new directions. When her company fell victim to the economic downturn she turned to a new and highly successful career as a motivator and keynote speaker. She is also well-known as the founder of Second Chance, an innovative scheme to find employment for ex-prisoners.

Nothing ventured, nothing gained is the story of a risk-taker, who knows how to turn adversity to advantage. This entertaining and provocative book will inspire and encourage everyone who reads it to get more out of themselves.

PENGUIN – THE BEST AUSTRALIAN READING

More, Please Barry Humphries

The details of Barry Humphries' life are still amongst the best kept secrets of our time. Recent volumes devoted to his work and career shed very little, if any, light on this most private and circumspect of artistes. Hitherto, he has deliberately furnished his hardworking biographers with blatant mystifications and whimsical fictions.

In consequence the revelations and confessions contained in this book will astonish his growing international public with their novelty and in no way echo the amiable, but wildly inaccurate, narratives of his recent memoralists. Here, at last, and in his own lapidary prose, is his account of his life up to the present.

More, Please was his first utterance and they are the two words that will inevitably spring to the lips of all those who read this book.

Conversations in Cabs Jim McClelland

In this new collection of jottings from his *Sydney Morning Herald* column, Jim McClelland ranges over subjects as diverse as the sinister art of function creep, our passion for noise, the economic rationalist religion, felophilia, and the virtues of ageing.